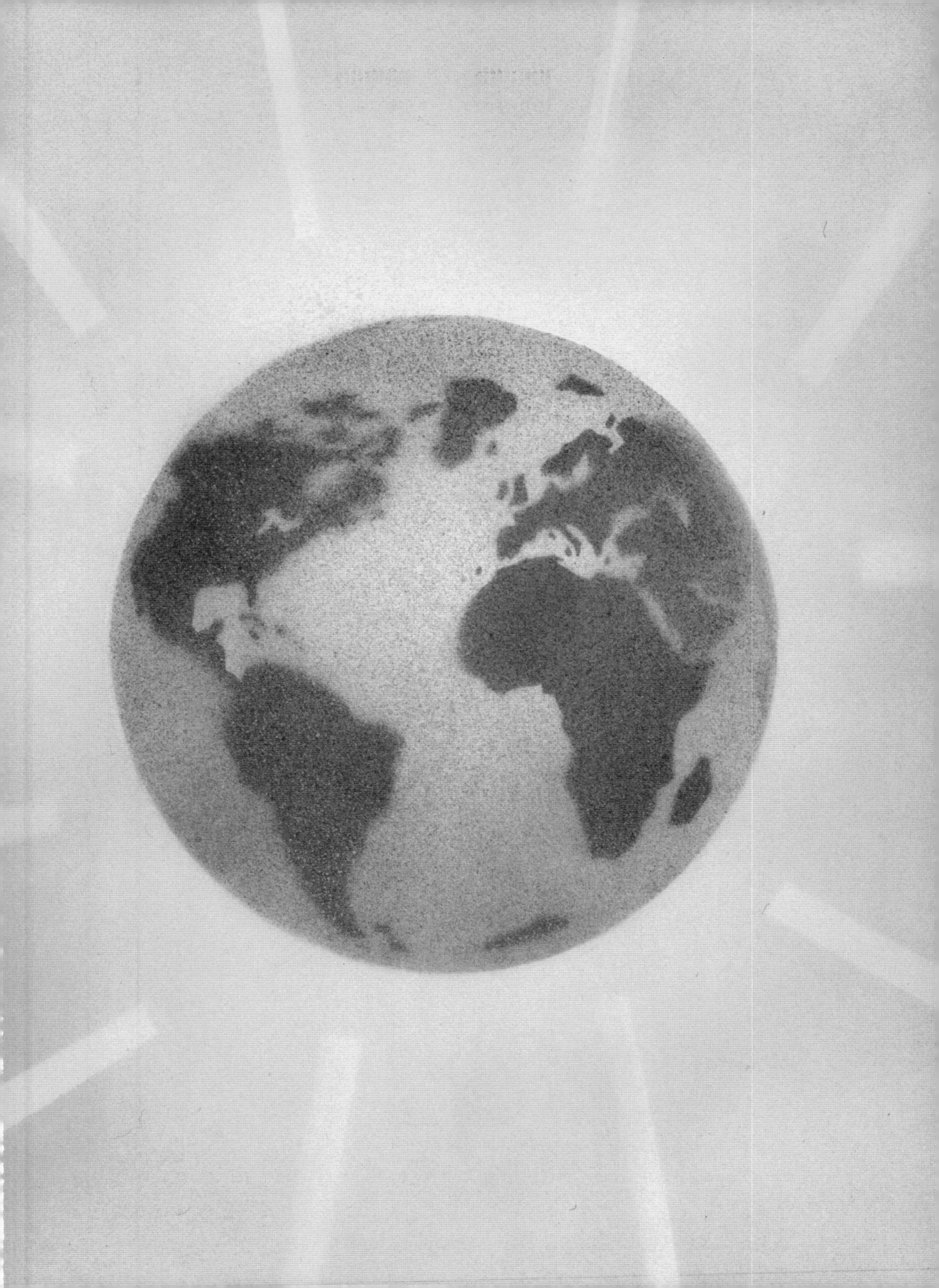

ISBN 1-891830-14-7
1. Kuper, Peter. 2. Art / Illustration.
3. Comics / Graphic Novels.

Top Shelf Productions, Inc.
PO Box 1282
Marietta, GA 30061-1282, USA
www.topshelfcomix.com
Book design by Peter Kuper and Brett Warnock.
Production Assistance by Laird Ogden.
Edited by Chris Staros and Brett Warnock.
Speechless logo design by Craig Thompson.
Fonts: Base-9 and Base-12 Serif by Zuzana Licko/Emigre.

Published in 2001 by Top Shelf Productions, Inc.

Printed in China

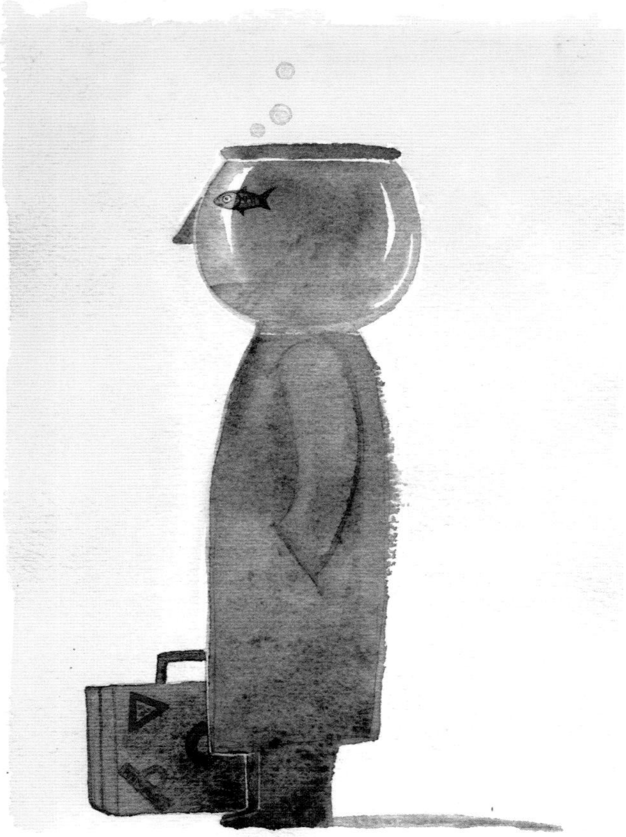

Above: *Trip's Over*, Unpublished, 1992.
Previous page: *World Weary*, Unpublished, 1991.
Front cover: *Global Warning*, published by Dark Horse, 1993.
Back cover: *Art Watchdog*, Unpublished cover commissioned by the *New Yorker*, 1993.

SPEECHLESS

For my parents, Alan and Ginger, for giving a hoot,
and my daughter, Emily, for being one.

Endless thanks and appreciation to a large number of people who helped make this book possible: to my wife Betty for always supporting my choices; Laird Ogden for his undying assistance throughout; Emily Russell for tremendous editing skills and a long list of great suggestions; Gahan Wilson for taking the time to write so eloquently; Seth Tobocman for inspiring so many things; Anthony Stonier for pointing me towards Kafka; all the art directors, editors and publishers who gave me the chance to get my work out there. Particular thanks to Brett and Chris at Top Shelf for demonstrating their love of the form so far beyond words, by sticking out their necks to produce *Speechless* so beautifully.

CONTENTS

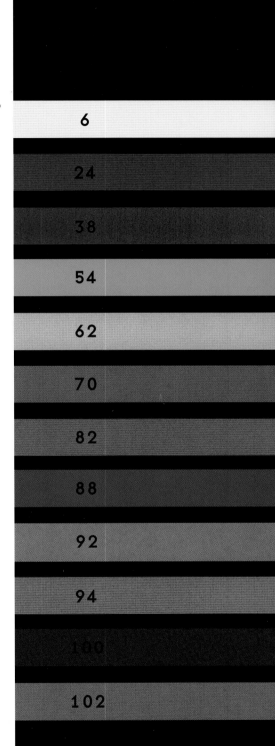

INTRODUCTION

Peter Kuper is an artist who has dared to work in the difficult and demanding tradition founded and developed by two of cartooning's most legendary and brilliant practitioners: Windsor McCay, the creator of *Little Nemo* and George Herriman, the creator of *Krazy Kat*. The remarkable thing is that he has not only succeeded in meeting that tradition's demands, he is—as the contents of this book will clearly demonstrate—in the process of expanding them.

Like McCay and Herriman, Kuper is not satisfied with merely presenting a series of illustrated panels which are only connected by the narrative thread; he insists on joining them graphically so that they spill into one another, reconnect in unexpected ways and otherwise manage to violate their seemingly serial nature in an Einsteinian fashion. Reader/viewers find themselves—all of a sudden—shocked into realizing that they hold in their hands an entire page, or two facing pages, or even a whole series of vitally connected pages which form a profoundly unified work of art.

Once, someone asked Cezanne how he went about producing a picture, and he told them one must paint the whole thing simultaneously. This is what McCay and Herriman and Kuper do. Everything is part of everything else, all elements spontaneously arise, and space is time and time is space. It beats 3-D comics all to hell.

Kuper's preference for urban locations plays into this intense interrelationship between the parts of his work, as cities more or less force their inhabitants to be aware of, and skillfully interact with, the elements of their environment. Barring grizzlies and overly territorial canines, one can afford to dreamily wander along a country pathway, but the city offers a constant multitude of factors. From challengingly-timed stoplights and ankle-twisting potholes, to potentially lethal muggers and sidewalk invasions by taxis, they must all be subconsciously apprehended if one is to complete a trip to the deli undamaged.

All this plays to what I think is essentially Kuper's main message, which is that we should open our eyes and keep alert since this is a very dangerous world. He is very rightly concerned about us and wants to help us, and I really do believe that you will find that buying this book and experiencing his art will genuinely increase your chances of survival.

And, as a bonus, you will find it hilariously funny.

Gahan Wilson is a cartoonist, illustrator and author whose work appears regularly in the *New Yorker* and *Playboy*, among many others. He is currently working on a show airing on Showtime, as well as other film and television projects.

Gahan Wilson
New York, 2000

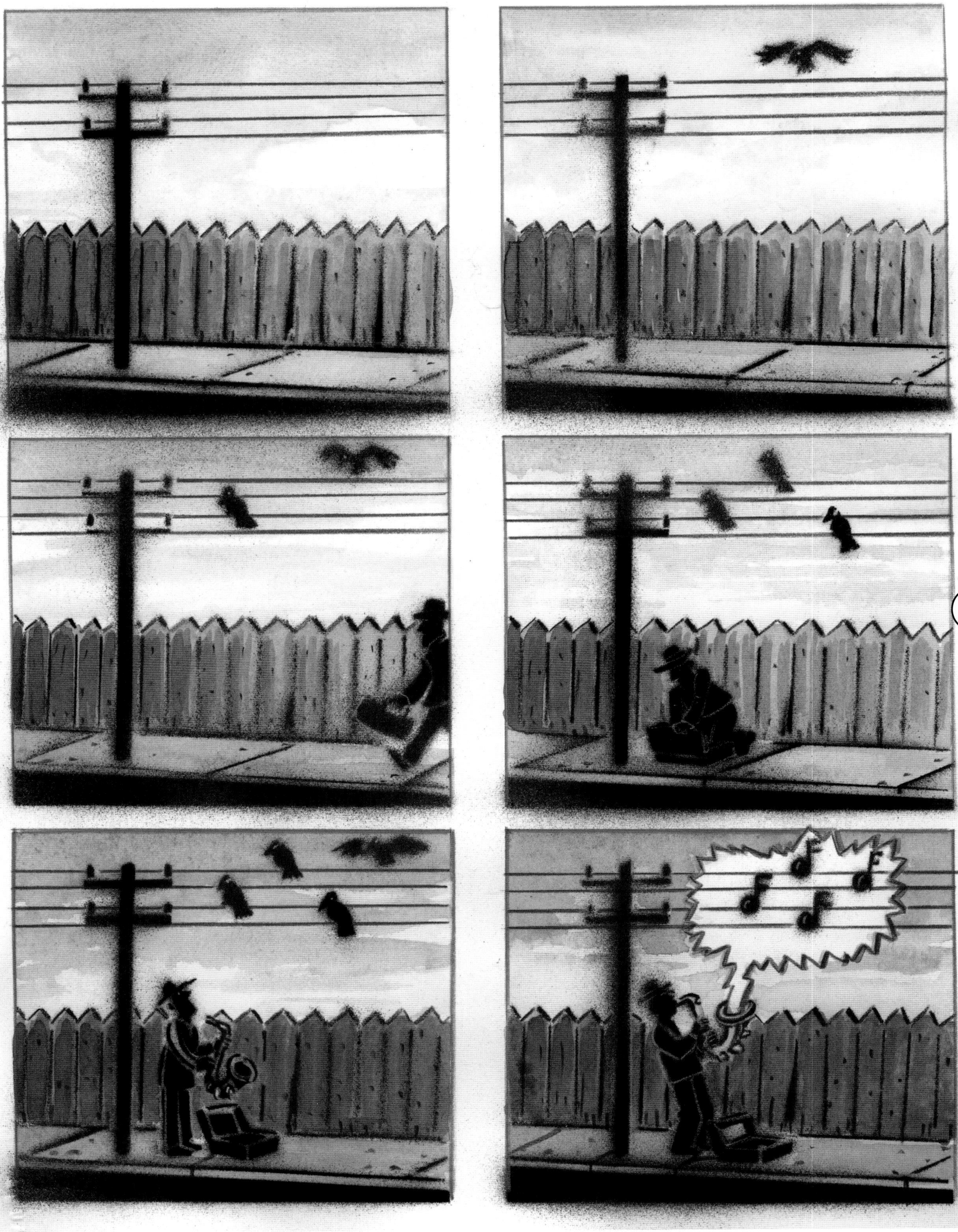

Bird, published in *Pulse!* magazine, 1994.

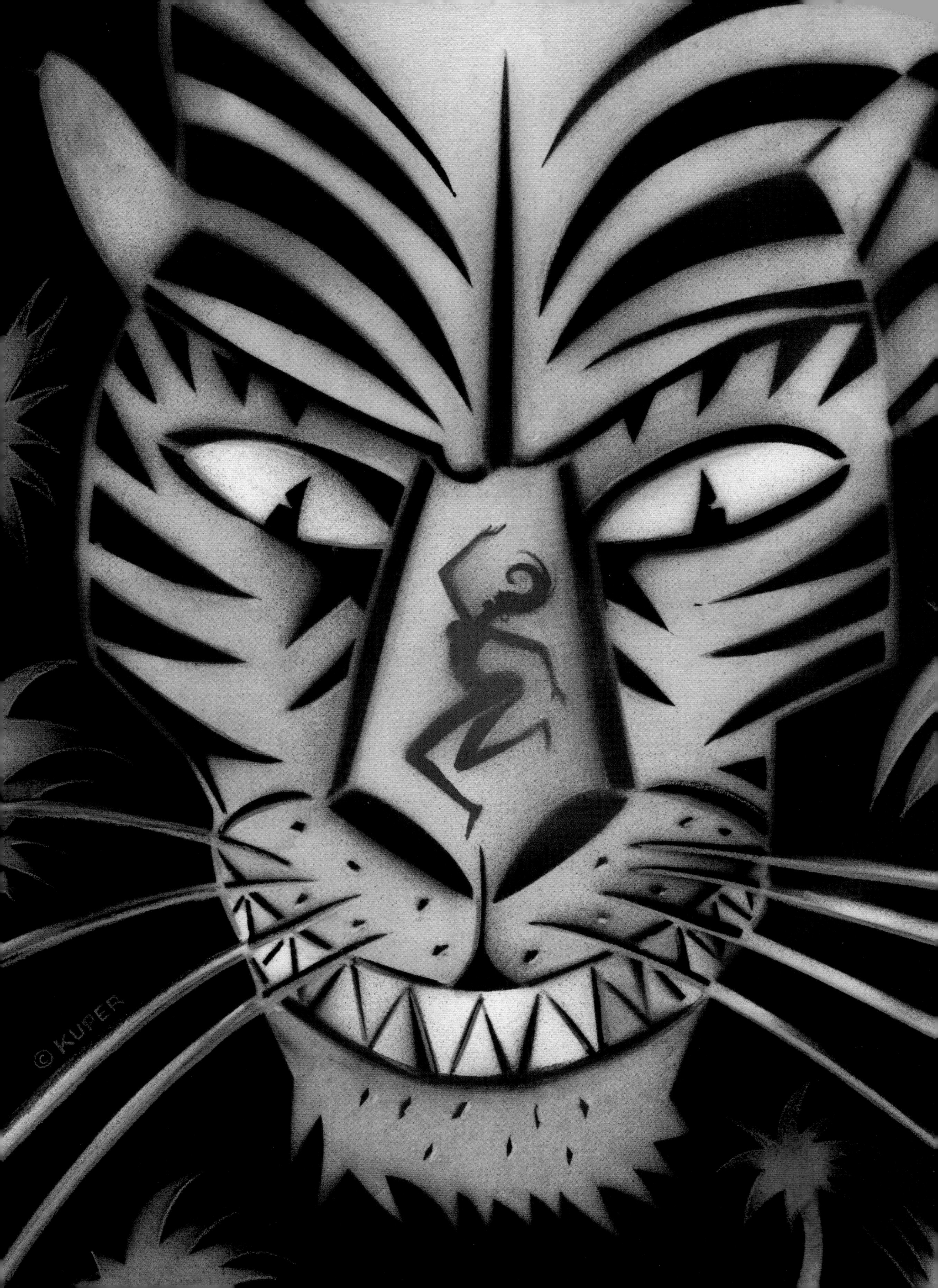
© KUPER

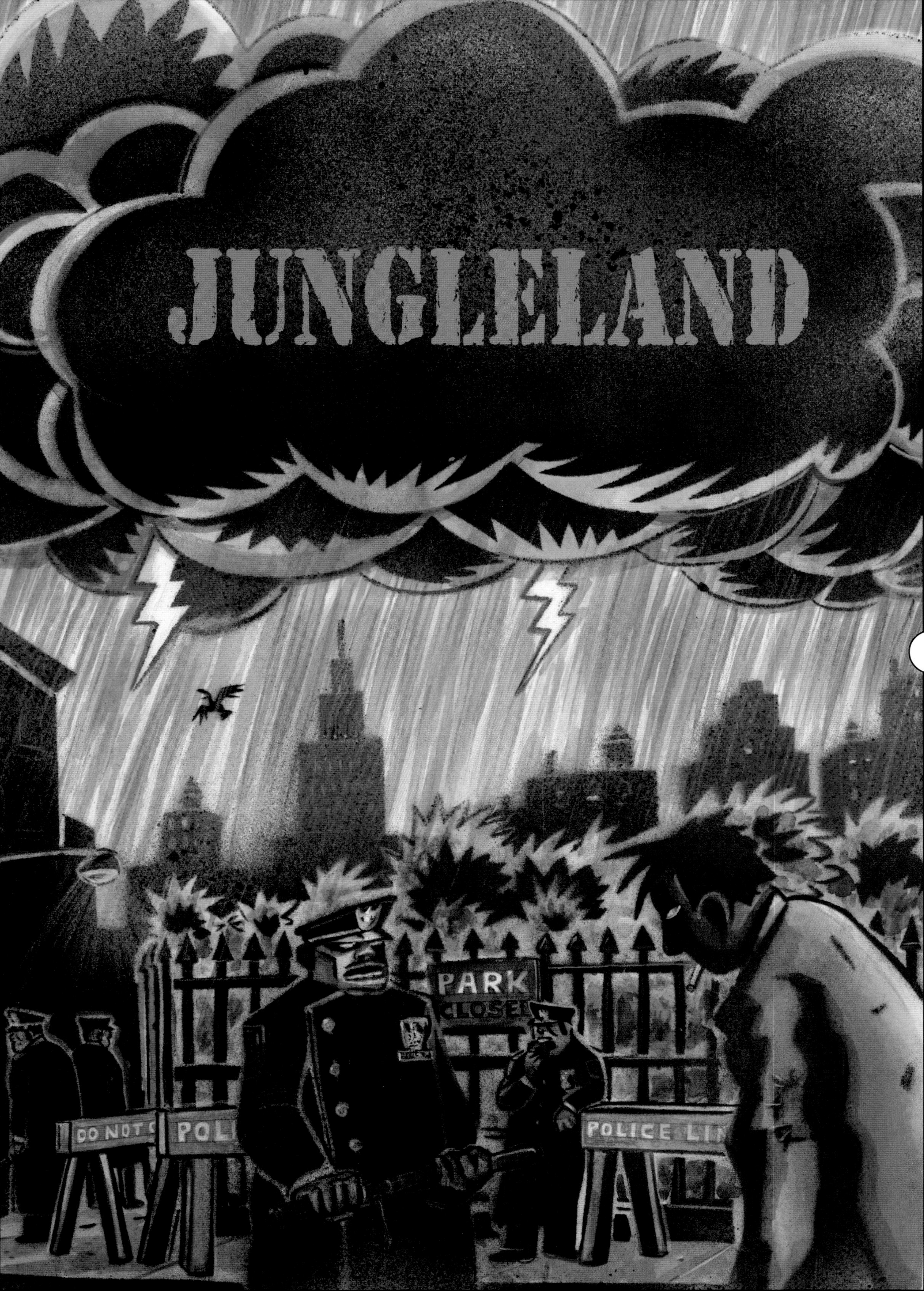
JUNGLELAND
PARK
CLOSE
DO NOT
POLI
POLICE LI

Jungleland appeared in black and white in *World War 3*, 1991.
Facing page: cover of *Aesop's Fables* published by Fantagraphics Books, 1992.

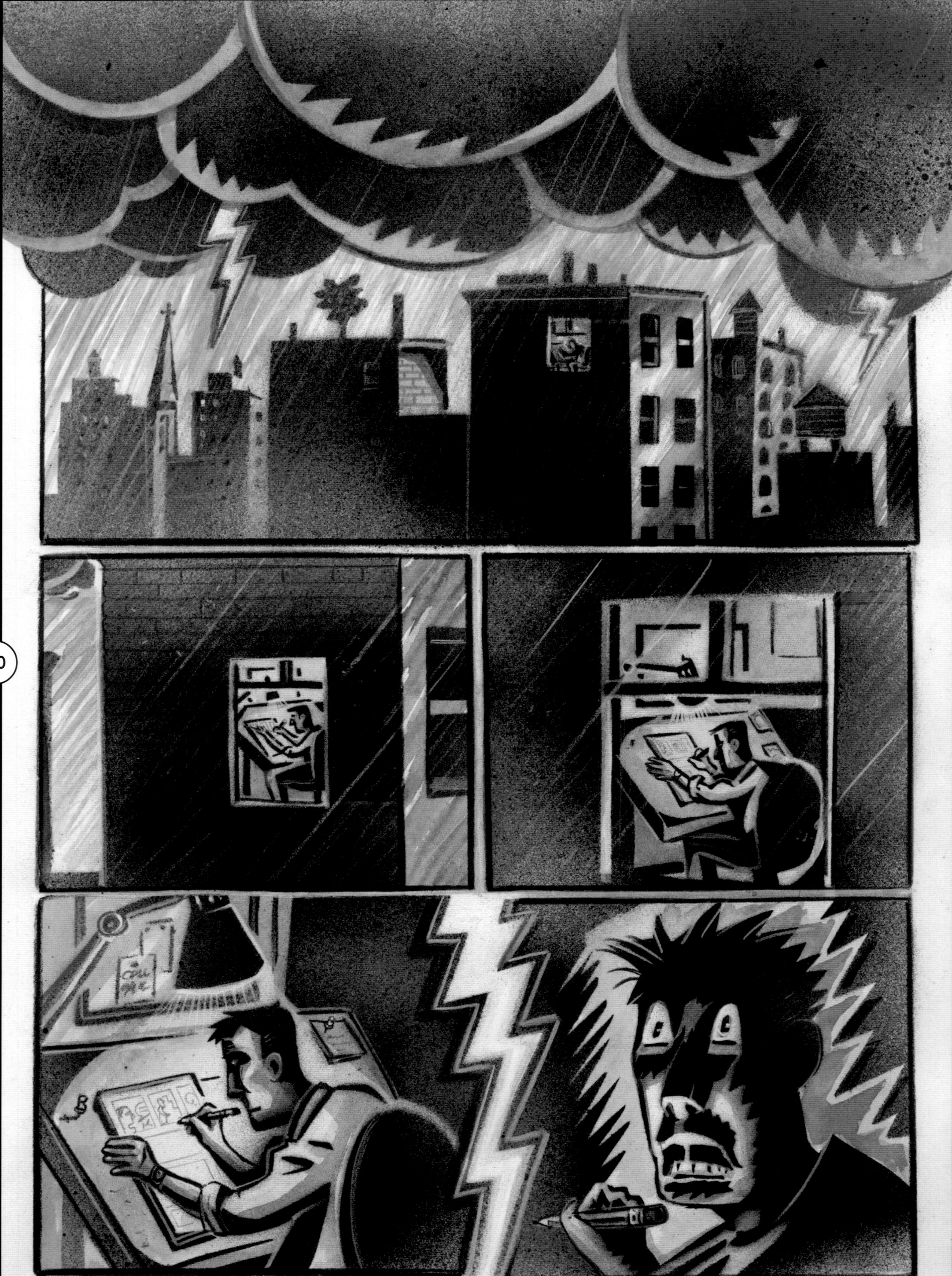

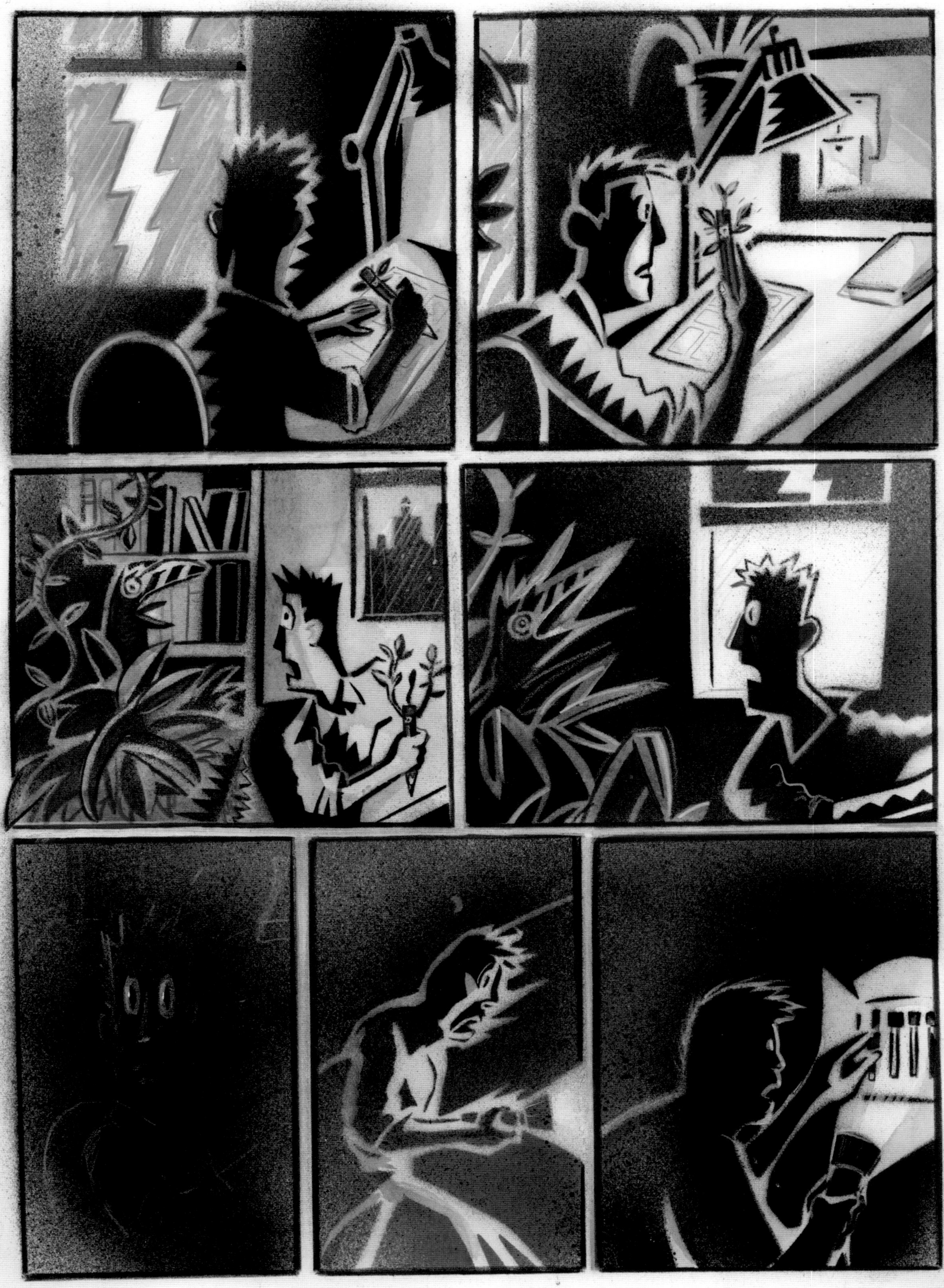

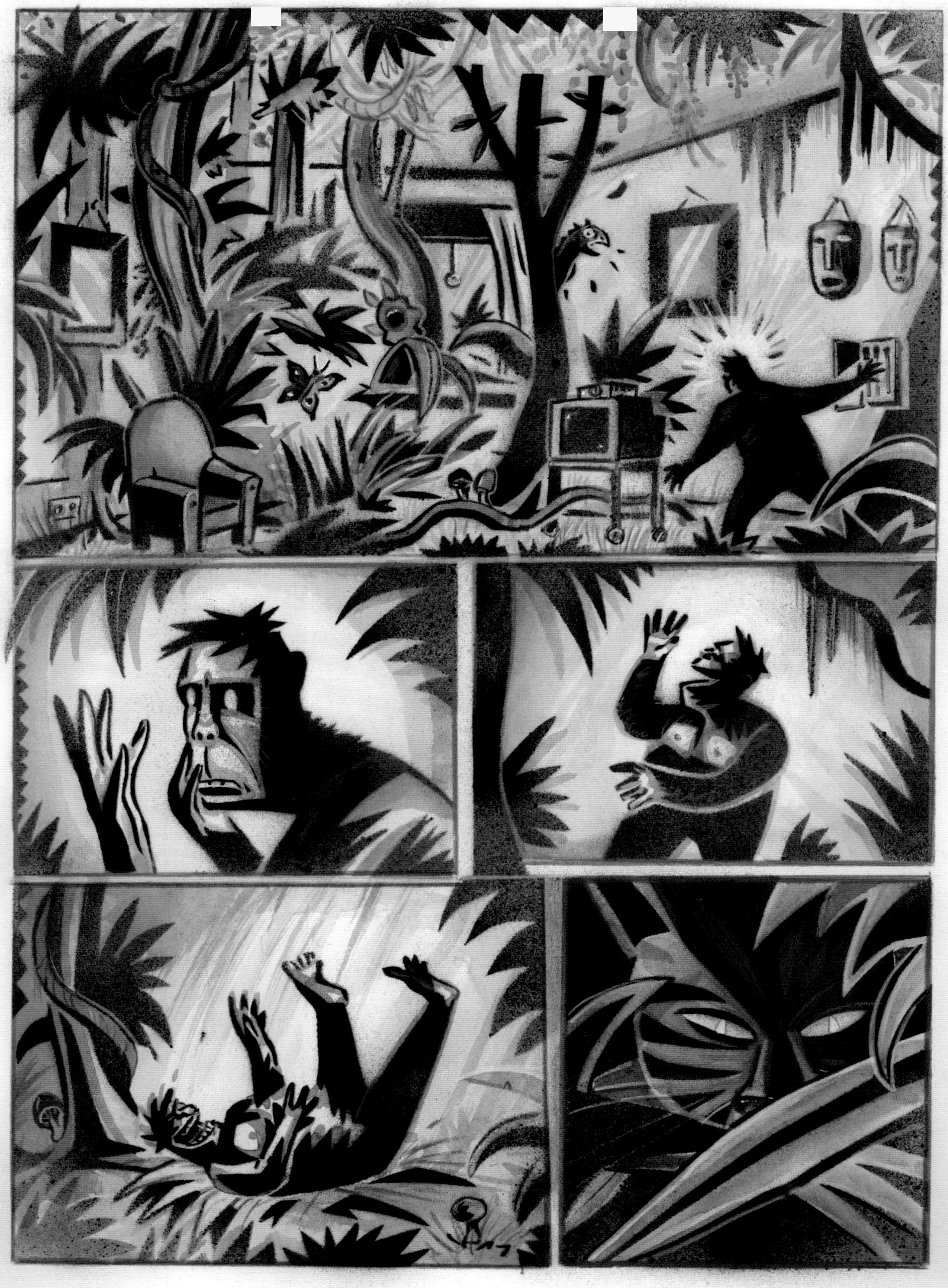

12

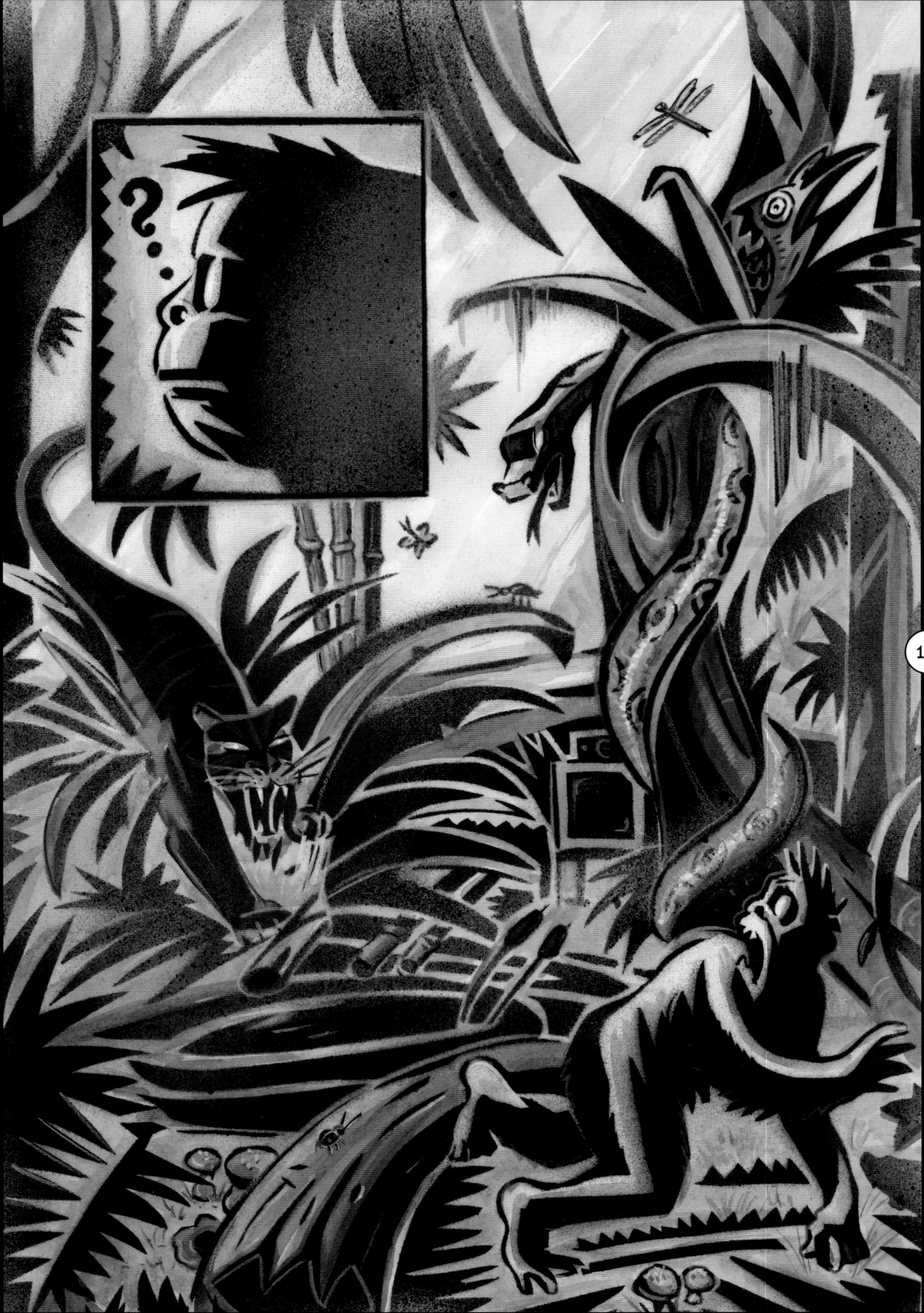
?

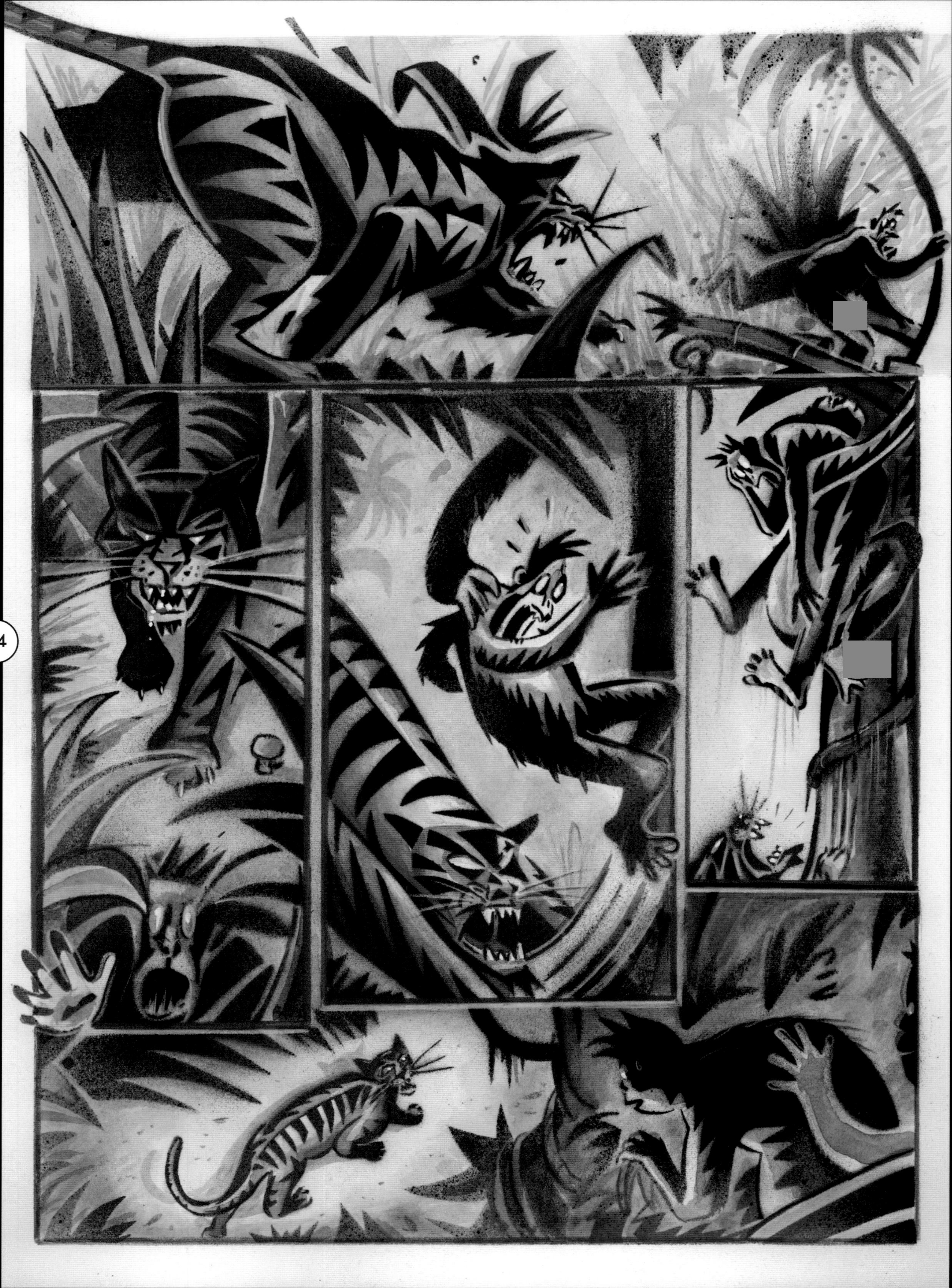

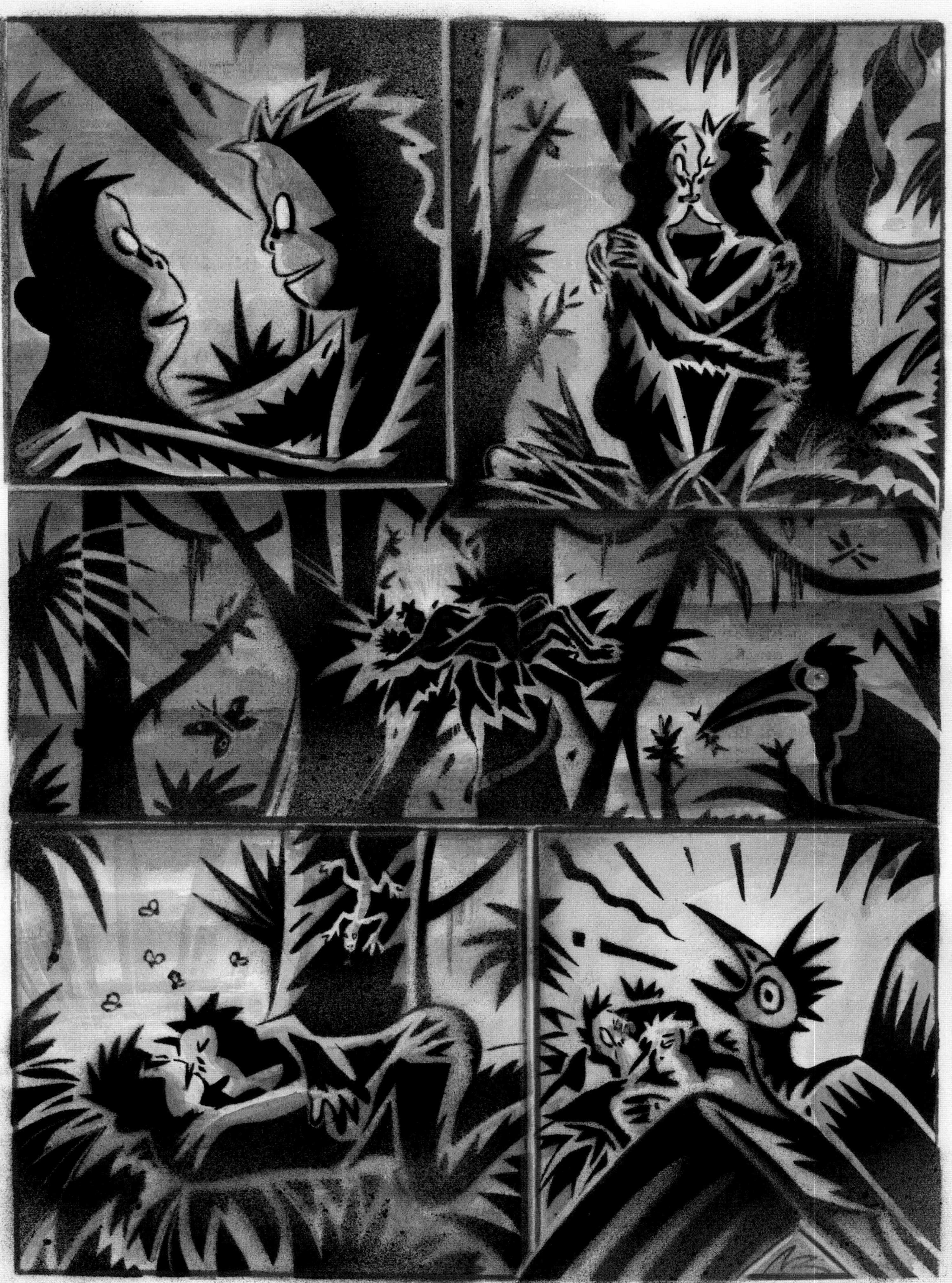

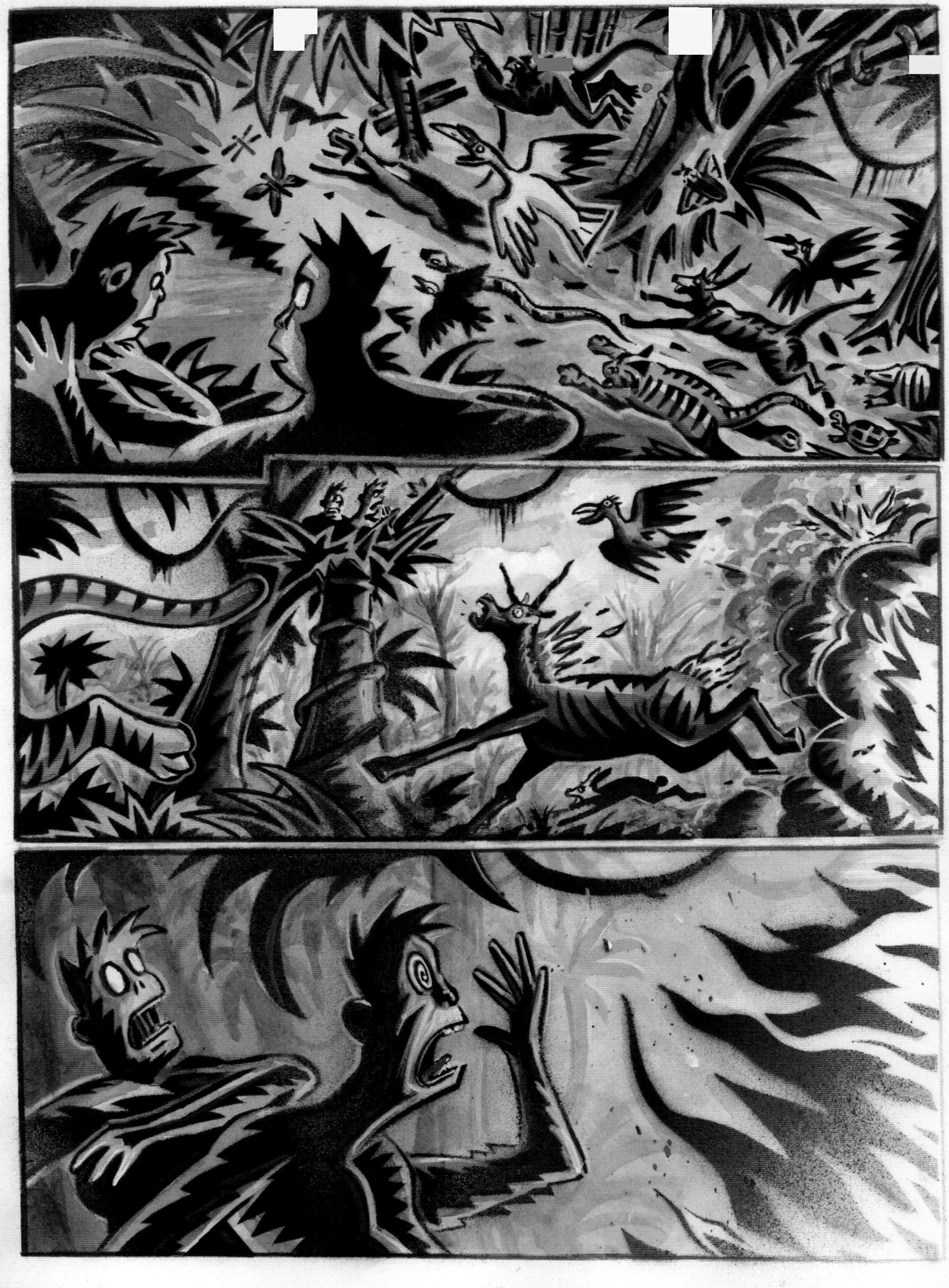

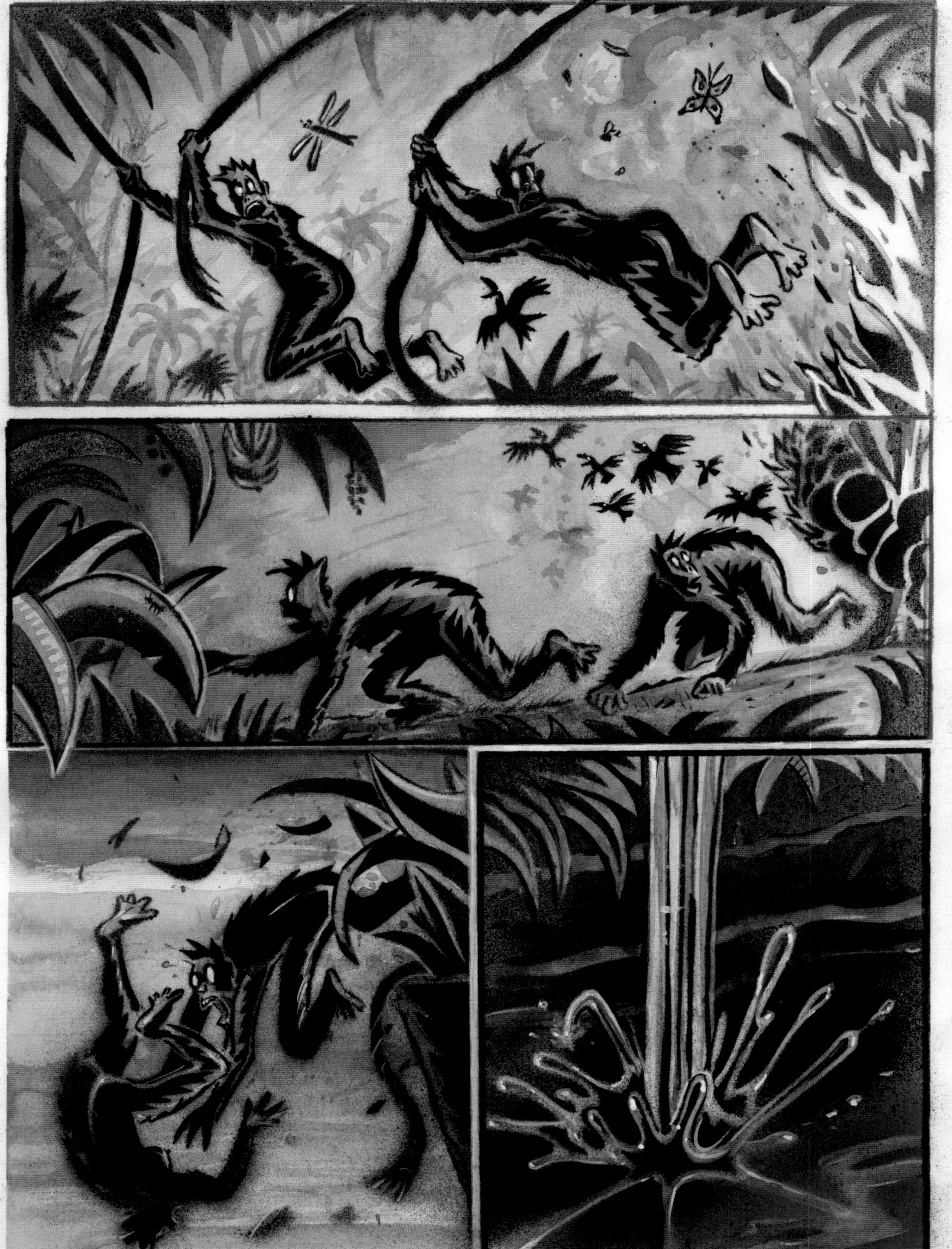

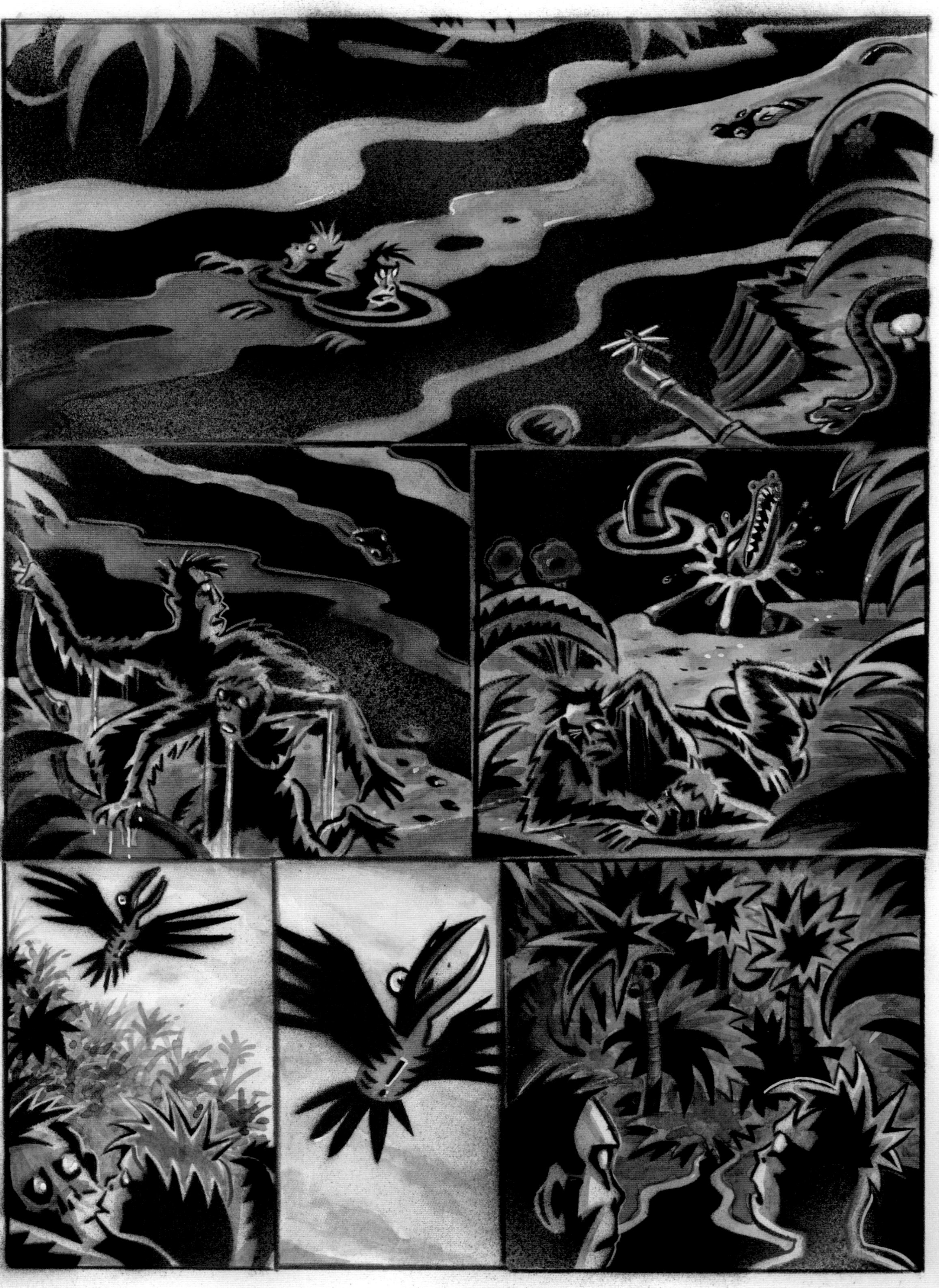

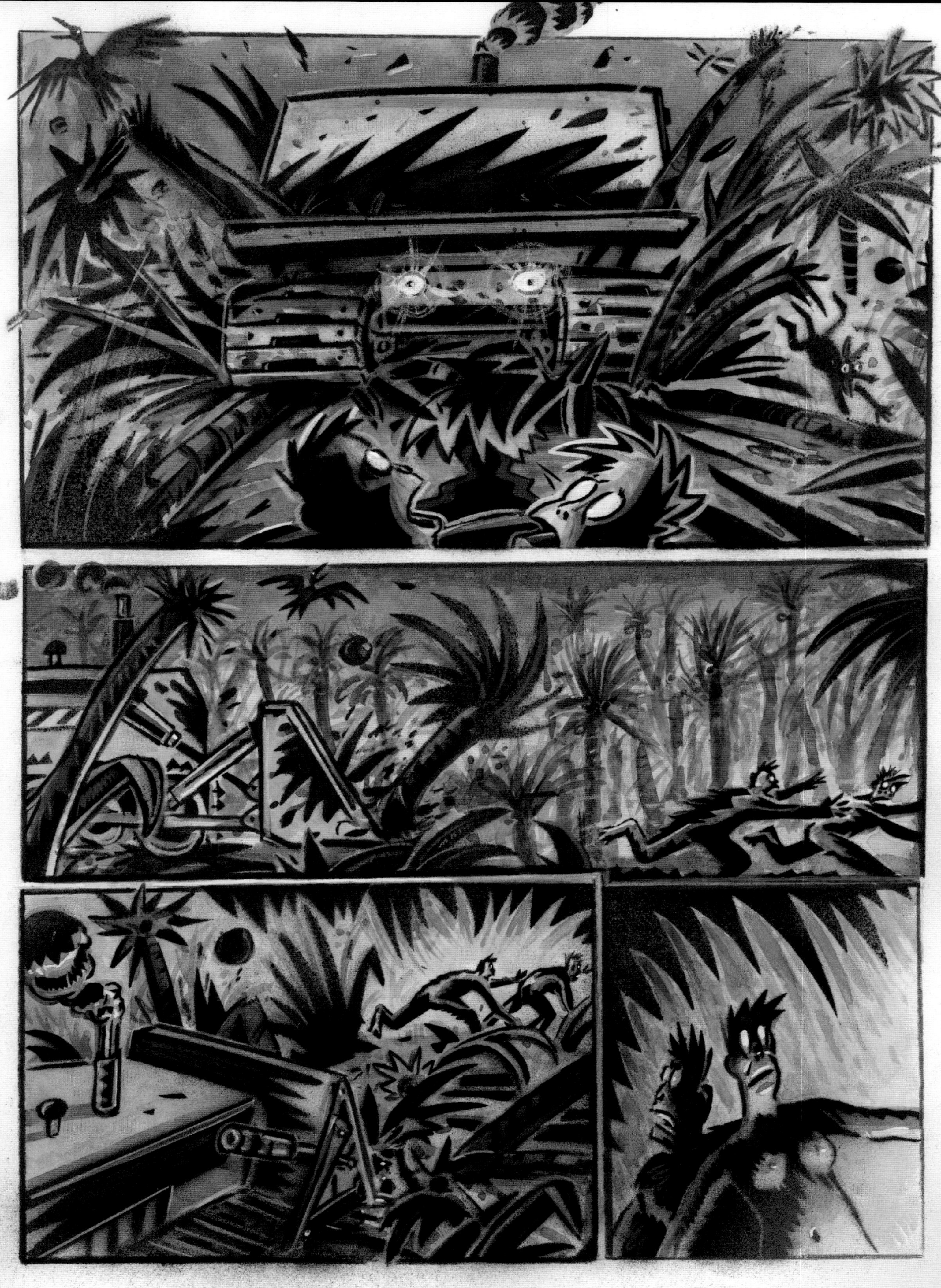

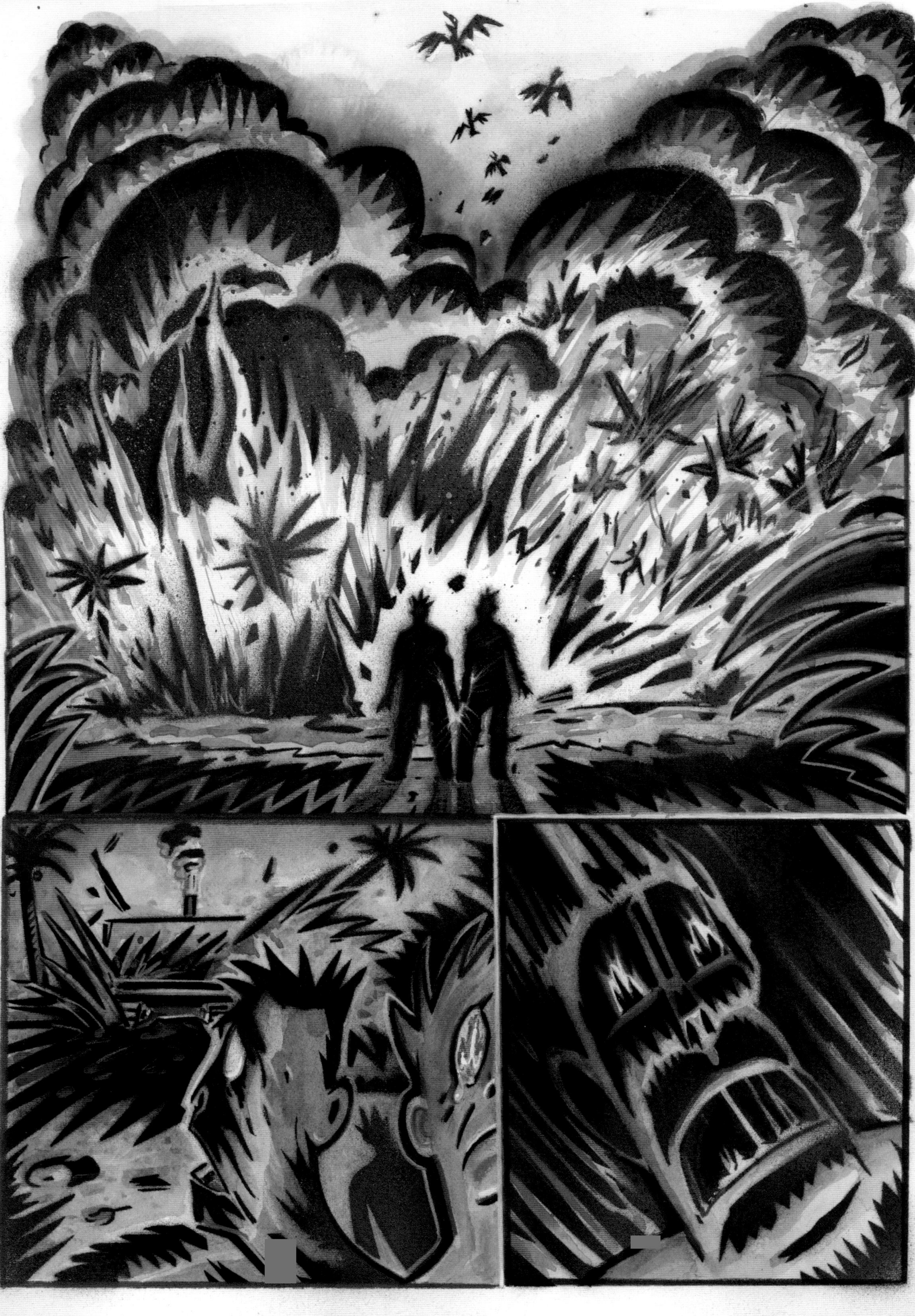

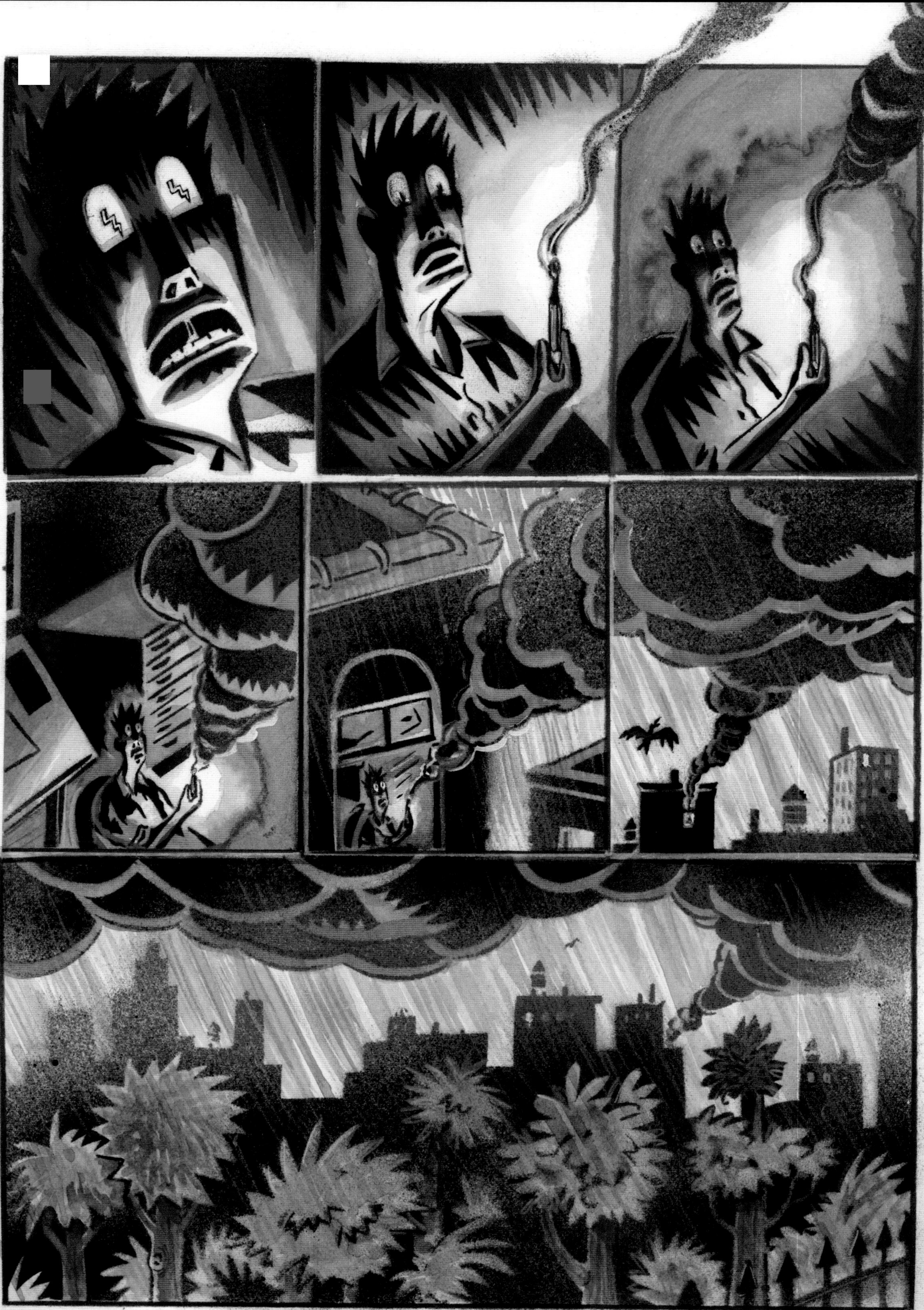

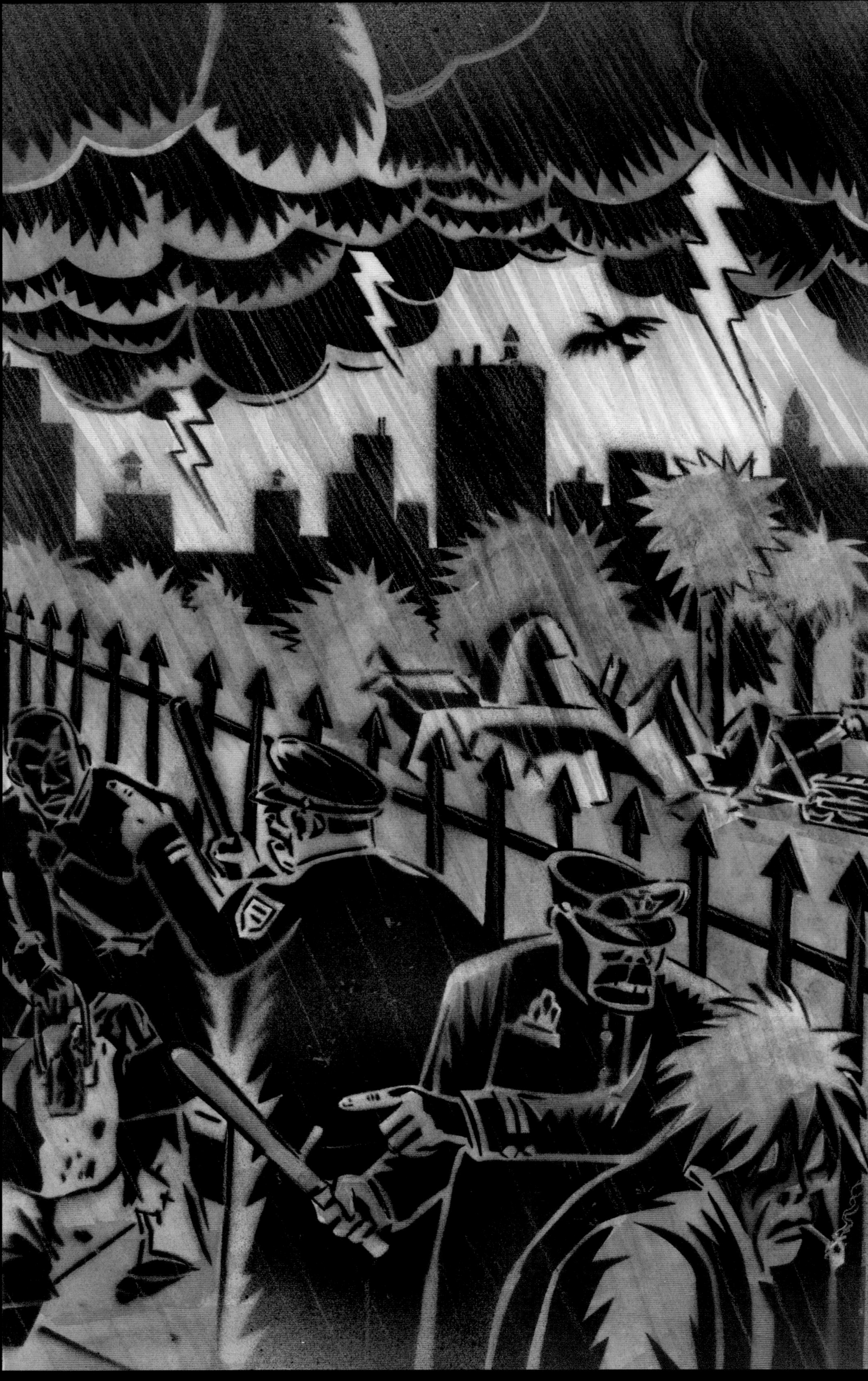

The End

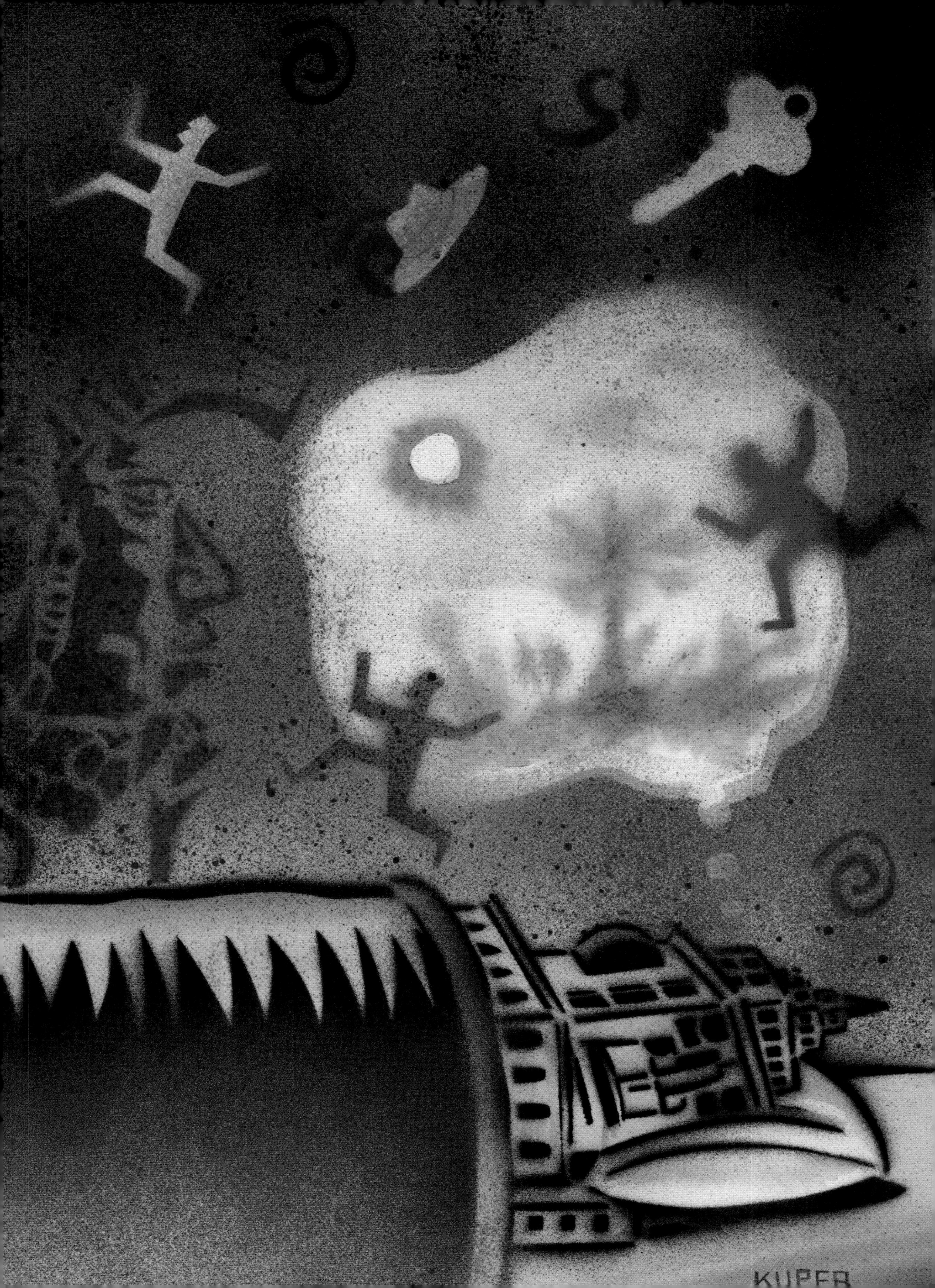
KUPER

NEW YORK NEW YORK

2

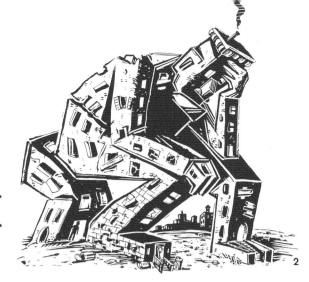

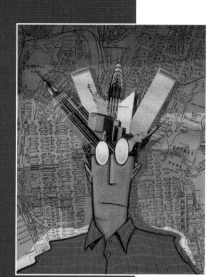

If I have a muse in my career, it would have to be this city. Perhaps *siren* is a better description, however, as the powerful calling that drew me here—and continues to seduce me—has always been just as likely to dash my head against the unforgiving pavement.

The city is ever full of mystery and allure, engaging me as if I'd only just arrived. After 23 years, I still find it surprisingly inscrutable. Like many artists before me, I will spend my days trying to express this fascination, hoping to capture the wonder that New York incites.

A walk down Broadway is certain to include various degrees of awe, excitement, horror and amusement. Of course, this can prove to be daunting when all I want is coffee to go and a bagel with a schmear.

1

I've been down on the farm and I don't like it.
I'm a city girl from the word go.
KUPER

3

Previous Page: Cover, *New York Mix*, 1992.

1. Cover, *New York, New York*, a collection of Kuper's comics published by Fantagraphics Books, 1987.

2. Cover, the *Baffler*, 1995.

3. Cover, *Duplex Planet* #6, 1994.

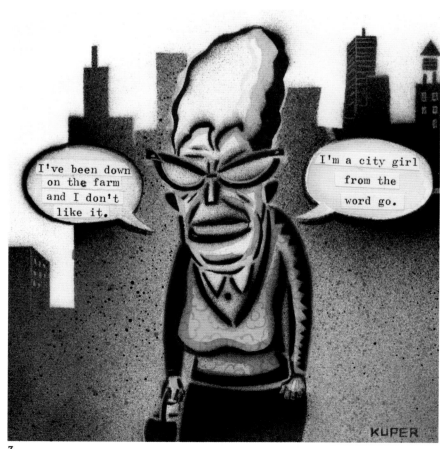

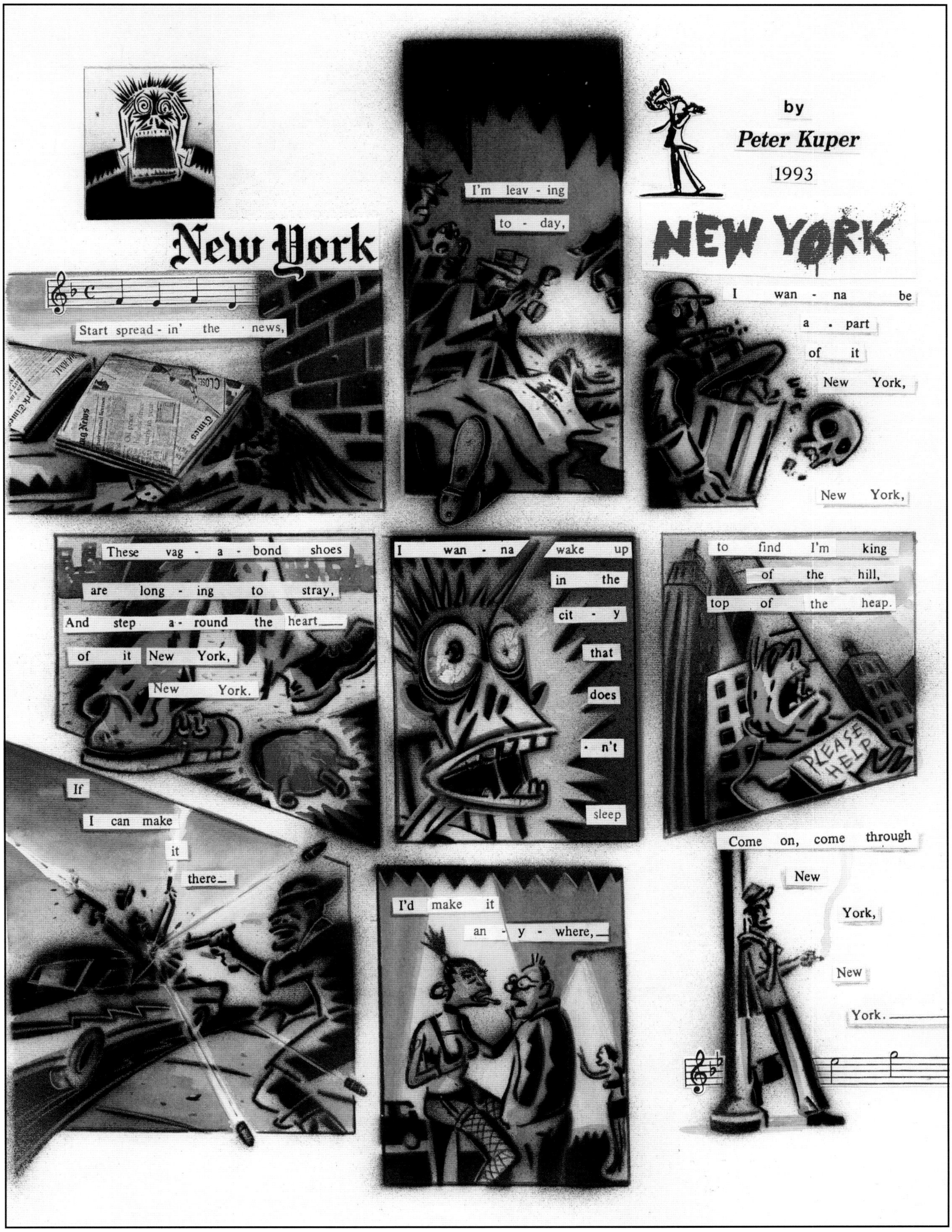

by
Peter Kuper
1993
New York
NEW YORK
Start spread - in' the news,
I'm leav - ing
to - day,
I wan - na be
a part
of it
New York,
New York,
These vag - a - bond shoes
are long - ing to stray,
And step a - round the heart___
of it New York,
New York.
I wan - na wake up
in the
cit - y
that
does
- n't
sleep
to find I'm king
of the hill,
top of the heap.
PLEASE HELP
If
I can make
it
there___
I'd make it
an - y - where,___
Come on, come through
New
York,
New
York.___

New York, New York,
published in *Pulse!* magazine, 1993.

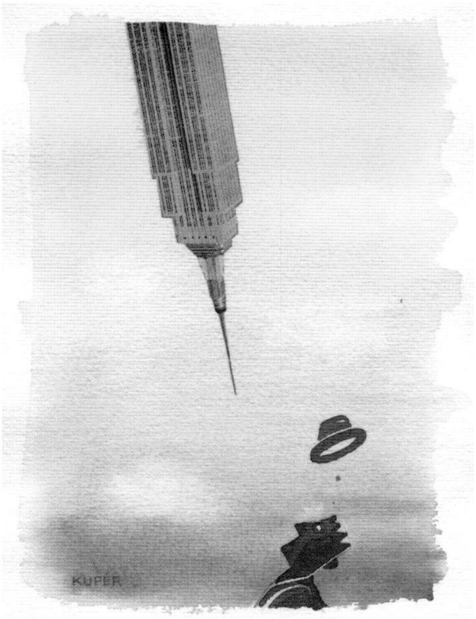
KUPER

1

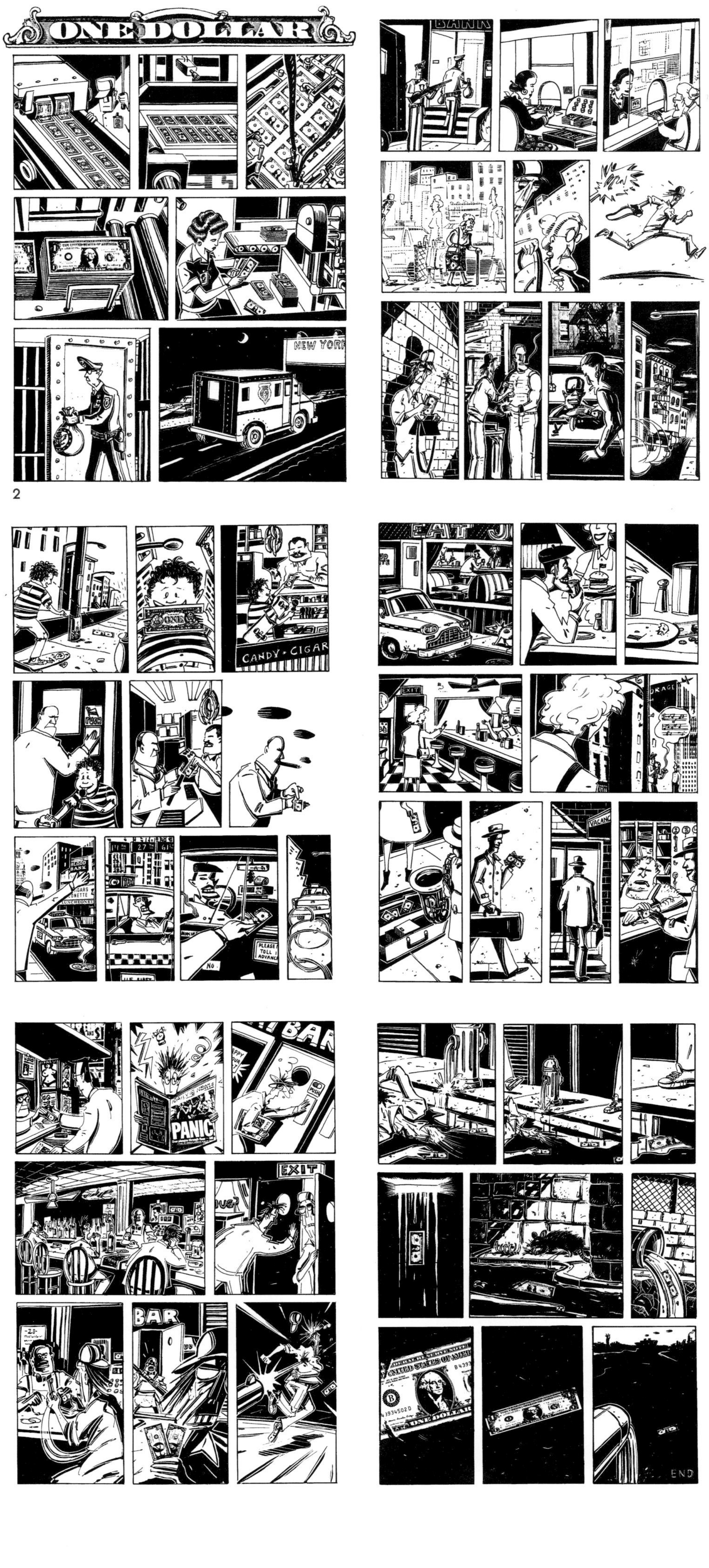
ONE DOLLAR
BANK
NEW YORK
CANDY • CIGAR
EXIT
VACANCY
PLEASE TOLL ADVANCE
PANIC
EXIT
BAR
BAR
END

2

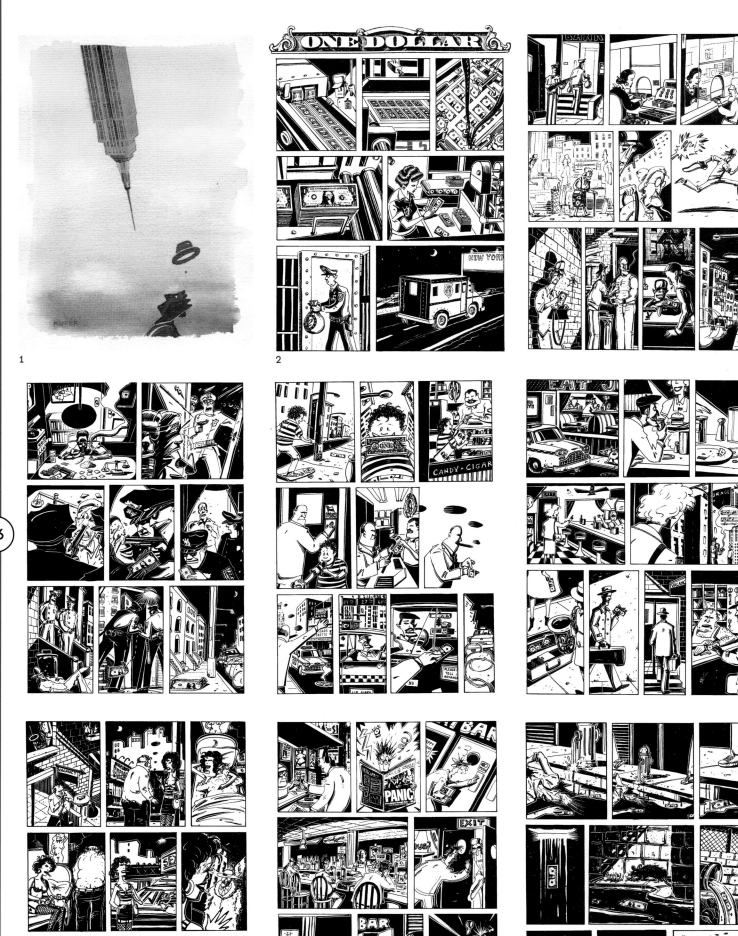

1. Unpublished sketchbook page, 1994.
2. *One Dollar*, published in *Heavy Metal*, 1988.

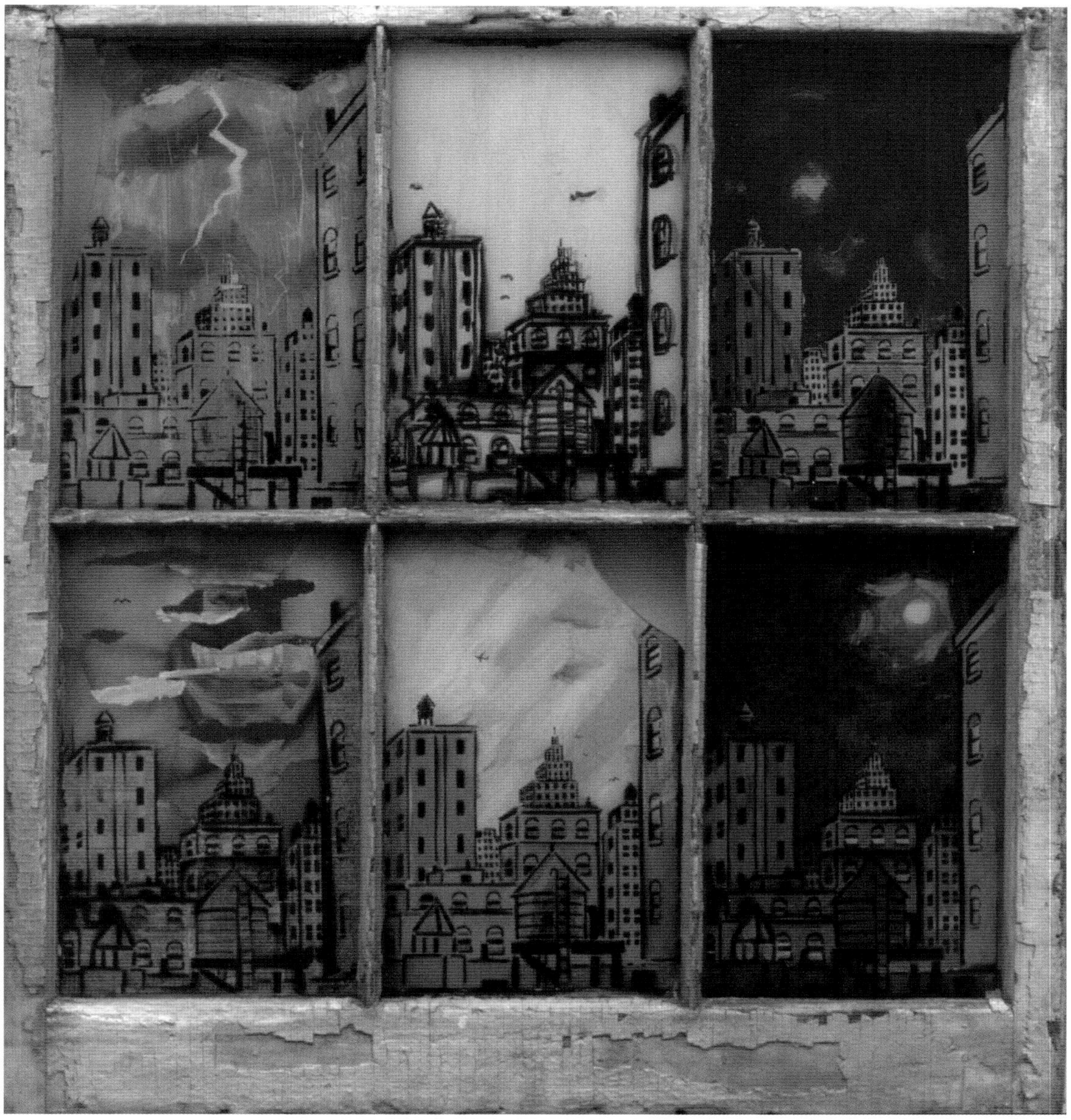

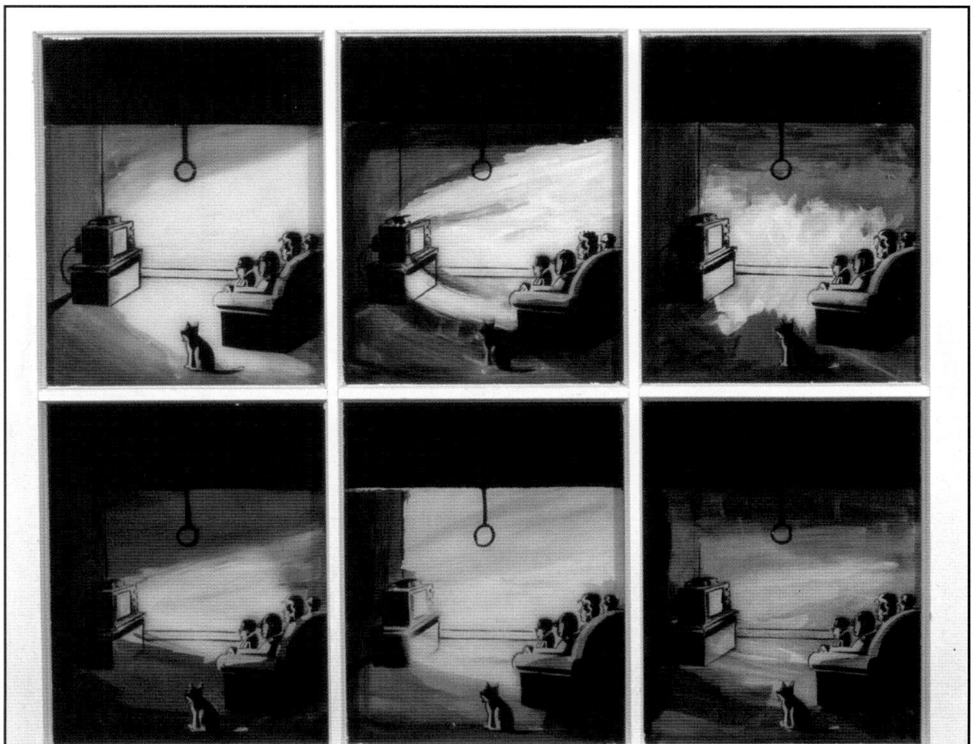

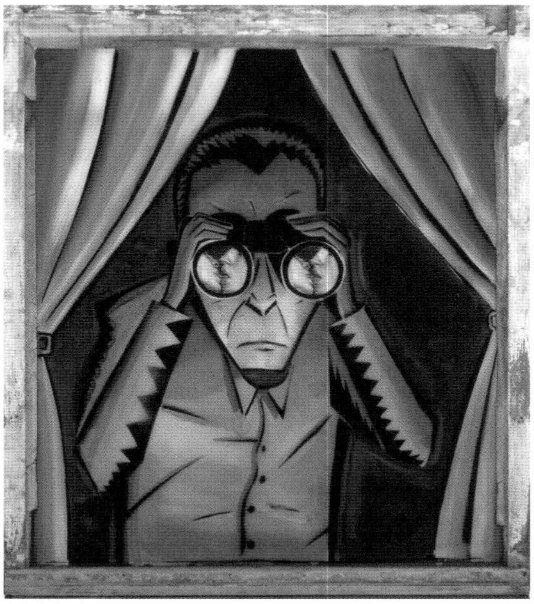

In 1993, I began producing a series of paintings on discarded windows after noting the resemblance of the frames to comic strip panels. Painting in layers on the back of the glass also mirrored the process of creating animation cels. For inspiration, all I had to do was look out my window.

Top: *Six Hours*, Unpublished, 1993.
Above: *Nuclear Family*, Unpublished, 1993.
Right: *Busy Bodies*, published in *Poz* magazine, 1994.

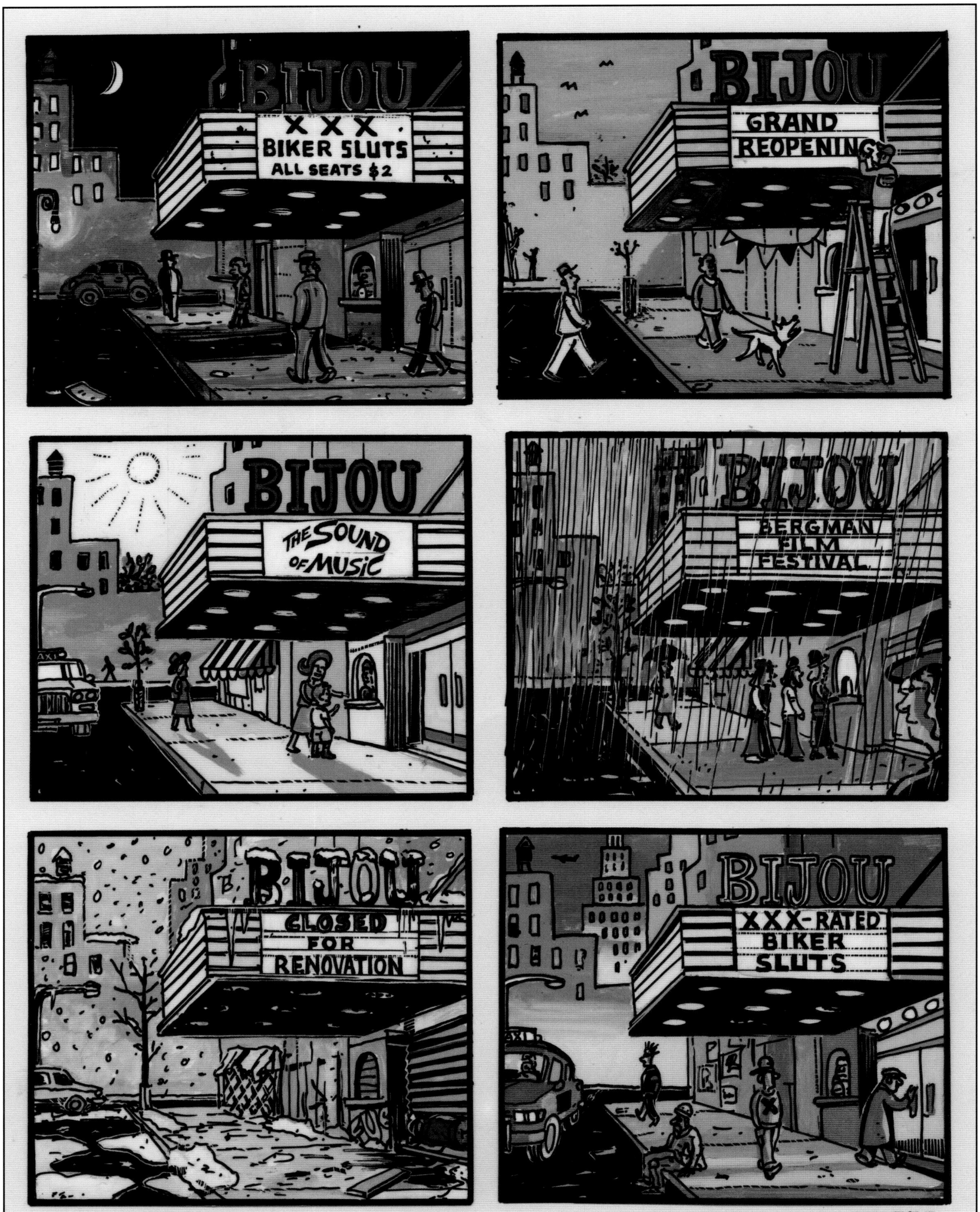

BIJOU
XXX
BIKER SLUTS
ALL SEATS $2
BIJOU
GRAND
REOPENING
BIJOU
THE SOUND OF MUSIC
BIJOU
BERGMAN
FILM
FESTIVAL
BIJOU
CLOSED
FOR
RENOVATION
BIJOU
XXX-RATED
BIKER
SLUTS
1998
KUPER

Sinema City, Unpublished, commissioned by the *New Yorker*, 1998.

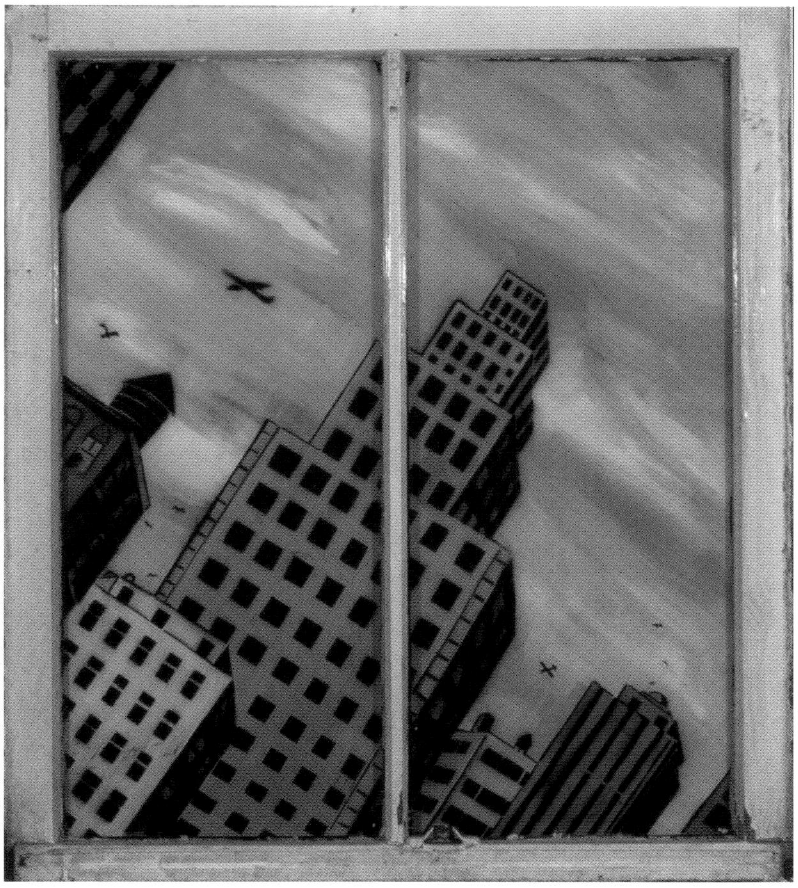

Above: *Vertigo*, Unpublished, 1993.
Below: Unpublished sketchbook page, 1986.
Right: *My Checker Past*, New York Daily News, 1999.

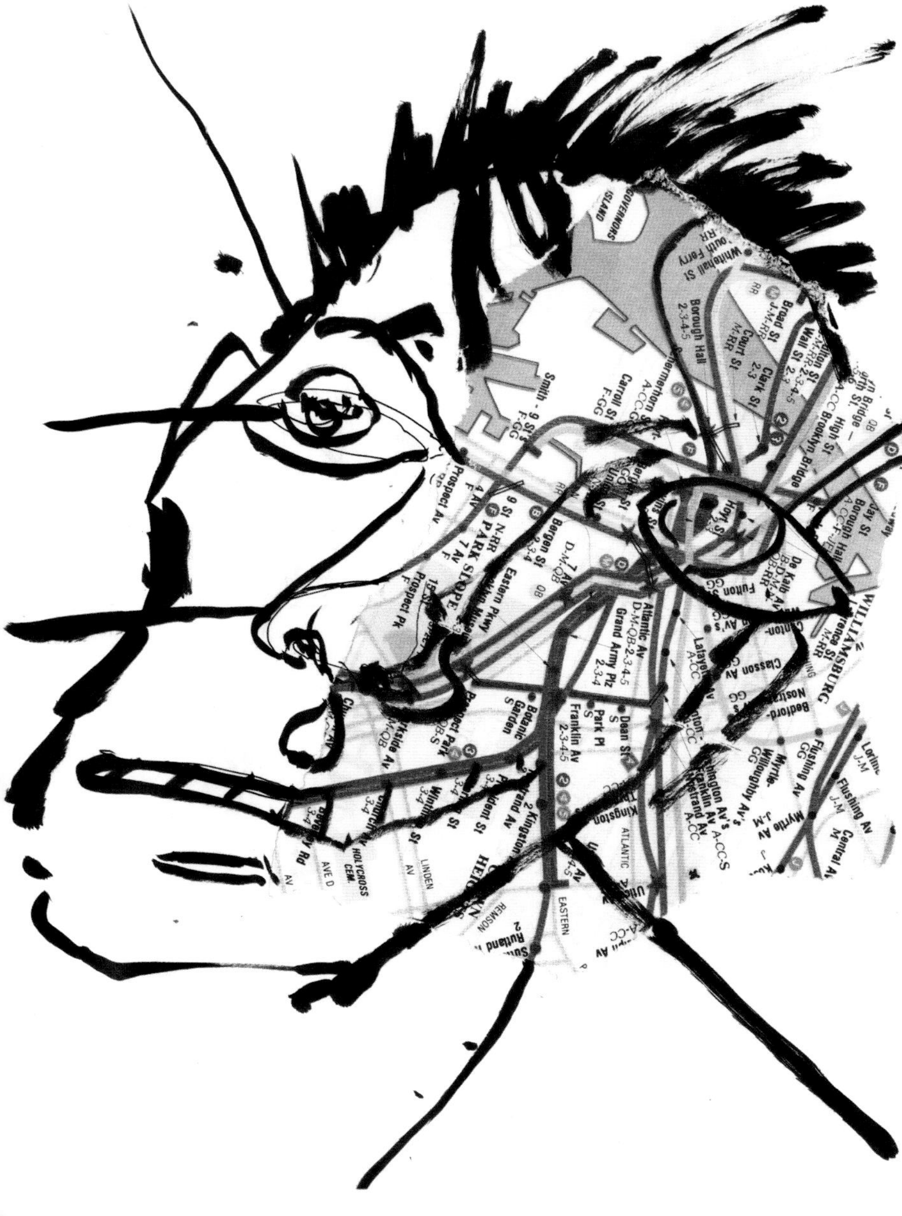

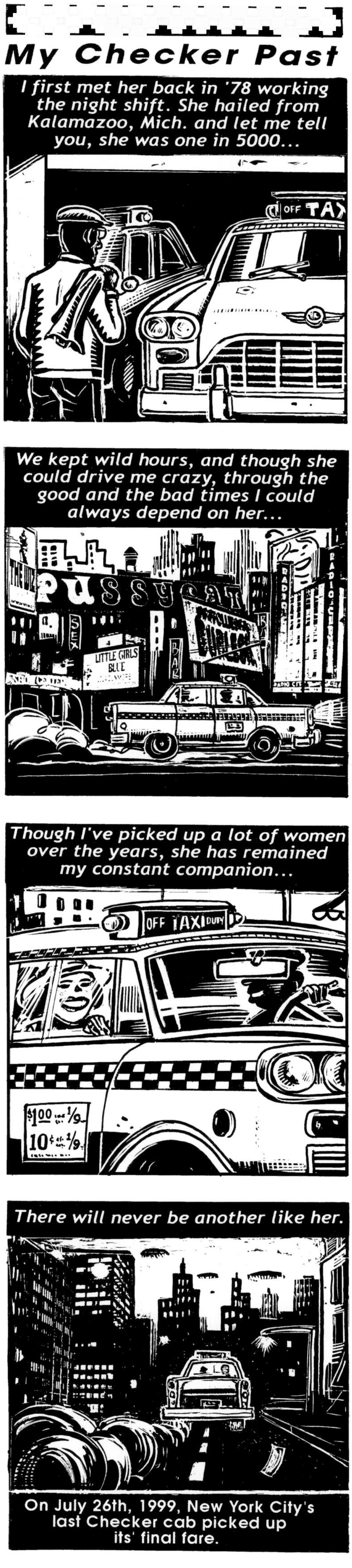

My Checker Past
I first met her back in '78 working the night shift. She hailed from Kalamazoo, Mich. and let me tell you, she was one in 5000...
OFF TAX
We kept wild hours, and though she could drive me crazy, through the good and the bad times I could always depend on her...
PUSSYCAT
SEX
LITTLE GIRLS BLUE
RADIO
Though I've picked up a lot of women over the years, she has remained my constant companion...
OFF TAXI DUTY
There will never be another like her.
On July 26th, 1999, New York City's last Checker cab picked up its' final fare.

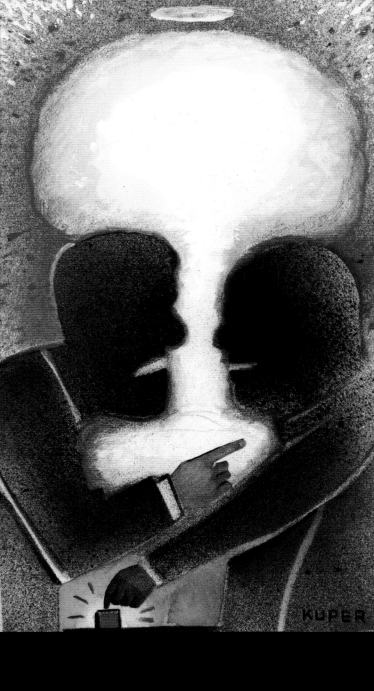

KUPER

on Time, 1999

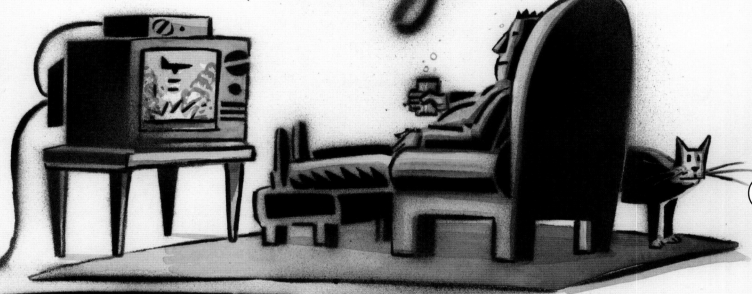

Bombs Away, published in *Heavy Metal*, 1991.

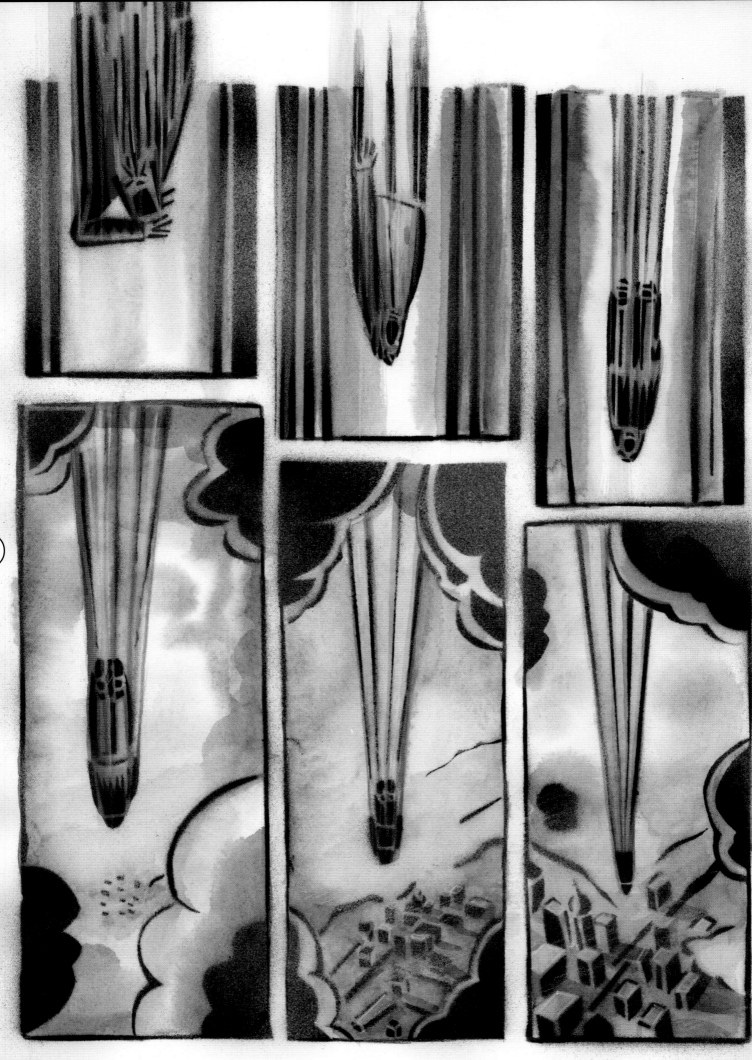

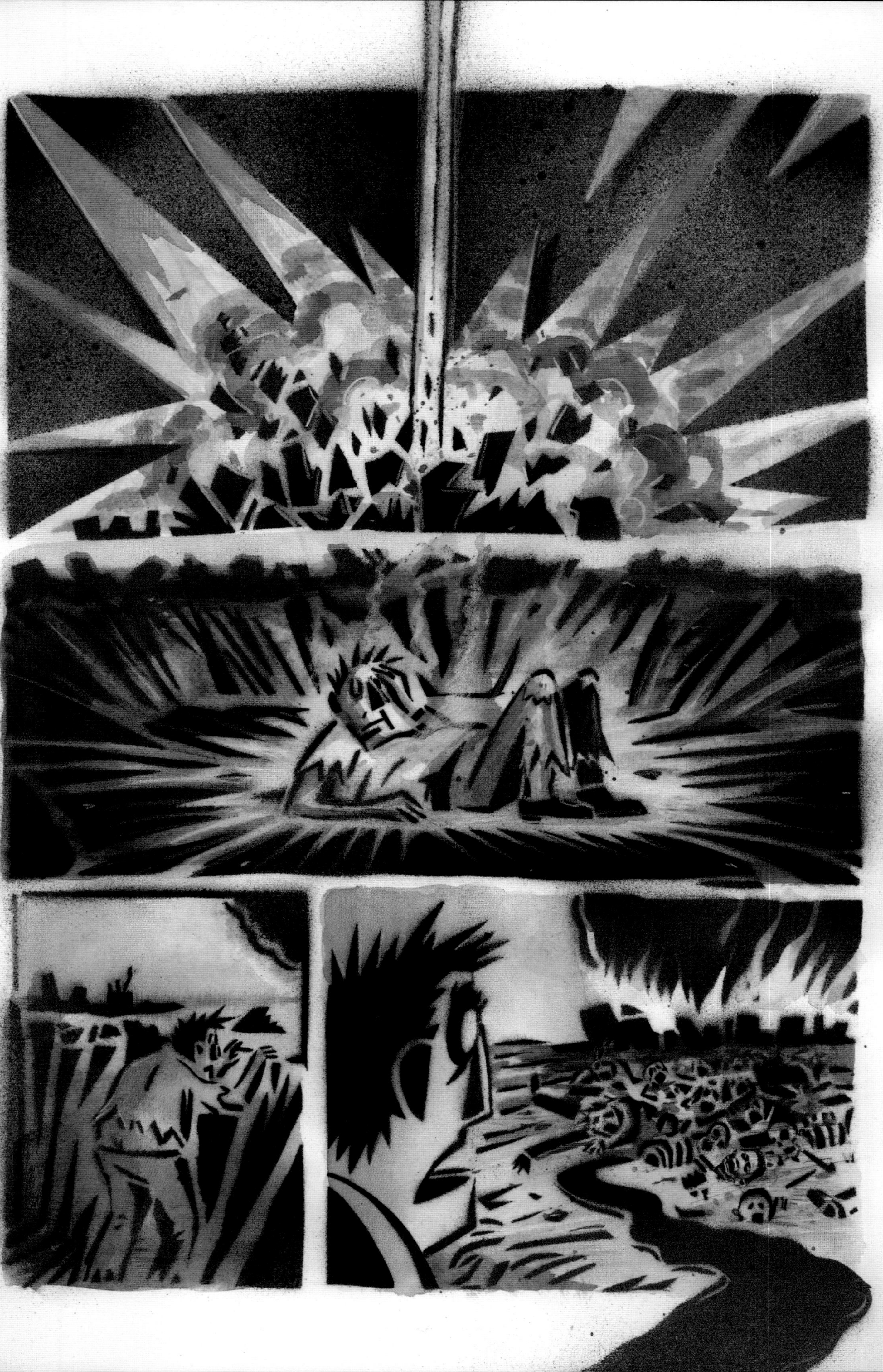

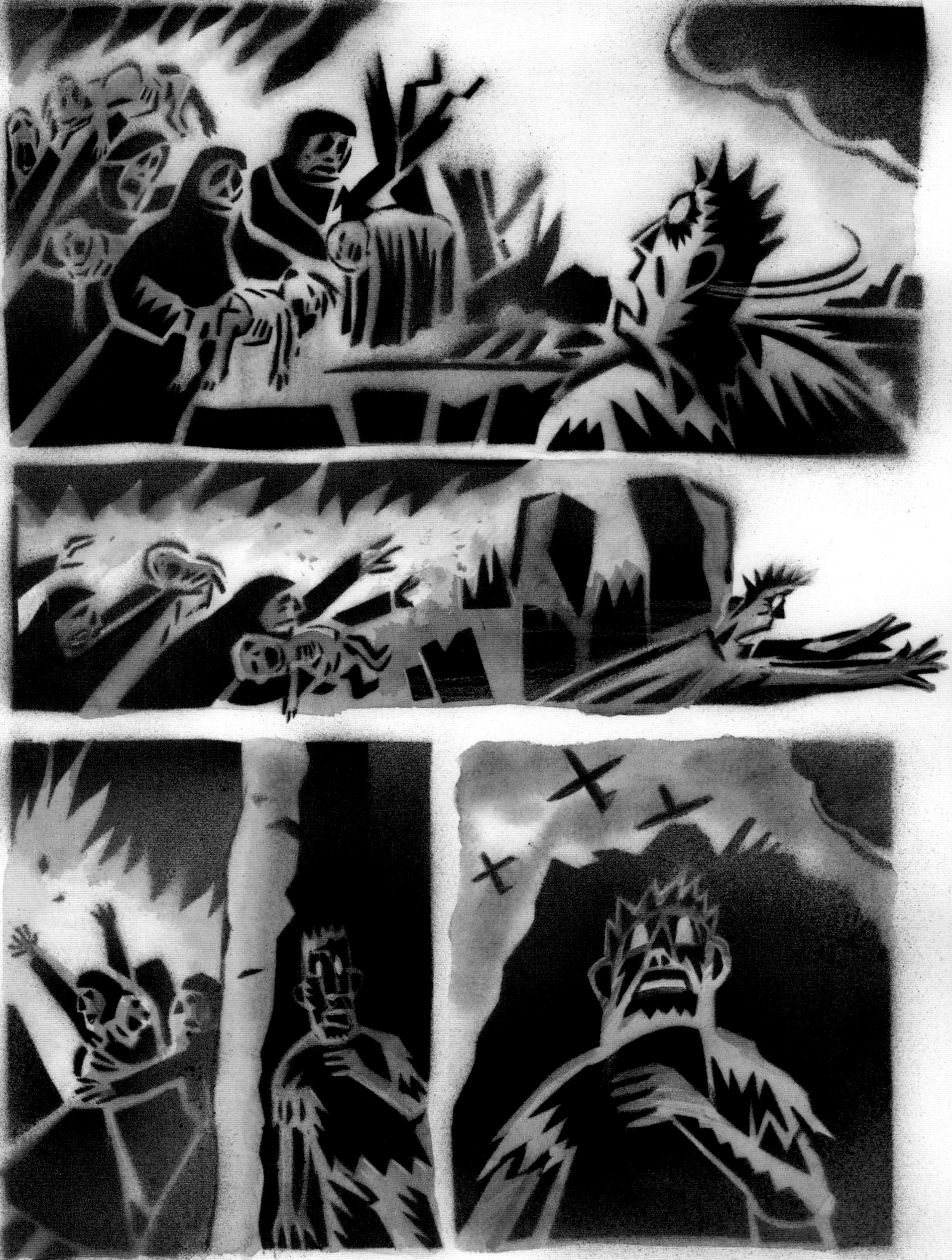

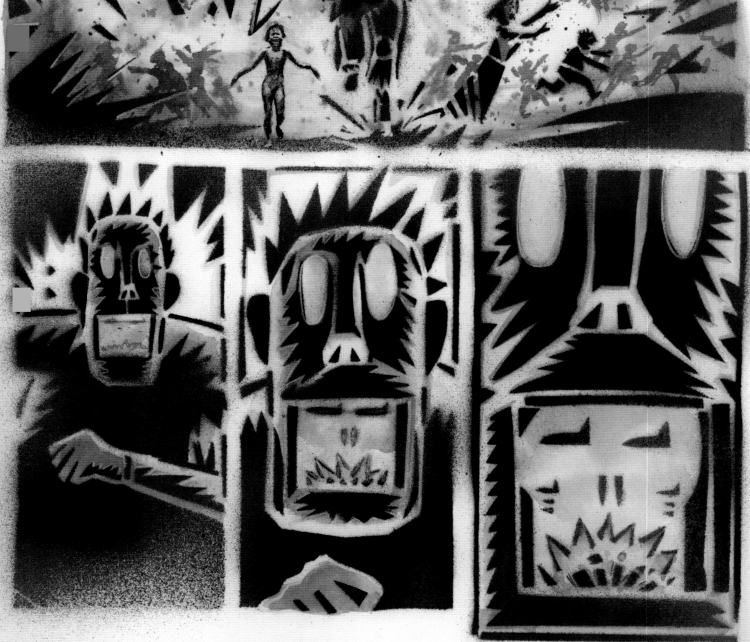

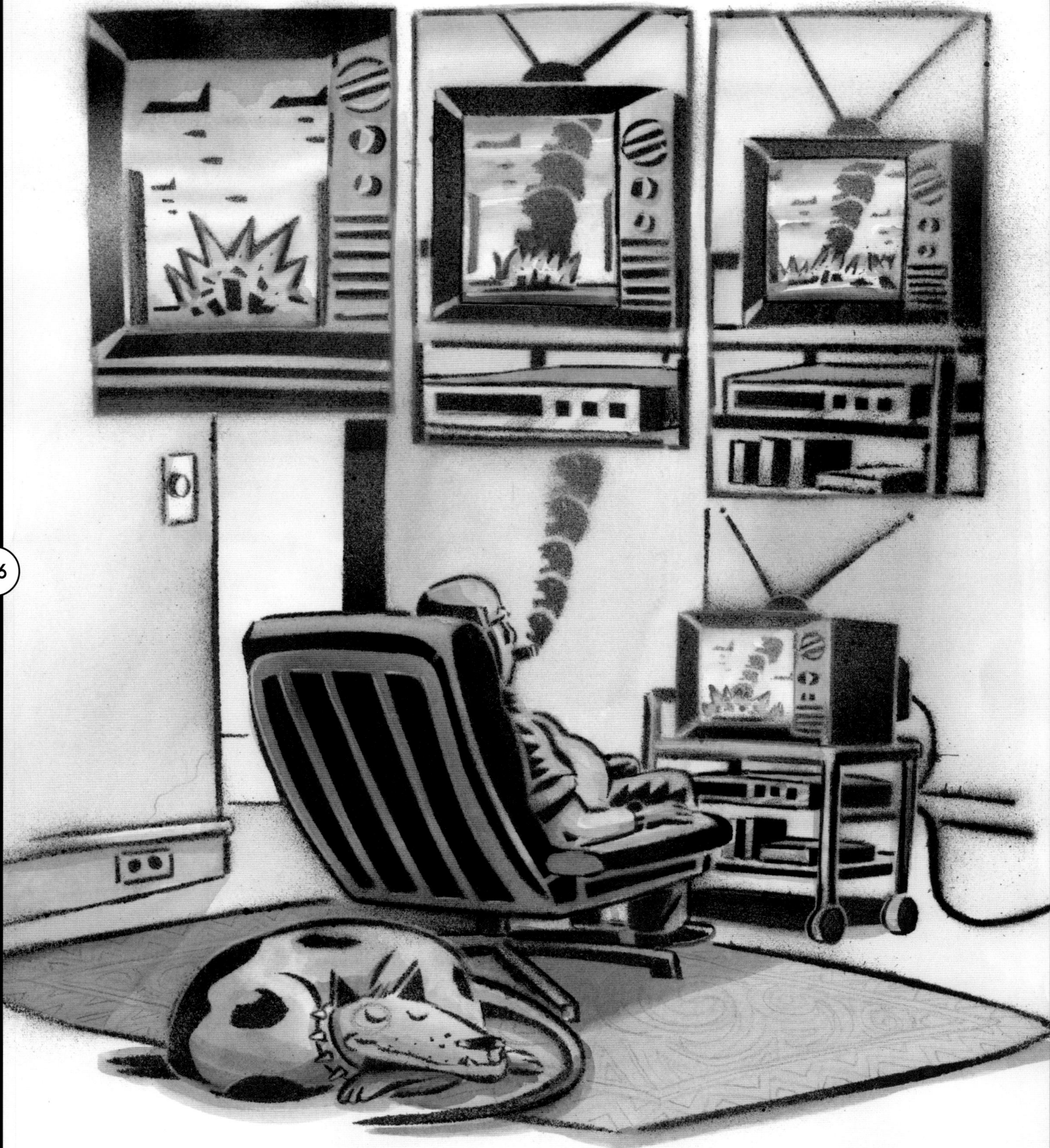

SEND IN THE MARINES

OPERATION POTATOE PEEL

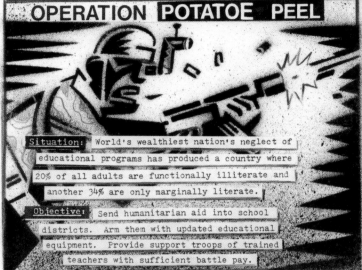

Situation: World's wealthiest nation's neglect of educational programs has produced a country where 20% of all adults are functionally illiterate and another 34% are only marginally literate.

Objective: Send humanitarian aid into school districts. Arm them with updated educational equipment. Provide support troops of trained teachers with sufficient battle pay.

OPERATION MARLBORO MAN

Situation: Large independent nation locked in the stranglehold of multinational corporations that

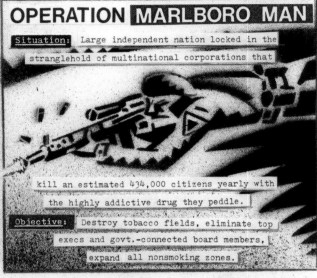

kill an estimated 434,000 citizens yearly with the highly addictive drug they peddle.

Objective: Destroy tobacco fields, eliminate top execs and govt.-connected board members, expand all nonsmoking zones.

OPERATION CARDBOARD BOX

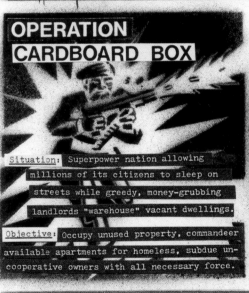

Situation: Superpower nation allowing millions of its citizens to sleep on streets while greedy, money-grubbing landlords "warehouse" vacant dwellings.

Objective: Occupy unused property, commandeer available apartments for homeless, subdue uncooperative owners with all necessary force.

OPERATION SOUND BODY

Situation: Highly industrialized country has 37 million citizens without health

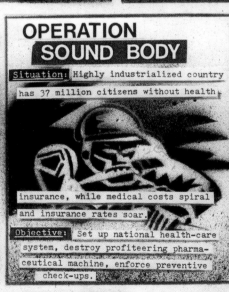

insurance, while medical costs spiral and insurance rates soar.

Objective: Set up national health-care system, destroy profiteering pharmaceutical machine, enforce preventive check-ups.

OPERATION FAMILY VALUES

Situation: Fanatical religious minority trying to control

nation's women and gays through terrorism and ignorance.

Objective: Secure clinic facilities, provide educational materials to populace, maintain separation of church and state.

OPERATION DESERT TESTING

Situation: Group of govt.-supported mad scientists in cahoots with industry are releasing nuclear substances into the atmosphere. Under the guise of "national security" they are radiating their own citizens.

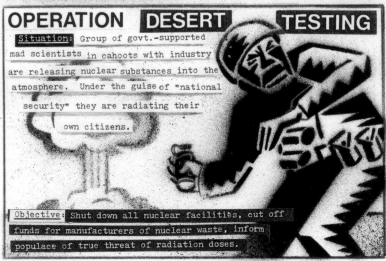

Objective: Shut down all nuclear facilities, cut off funds for manufacturers of nuclear waste, inform populace of true threat of radiation doses.

OPERATION SELF-DESTRUCT

Situation: Once powerful nation being destroyed by military junta who are draining country's resources for munitions manufacturers' gains.

Objective: Dismantle military-industrial complex, redirect funds to desperately needed social programs and infrastructure repair.

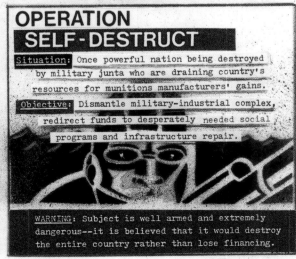

WARNING: Subject is well armed and extremely dangerous--it is believed that it would destroy the entire country rather than lose financing.

©1992

PETER KUPER

Send in the Marines, published in the *Village Voice,* 1992.

Art by James Romberger

WORLD WAR 3

The following is a modified version of an essay published in the *American Institute of Graphic Arts Journal*, 1993.

In 1979, frustrated by the lack of outlets for political graphics and comics, Seth Tobocman and I decided to form our own magazine. With the hostage crisis in Iran, the threat of nuclear conflict, and Ronald Reagan running for president, *World War 3 Illustrated* seemed like an appropriate title.

WW3 follows in the tradition of polemical magazines such as the *Masses*, but it is also a child of the underground comix of the sixties and seventies. Like many of those cartoonists, we're documenting events and experiences often overlooked by the mainstream media. The first couple of issues took on world concerns, but we realized very quickly that it wasn't necessary to look far beyond the streets of New York to find meaningful subject matter: the daily warfare waged by landlords evicting and gentrifying whole neighborhoods, police turning a blind eye to rampant drug dealing, and a government cutting aid to social service programs. With World War III, the event, taking place in our very own city, and casualties seen in almost every doorway, our first mission was to get *WW3*, the magazine, from the printer to the newsstand.

Distribution is always the most difficult aspect of any publishing venture, and we ran into a wall of resistance at every turn. Retailers considered the magazine too political to be placed with comics and too comic-bookish to sit with "serious" magazines. As a result, our first issues were distributed primarily by hand. The solution to this problem thankfully came in the form of Ruth Schwartz, who distributed alternative music (including records by The Dead Kennedys), and was not put off by controversial material. Through her company, Mordam Records, she began getting *WW3* into Tower Records, magazine racks and alternative bookshops, as well as into many of the traditional outlets for comics. Thus, *WW3* was able to expand from a small group of artists and an erratic publishing schedule, to dozens of contributors, a rotating editorial board, and bi-annual publication.

WORLD WAR 3
$2
Illustrated
FIRST ISSUE
Cola

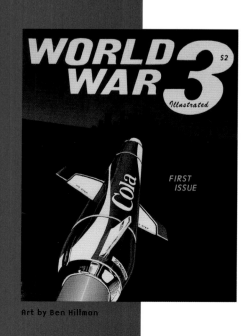

Art by Ben Hillman

Each issue of *WW3* begins with a meeting of possible contributors, who attend by invitation and word-of-mouth. Typical contributors include professional illustrators, writers and fine artists, first-time cartoonists, as well as anarchists and pacifists, squatters and homeowners, feminists, and people who would rather not be categorized. The focus of a given issue is determined by current events or topics that artists feel compelled to explore. Sometimes, no theme is set until the material itself suggests a direction. Previous issues have examined religion,

WORLD WAR 3

No. 2

$2

Illustrated

This issue: Twin Titans Threaten Earth!

Art by Seth Tobocman

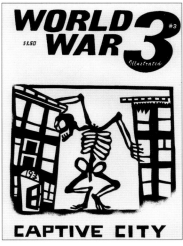

WORLD WAR 3

#3

$1.50

Illustrated

CAPTIVE CITY

Art by Michael Roman

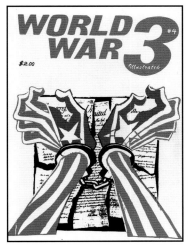

WORLD WAR 3

#4

$2.00

Illustrated

Art by Seth Tobocman

WORLD WAR 3

#5

Illustrated

Don't blame GOD

Art by Peter Kuper

WORLD WAR 3

#6

$2.00

Illustrated

Art by Seth Tobocman

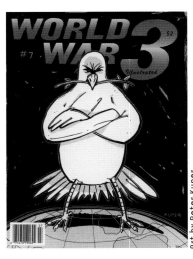

WORLD WAR 3

#7

$2

Illustrated

KUPER

Art by Peter Kuper

WORLD WAR 3

#8

$2.00

Illustrated

Art by Aki Fujiyoshi

WORLD WAR 3

#9

$2

Illustrated

FEDERAL RESERVE NOTE OF AMERICA

UNITED STATES

H50510499

WASHINGTON, D.C.

ONE

0499C

ONE DOLLAR

THE BUCK STOPS

Art by Peter Kuper

WORLD WAR 3

#10

$3

Illustrated

Art by Sue Coe

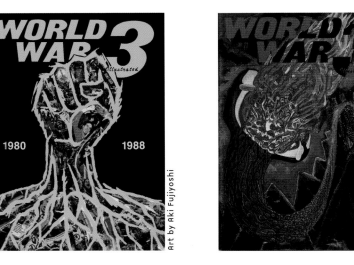

WORLD WAR 3

Illustrated

1980   1988

Art by Aki Fujiyoshi

WORLD WAR 3

Illustrated

THE RIOT ISSUE

Art by Helena Munninghoff

WORLD WAR 3

#12

Illustrated

$4.00

ECOLOGY HEALTH CRISIS

Art by James Romberger and Maguerite Van Cook

WORLD WAR 3
#13
Illustrated

Art by James Romberger

Art by Sabrina Jones

WORLD WAR 3
$3
#16
Illustrated
HERSTORIES

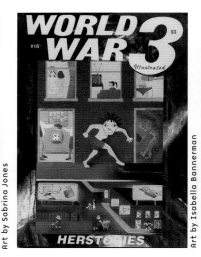

Art by Isabella Bannerman

#17

Art by Seth Tobocman

fascism, biohazards, and personal experiences ranging from the daily struggles of squatting a building, to the difficulties a woman can encounter simply taking a walk around the block.

A core of contributing editors oversee each issue from the first planning meeting to the last press check, and handle all of the grunt work in between. Although the magazine has become self-supporting, it is all produced on a voluntary basis, neither editors nor contributors receiving any pay for their efforts. It can takes five or six meetings to gather an issue together, and these range in tone from mutual enthusiasm to violent disagreement. Even though the subjects we're dealing with aren't neat little packages that can be tied up without strain, we join together with a shared goal. It's this group effort that has created 28 powerful issues over the last 21 years.

Although the covers of *WW3* are printed in color, the interiors have always been in black and white. Keeping our printing costs down has enabled us to keep *WW3* affordable for our readership. This has certain asthetic drawbacks, but even with the limitations of black and white newsprint, many artists have published some of their finest work to date in *WW3*. Eric Drooker's comics, which eventually took shape in his award-winning graphic novel *Flood!*, were first serialized in *WW3*. James Romberger, whose pastels are now in the permanent collection of New York's Metropolitan Museum of Art, could previously be viewed on our covers and interiors. We also published the first installment of his collaboration with David Wojnarowicz, nearly a decade before DC Comics released the completed work, *Seven Miles a Second*.

In addition to the magazine, *WW3* has acted as an artists' collective, producing and providing graphics for rallies, benefit art shows and activist organizations. In 1990, we mounted a *WW3* retrospective in San Francisco as part of a project opposing Mission Bay gentrification. During the Gulf War, *WW3* artists provided graphics for The Gulf Crisis T.V. Project, produced as an alternative to the sanitized mainstream news coverage of the war. We have also created a number of murals, including a 36-foot comic strip for the alternative Living Theater in New York.

It's no surprise that anyone interested in seeing graphic protests and commentary on the events that shape our lives will be sorely disappointed by the mainstream, which is usually 10 steps behind society's new ideas, problems, and solutions. Was rap music a viable art form only when MTV began broadcasting its videos? Did AIDS strike the heterosexual community only with Magic Johnson? In a world led by a myopic mainstream, the dialogues and debates found in the pages of *WW3* (and most other forms of protest) become even more vitally important. In the end, perhaps *WW3*'s greatest achievement has been its perseverance and ever expanding voice, while apathy was presumed to be the news. After over two decades of publication, *WW3* has not just maintained its vitality and immediacy, it thrives with a whole new generation of contributors and activism.

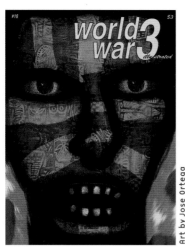

#18
$3
world war 3
illustrated

Art by Jose Ortega

WORLD WAR 3
#19
Illustrated
$3

Art by Sabrina Jones

WORLD WAR 3
#20
$3
Illustrated

Art by Peter Kuper

WORLD WAR 3
$3
Illustrated

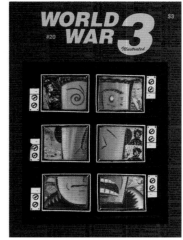

Art by Scott Cunningham

IMPORTANT!
WORLD WAR THREE ILLUSTRATED
AMERICA'S
LOVE AFFAIR
WITH
DECEPTION

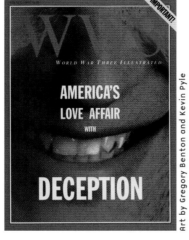

Art by Gregory Benton and Kevin Pyle

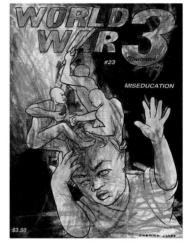

WORLD WAR 3
#23
Illustrated
MISEDUCATION
$3.50
SABRINA JONES

Art by Sabrina Jones

WORLD WAR 3
Illustrated

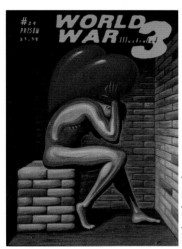

Art by Eric Drooker

WORLD WAR 3
Illustrated
freaks, cults, saints and revelations...

Art by Gig Wailgum

WORLD WAR 3
#26
$3.50
Illustrated
female complaints

Art by Sabrina Jones

WORLD WAR 3
#27
$3.50
Illustrated
LAND AND LIBERTY

Art by Jordan Worley

WORLD WAR 3
28
$ 3.50
Illustrated
WAR
and
GENOCIDE

Art by Miro Stefanovic'

WORLD WAR 3
Illustrated
JARDIN DE LA ESPERANZA

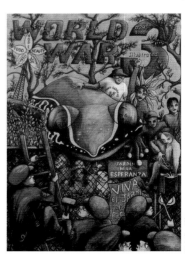

Art by Fly

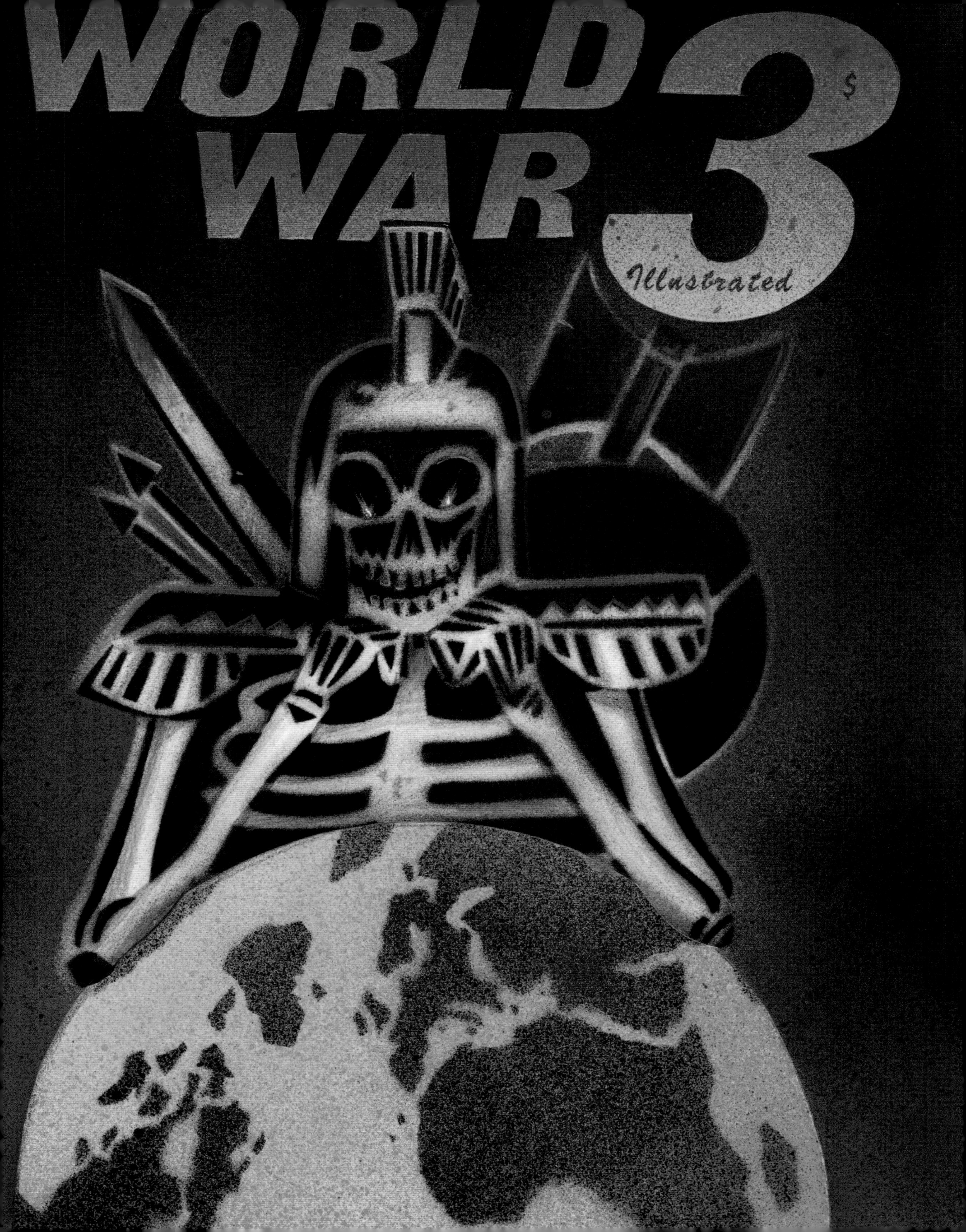
WORLD WAR 3
$
Illustrated

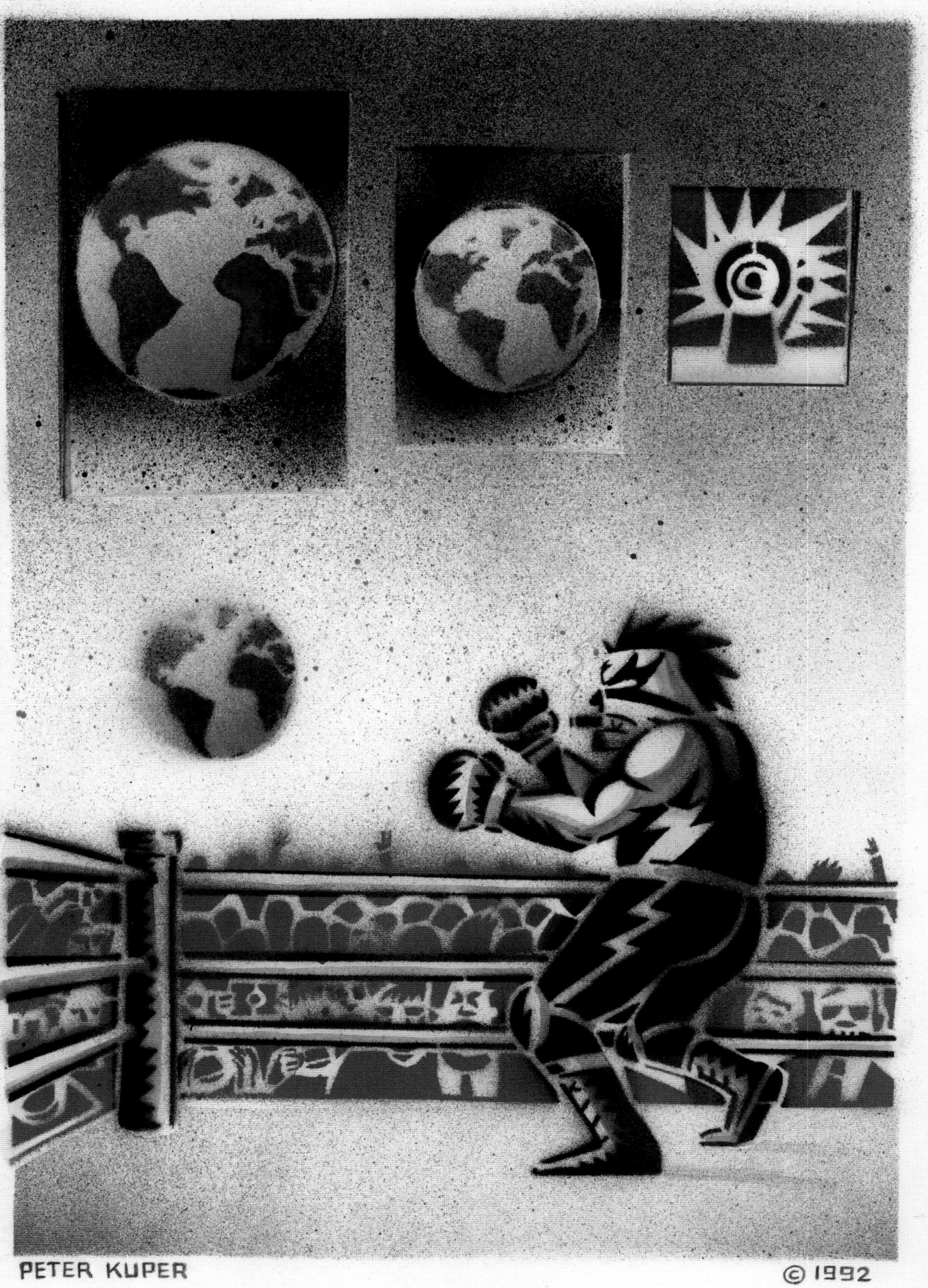
PETER KUPER
© 1992

Above: *TKO*, published in *Heavy Metal*, 1992.
Facing page: Cover of *World War 3* #14, "Gulf War" issue, 1991.

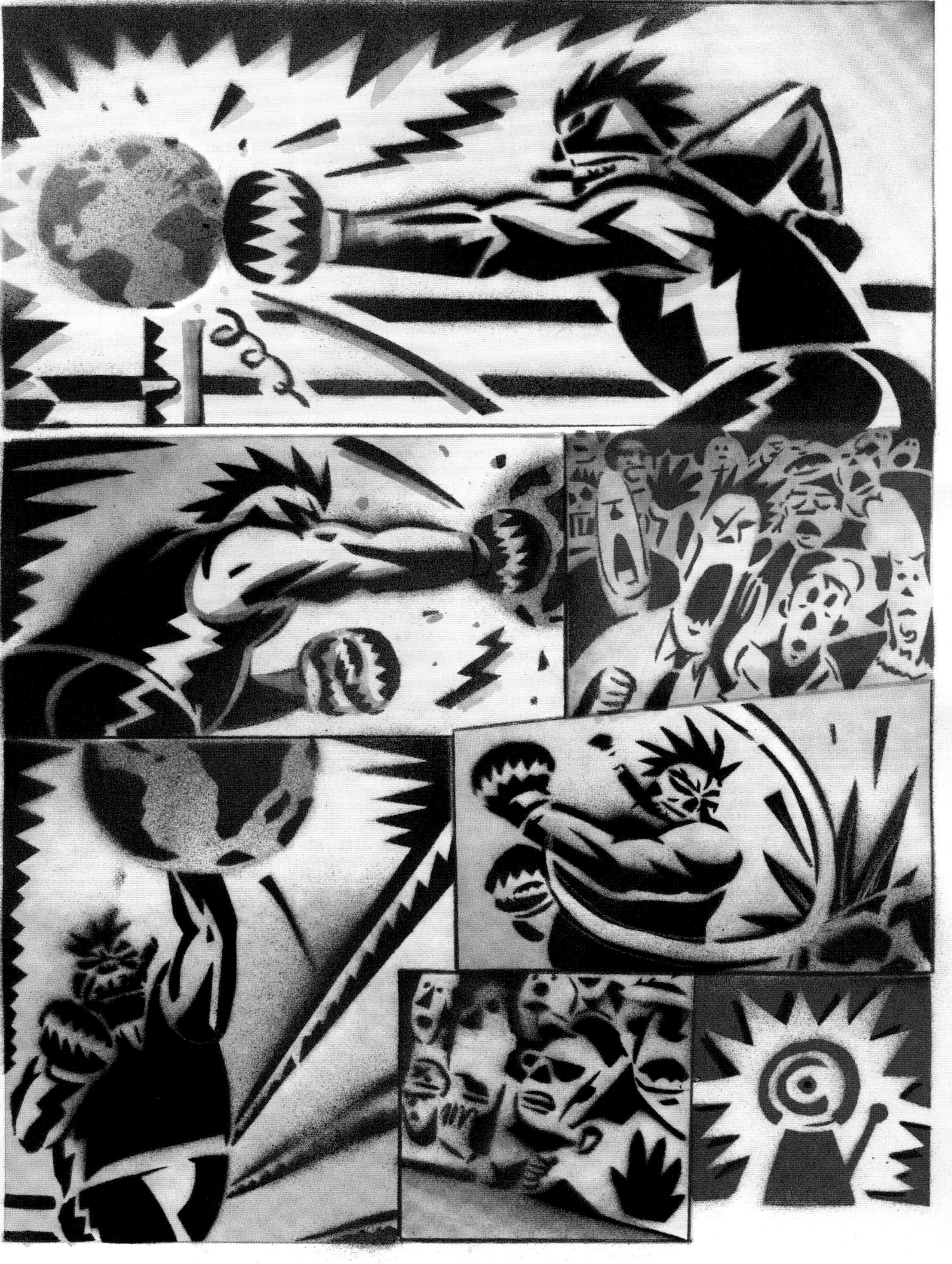

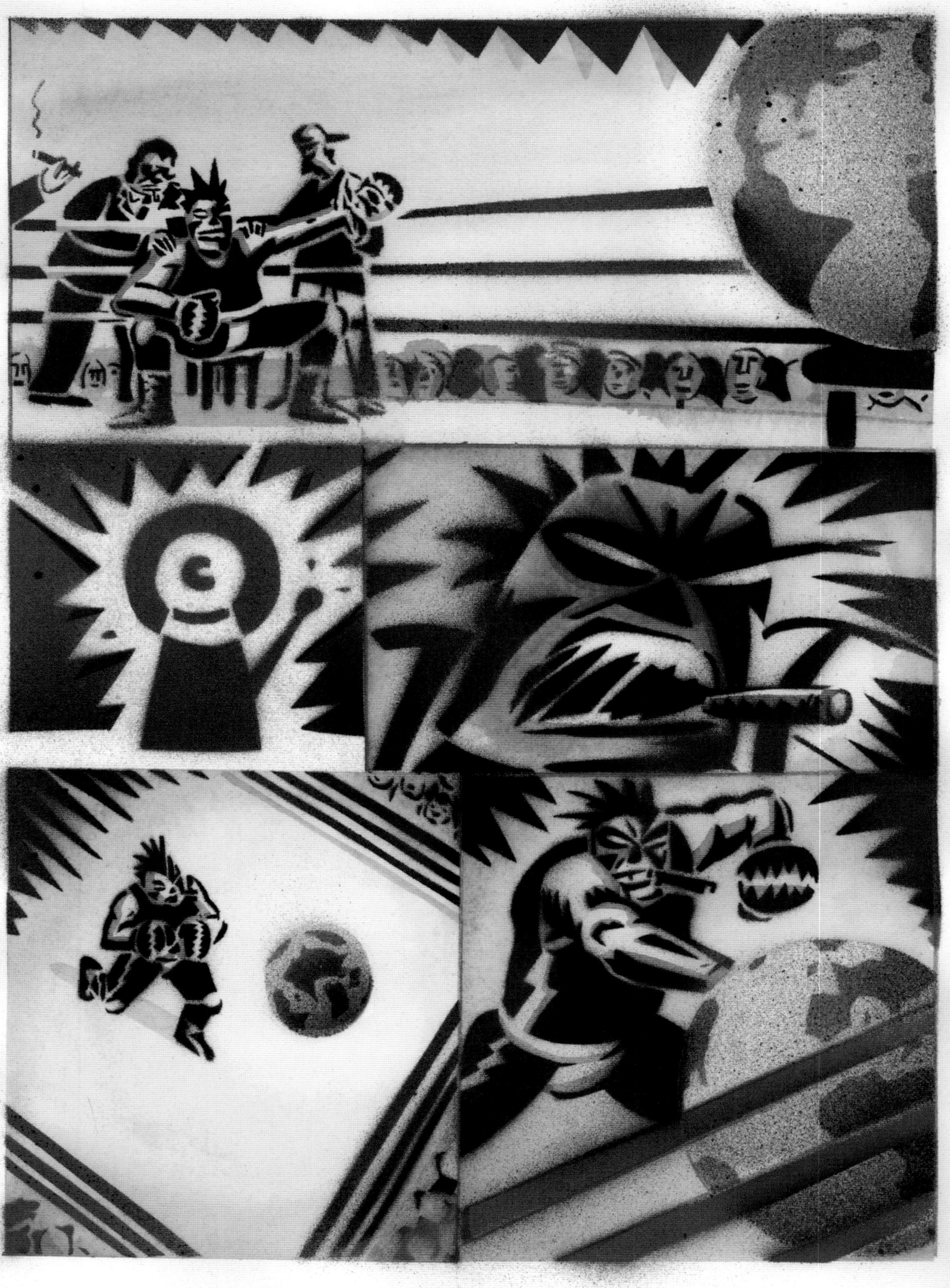

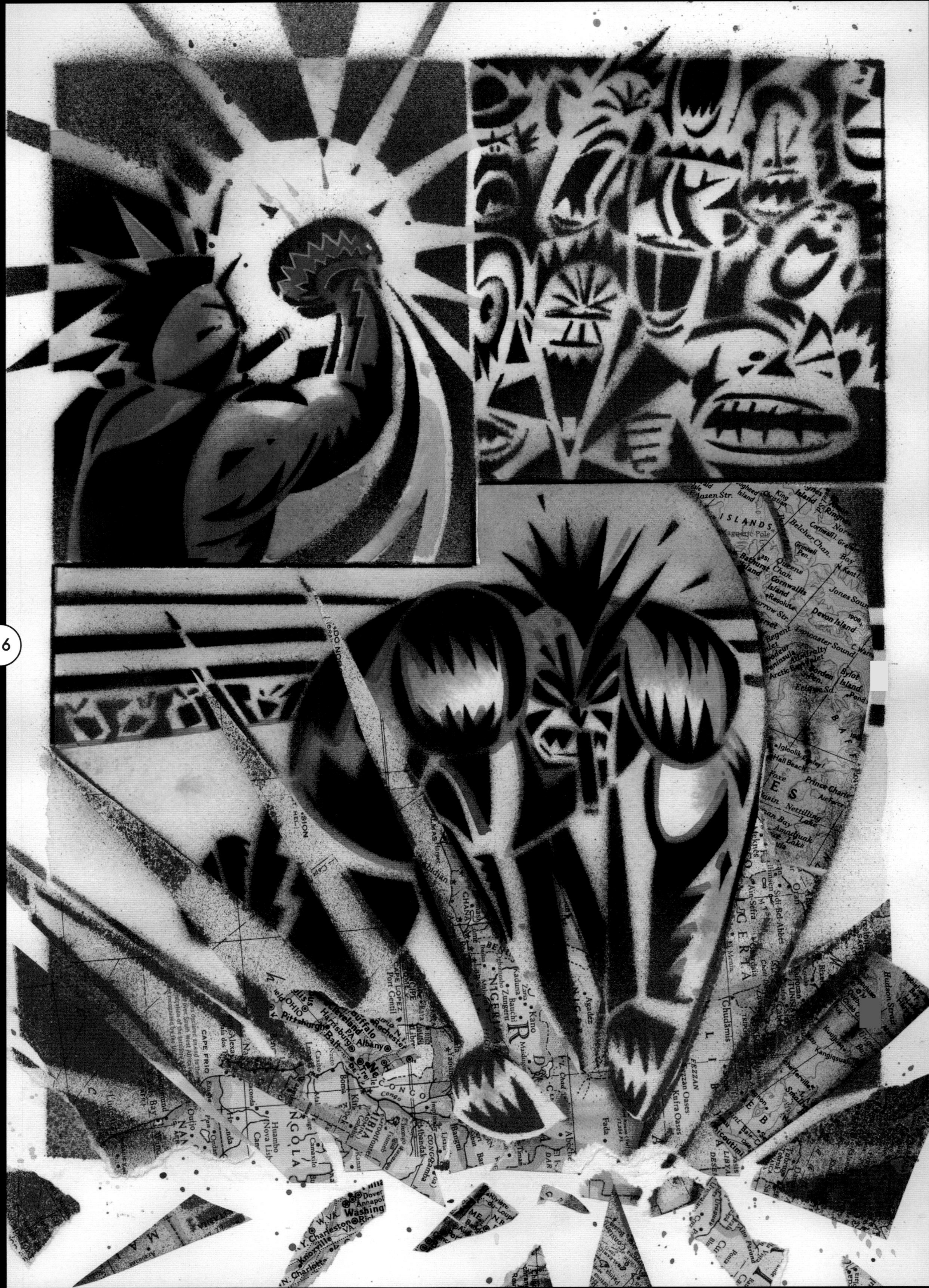
ISLANDS
Magnetic Pole
Belcher Chan.
Bathurst Island
Queens Chan.
Cornwallis Island
Resolute
Barrow Str.
Jones Sound
Devon Island
Lancaster Sound
Regent
Bylot Island
Igloolik
Hall Beach
Prince Charles
Nettilling Lake
Amadjuak Lake
Chudamis
FEZZAN
Kufra Oases
NIGERIA
Kano
Zaria
Bauchi
Agadez
Buffalo
Rochester
Cleveland
Pittsburgh
Harrisburg
Albany
CONGO
ANGOLA
Huambo
CAPE FRIO
Charleston
Knoxville
Washington
Dover
Annapolis

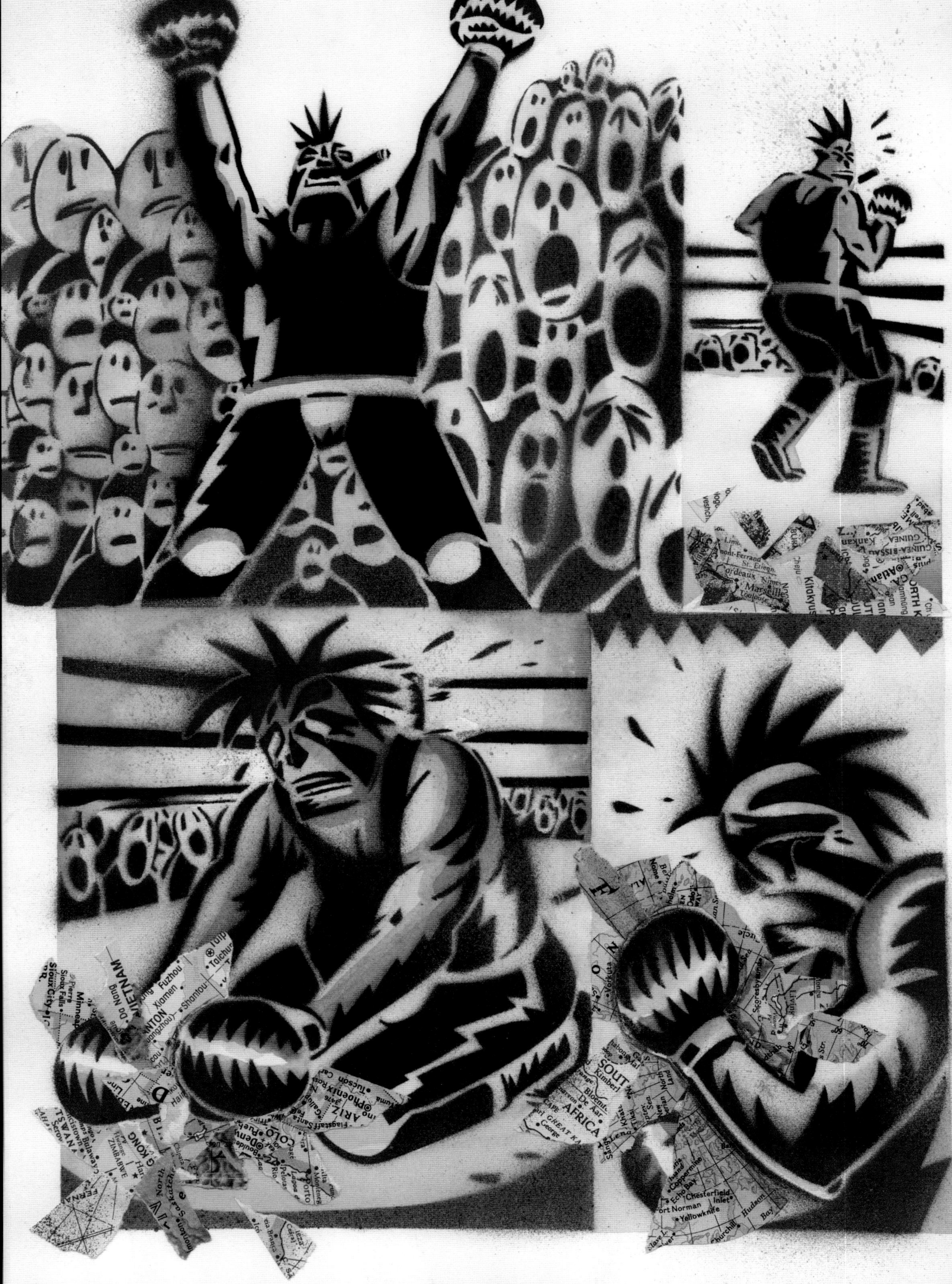

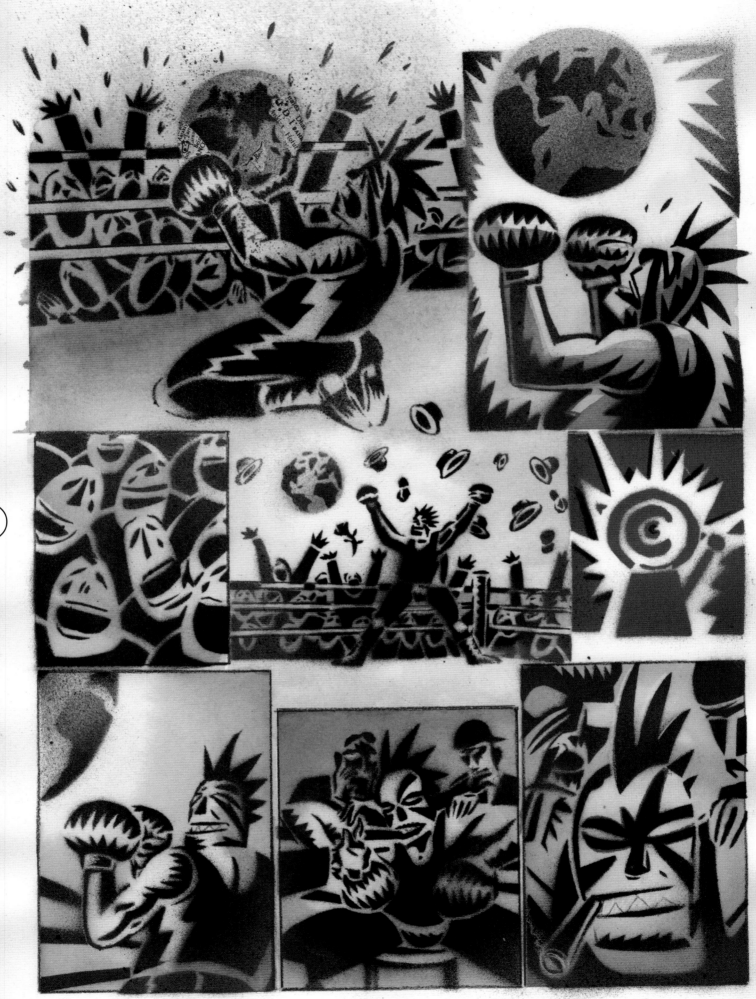

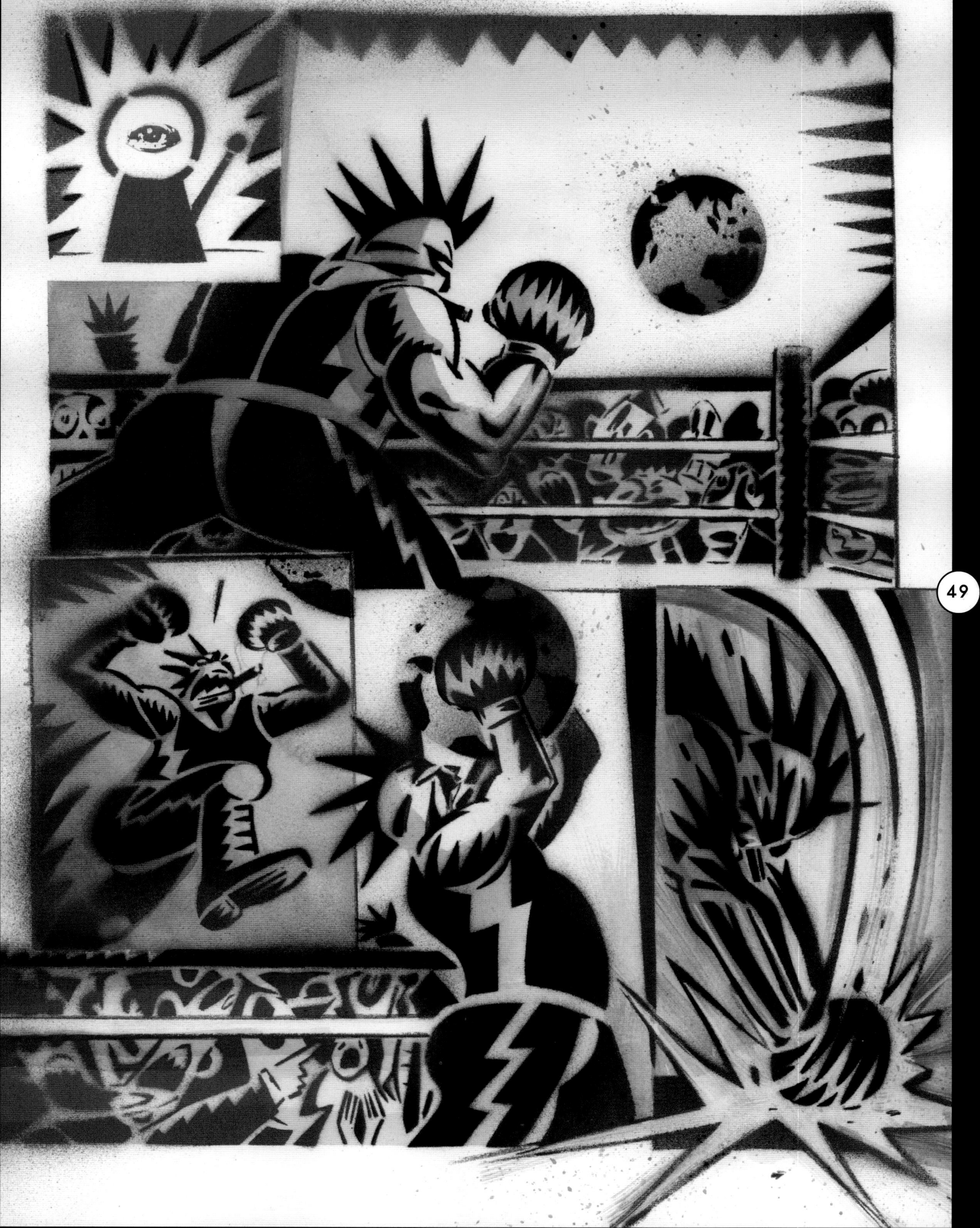

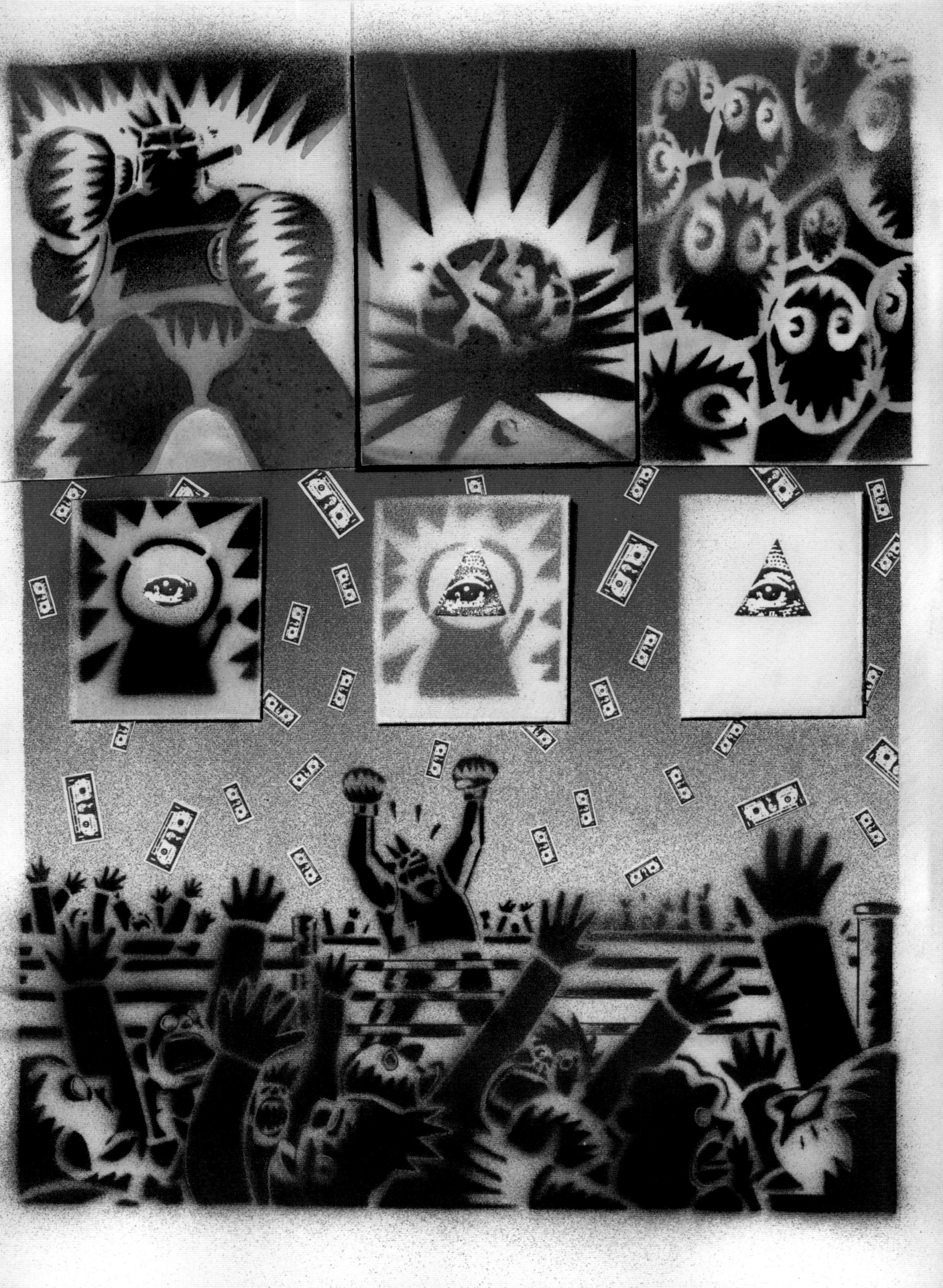

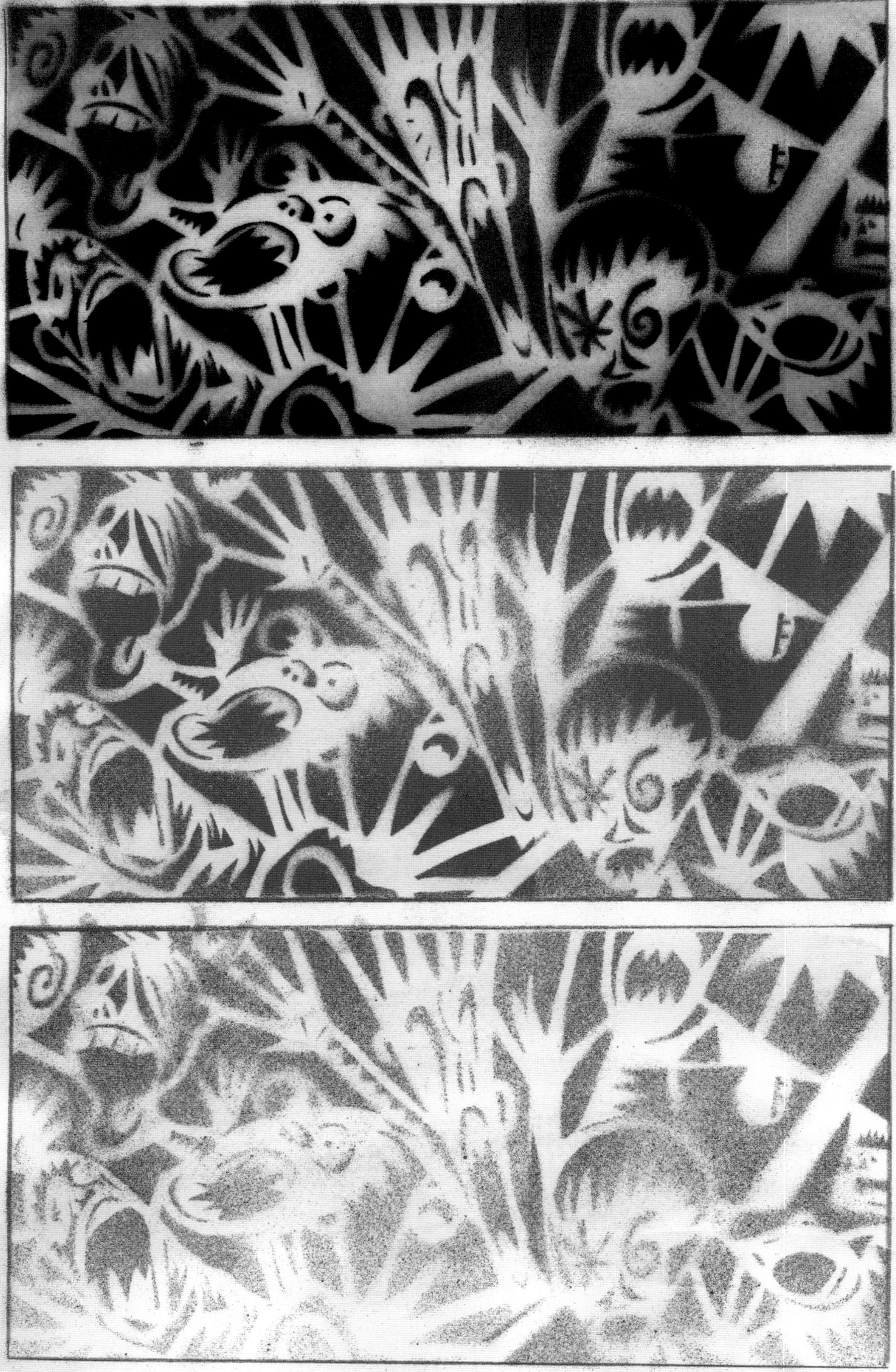

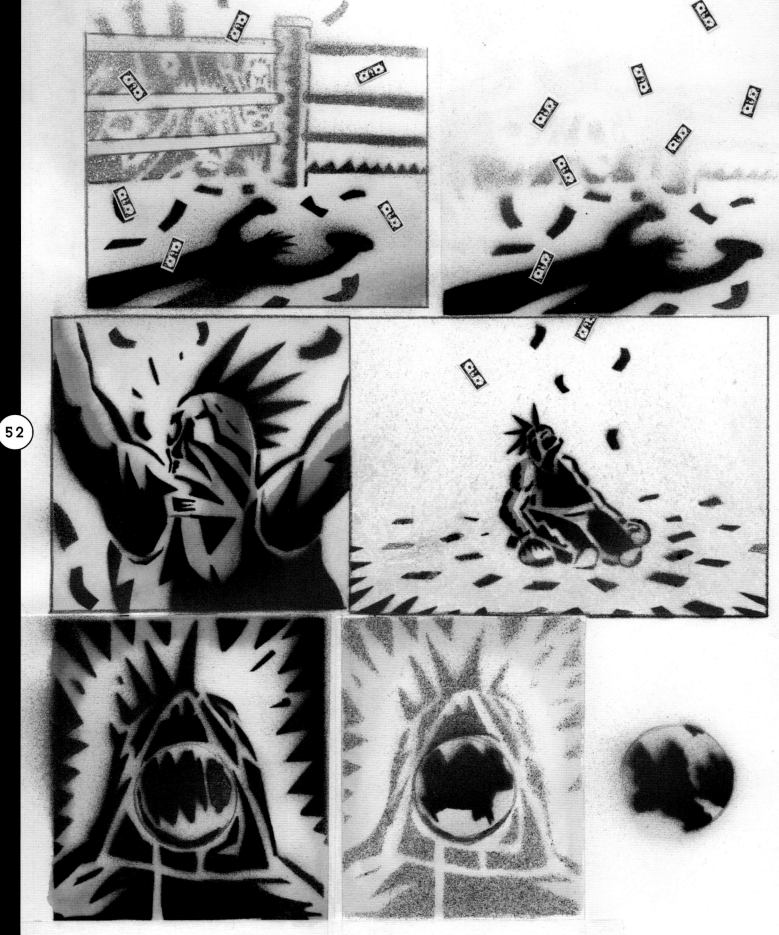

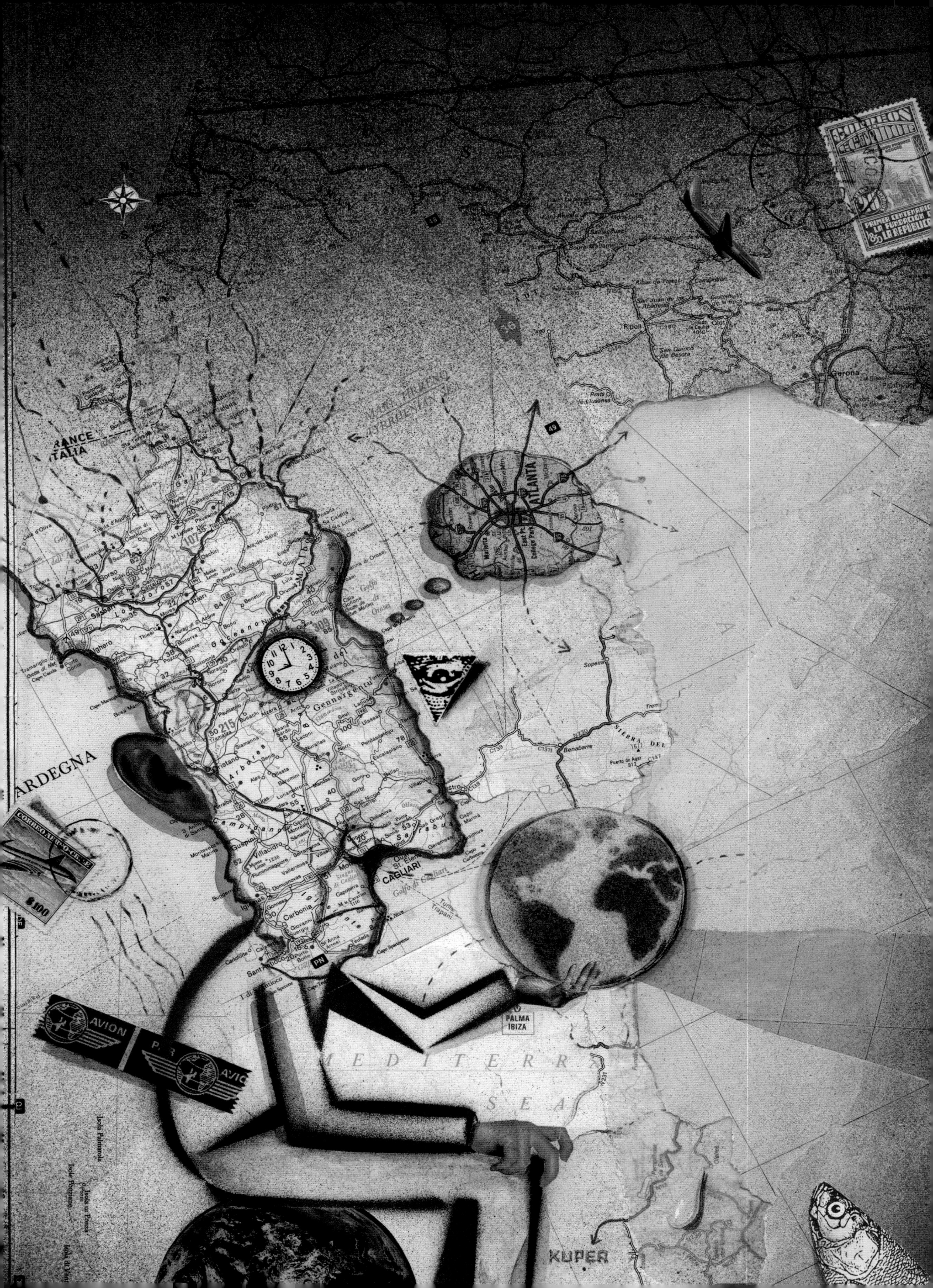

RANCE
ITALIA
ARDEGNA
ATLANTA
Gennargentu
CAGLIARI
SIERRA DEL
Benabarre
Gerona
CORREO AEREO
PALMA
IBIZA
AVION
PAR AVION
M E D I T E R R
S E A
KUPER

COMICS TRIPS

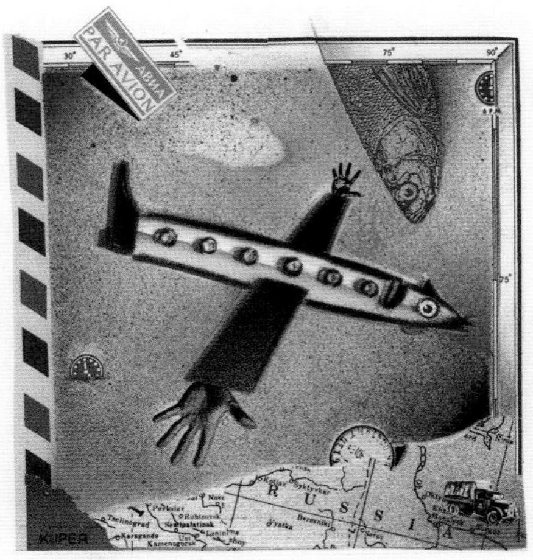
PAR AVION
KUPER

Illustration, the *New York Times*, 1993.

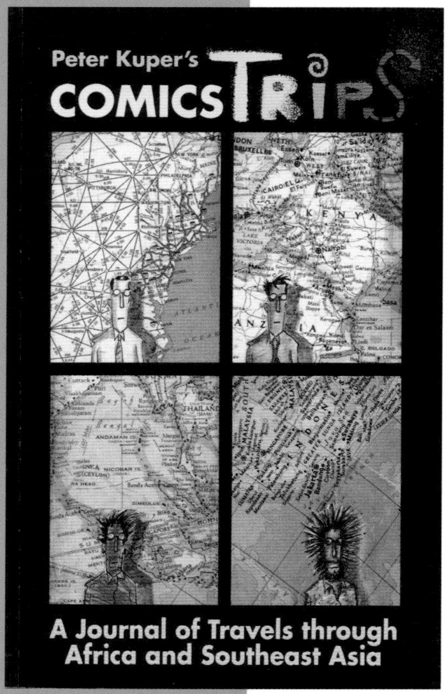
Peter Kuper's
COMICS TRIPS
A Journal of Travels through Africa and Southeast Asia

Comics Trips bookcover, published by Tundra, collecting work produced on an eight month trip around the world, 1992.

I have planned many trips abroad under the false pretense of "taking a vacation." That veneer is usually stripped away as I awake disoriented around 17 hours into a 32-hour flight. Or as I'm sweltering, crushed three to a seat on a rickety bus, bouncing down a pot-holed road. Or as I attempt to swat flies from my face while bent over a putrid squat toilet. At that point, the reality creeps in that recycled airplane air, discomfort, and that incessant buzzing don't have the relaxing ring the word *vacation* implies. Comfort, as I formerly understood it, has been vanquished and replaced with experiencing the moment. Once this happens, I begin to shed my skin and replace it with a travel hide; redefining *vacation* to mean a trip away from routine and a break from the shackles that keep my brain stuck in a rut.

Of course, I don't just travel for the mental exercise. Having the opportunity to crouch next to mountain gorillas in Rwanda, join in a ceremonial feast in the wilds of New Guinea, and smell incense wafting down Jerusalem's ancient streets are among the most indelible experiences of my life. These trips have also inspired me to experiment in my sketchbook unhindered by any considerations of style or commerce. Joined with exposure to art from around the globe, these experiences have transformed my work.

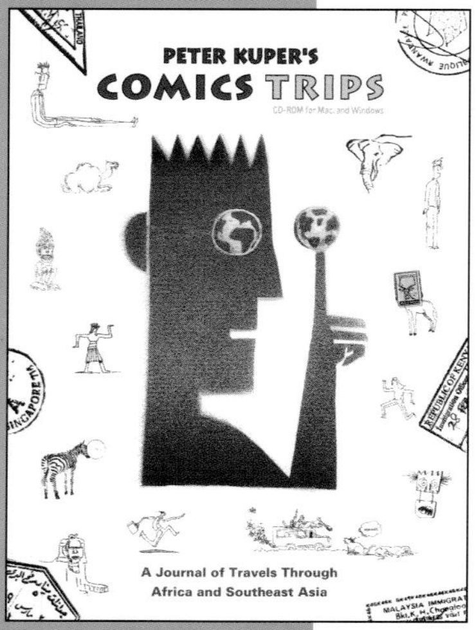
PETER KUPER'S
COMICS TRIPS
CD-ROM for Mac and Windows
A Journal of Travels Through Africa and Southeast Asia

Traveling imbues geographic lines with a reality maps alone can never express. It turns foreign places with hard to pronounce names into 3-dimensional realities, with personal significance far beyond news headlines. Traveling can also be very empowering, since you discover that your behavior abroad can shape foreigners' perceptions of your entire country. And you'll become painfully aware of the enormity of this responsibility as you contend with all the impressions left by your countrymen who preceded you.

Comics Trips CD ROM cover, published by Interlink, a Japanese company, collecting work produced on the eight month trip, with additional, animation, writing, photos, art, sound recordings, and original music. 1998.

Previous page: *All Over The Map*, cover, *Village Voice*, Literary Supplement, 1994.

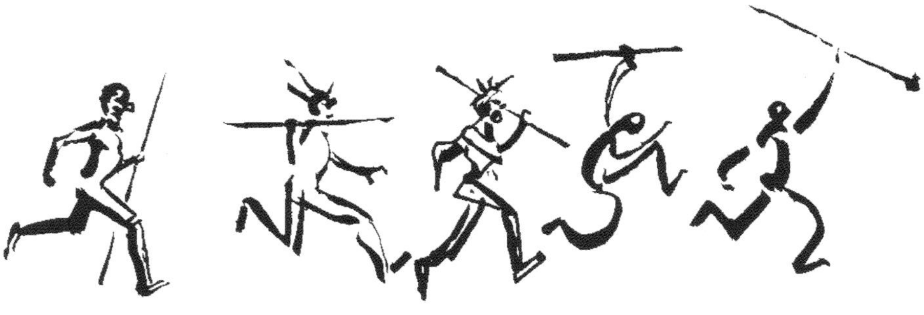

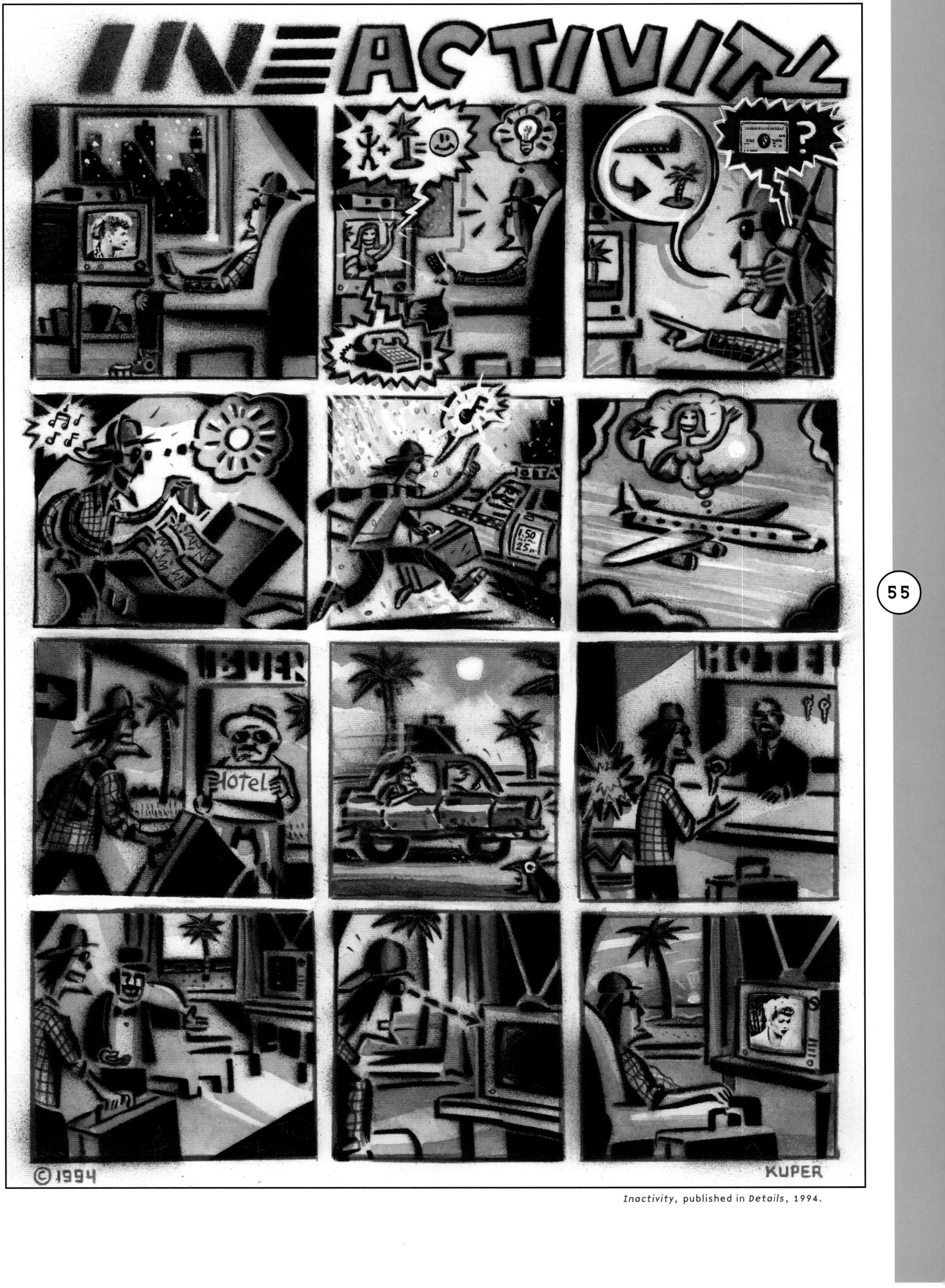
INACTIVITY
HOTEL
1.50
25
©1994
KUPER

Inactivity, published in *Details*, 1994.

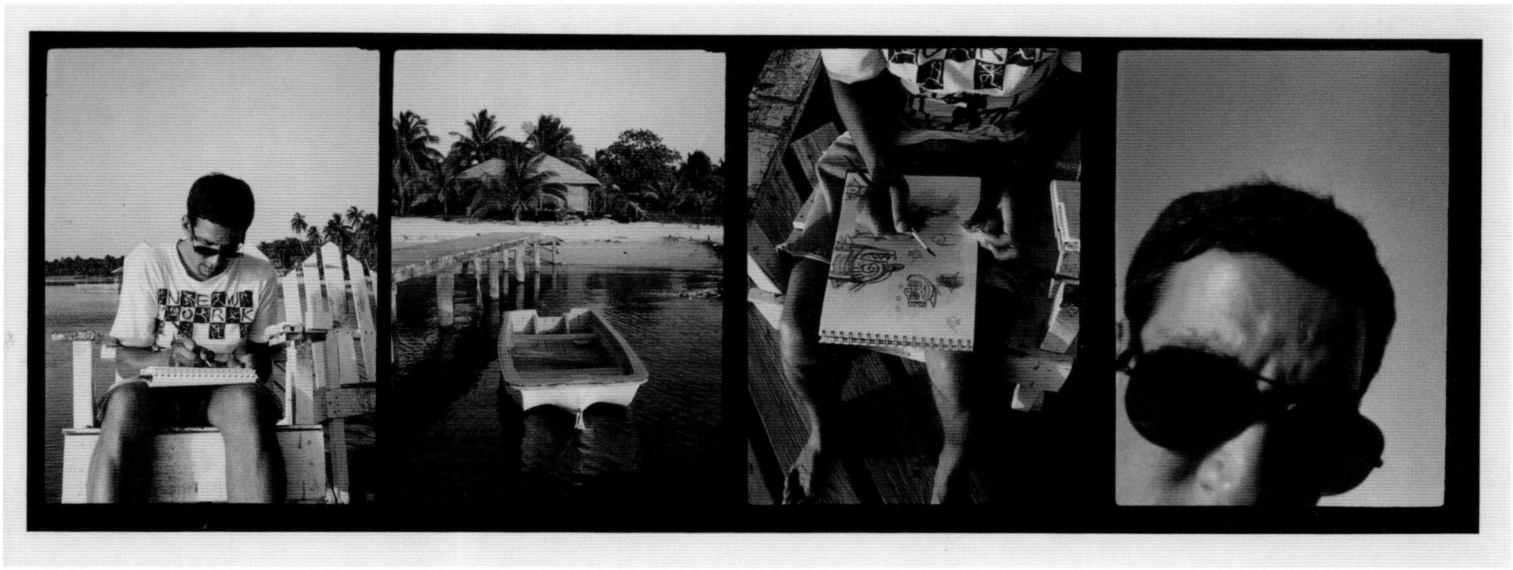

1

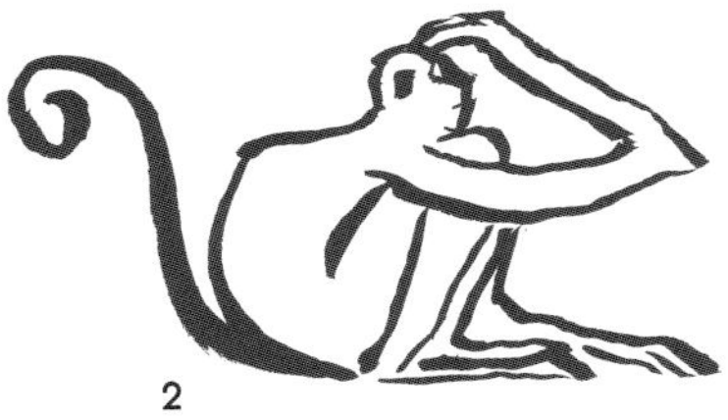

2

1. Kuper in Honduras, 1992, photographer: Mark E. Owen.

2. Honduras, 1992.

3. Irian Jaya, Indonesia, 1995.

4. Guatemala, 1992.

Opposite Page:

5. Mexico, 1987.

6. Bali, Indonesia, 1995.

7. Honduras, 1992.

8. Kenya, 1989.

9. Kuper in Irian Jaya, 1995, photographer: Mark E. Owen.

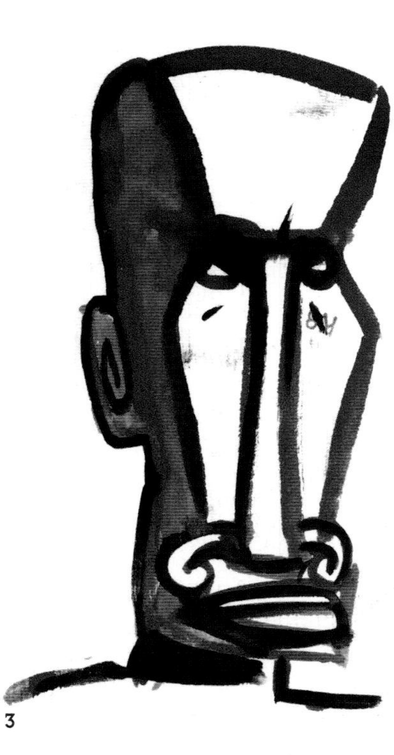

3

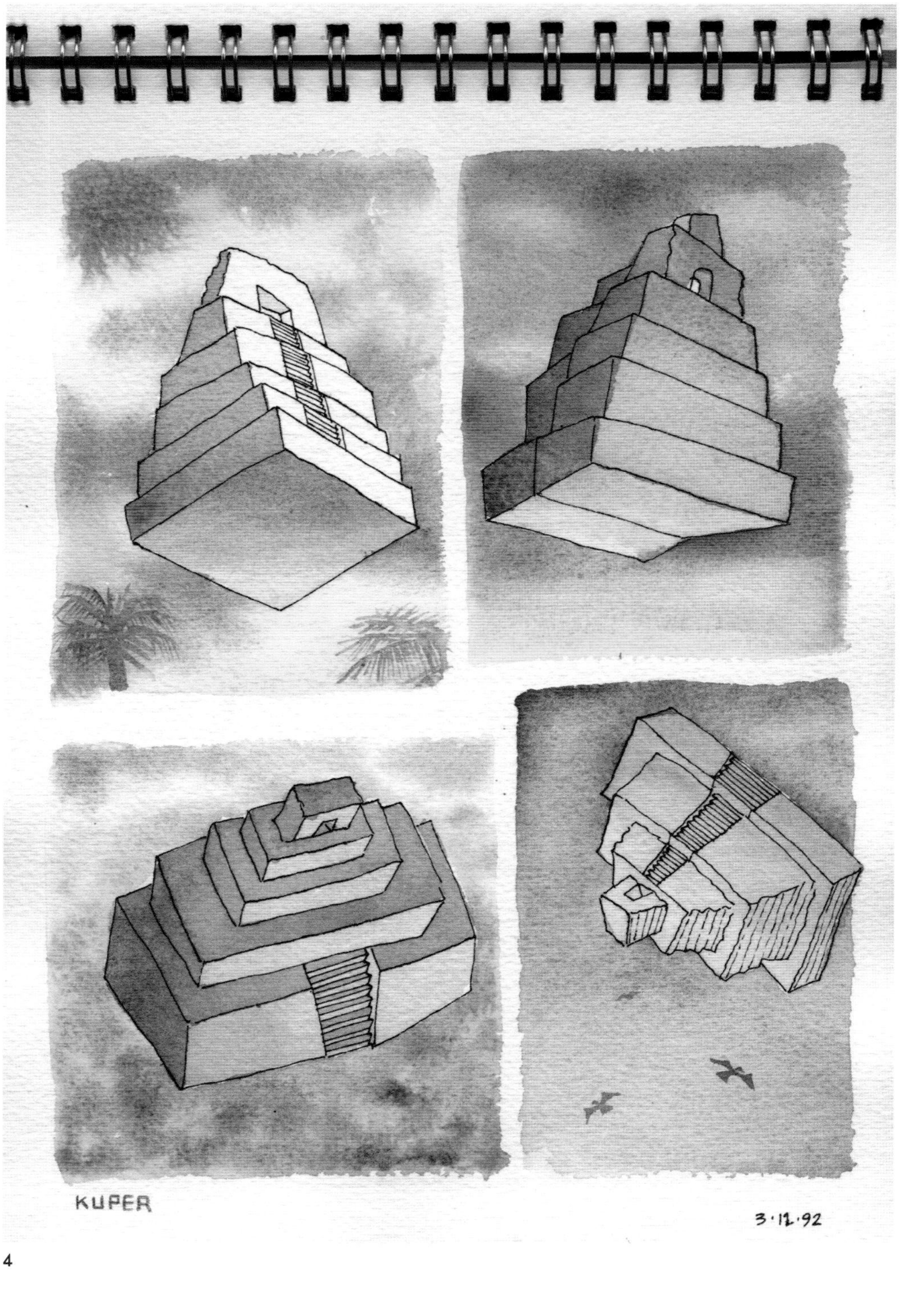
KUPER
3·12·92

4

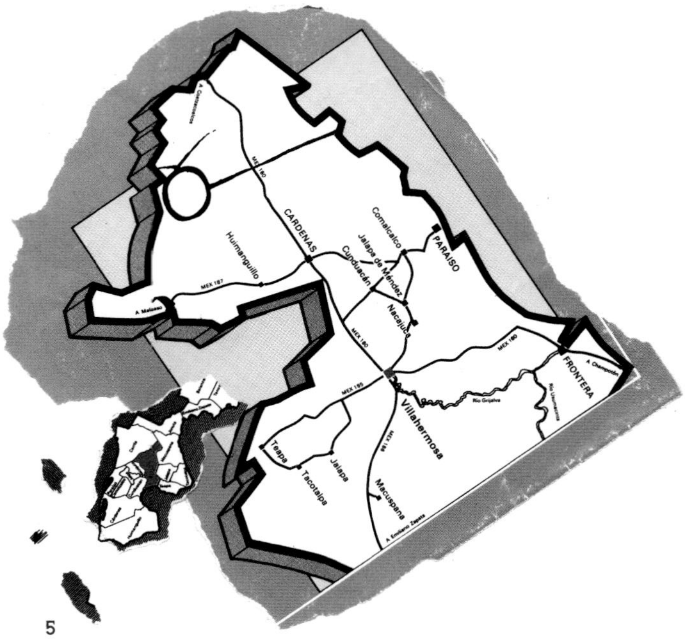
CARDENAS
Huimanguillo
Comalcalco
Jalpa de Méndez
Cunduacán
PARAISO
Nacajuca
FRONTERA
Villahermosa
Teapa
Tacotalpa
Jalapa
Macuspana

5

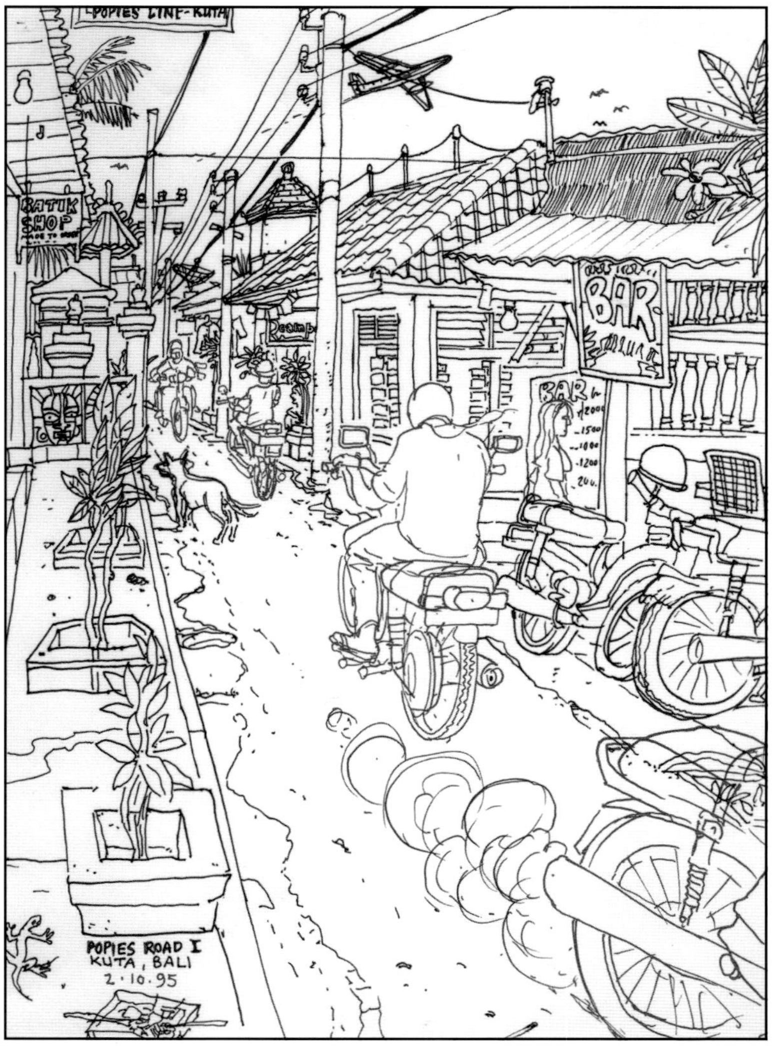
POPIES LINE-KUTA
BATIK SHOP
BAR
BAR
POPIES ROAD I
KUTA, BALI
2·10·95

6

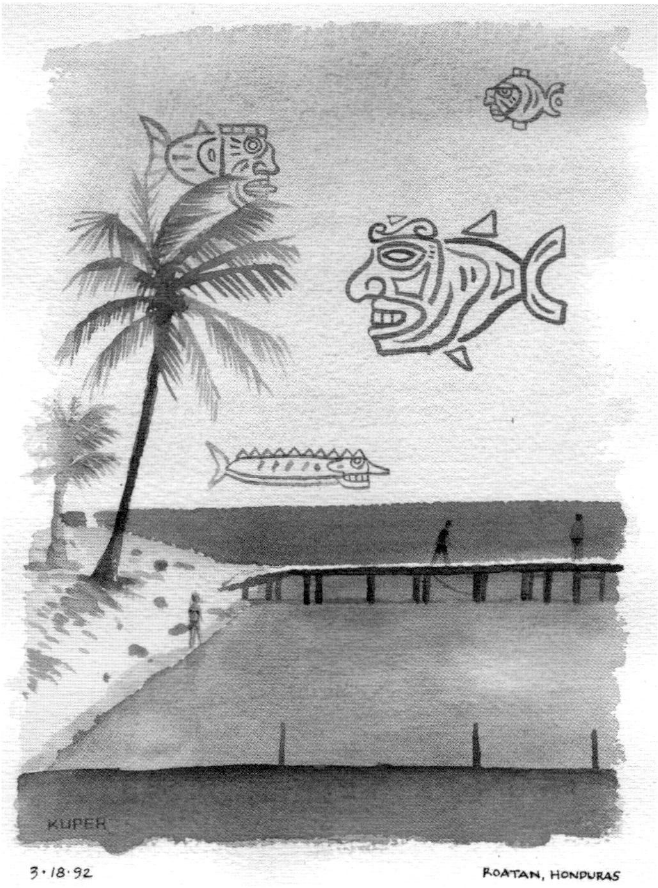
KUPER
3·18·92
ROATAN, HONDURAS

7

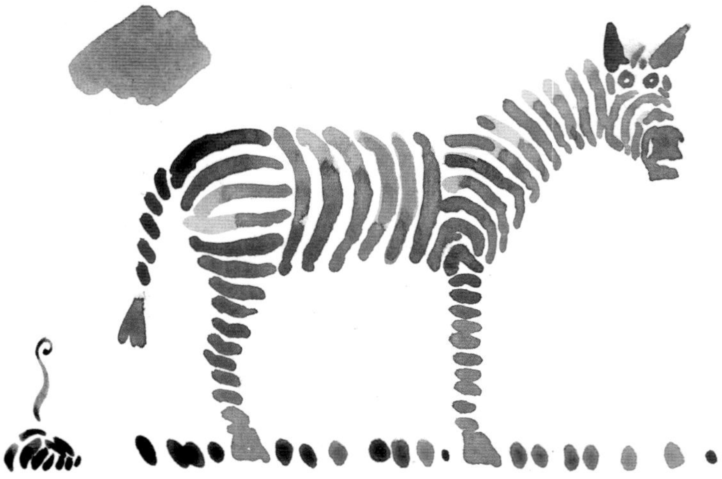

8

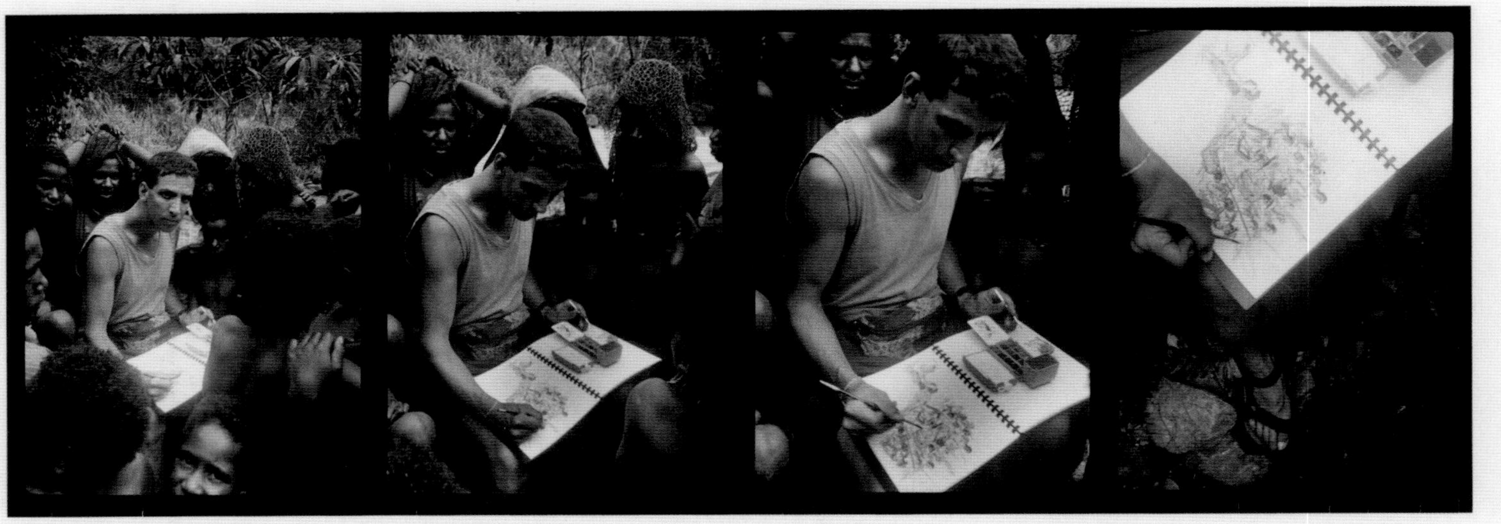

9

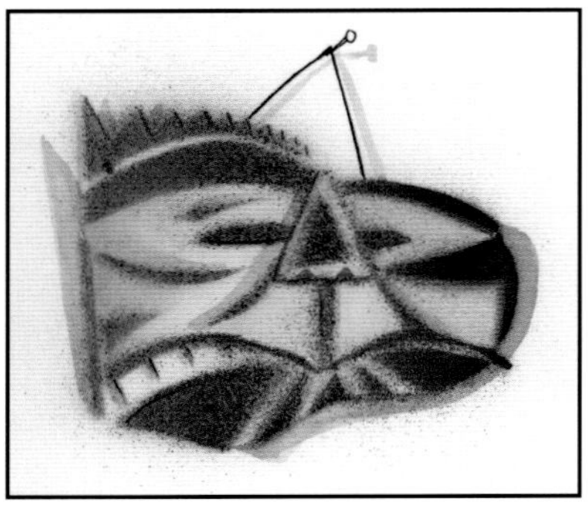

Bad Gyro Sandwich

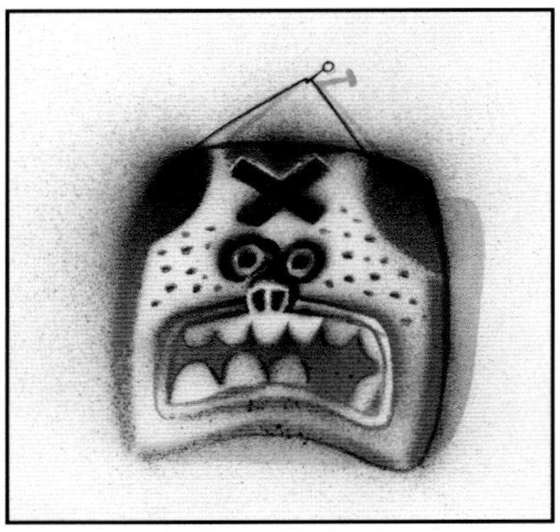

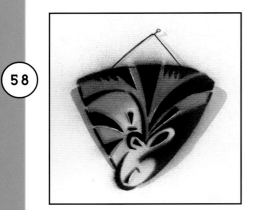

Flu Season

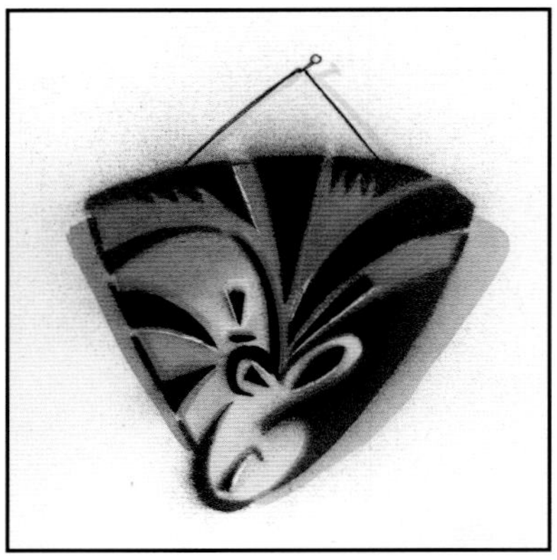

Unidentified Odor

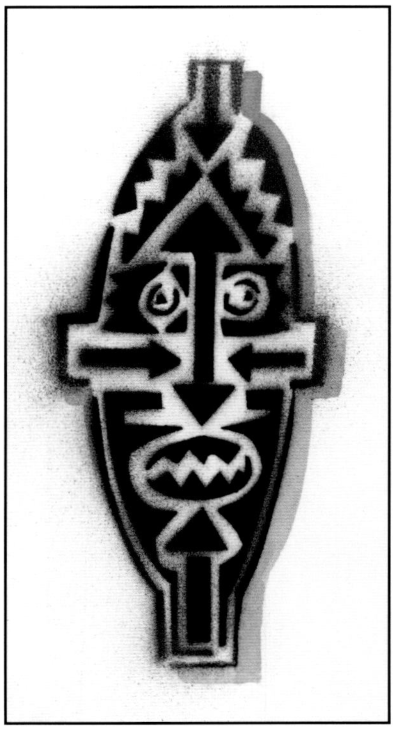

Parking Space Hunt

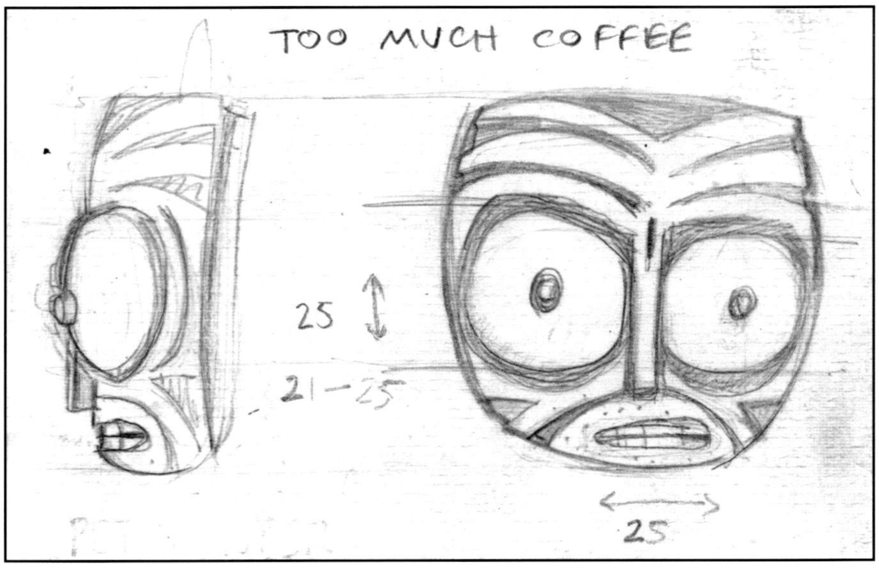
TOO MUCH COFFEE
25
21–25
25

One of twelve designs given to mask makers in Bali for carving...

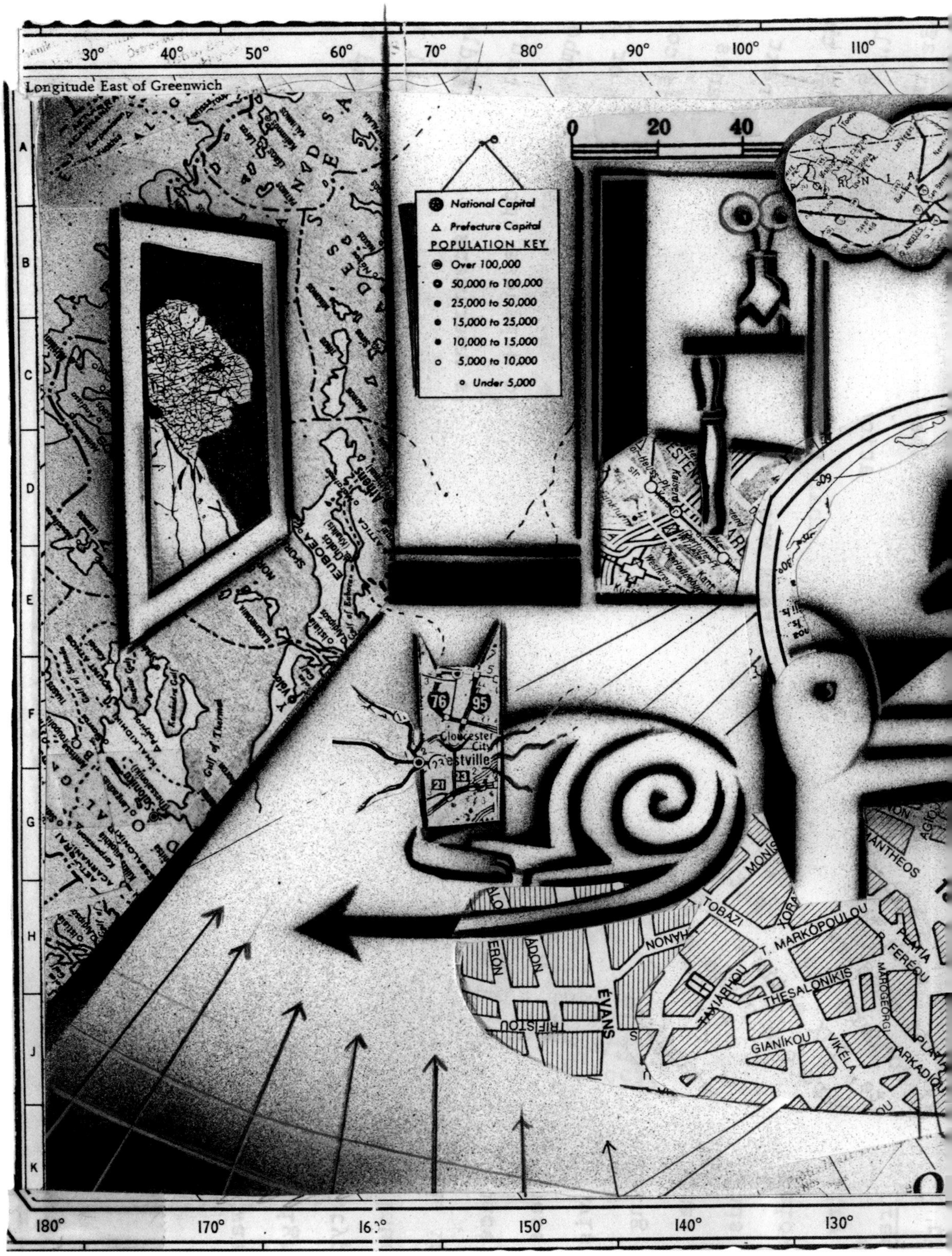
30° 40° 50° 60° 70° 80° 90° 100° 110°
Longitude East of Greenwich
0 20 40
National Capital
Prefecture Capital
POPULATION KEY
Over 100,000
50,000 to 100,000
25,000 to 50,000
15,000 to 25,000
10,000 to 15,000
5,000 to 10,000
Under 5,000
76
95
Gloucester City
Westville
T. MARKOPOULOU
THESALONIKIS
EVANS
VIKELA
180° 170° 150° 140° 130°

Atlas Shrugs, published in the *New York Times* Travel Section, 1992.

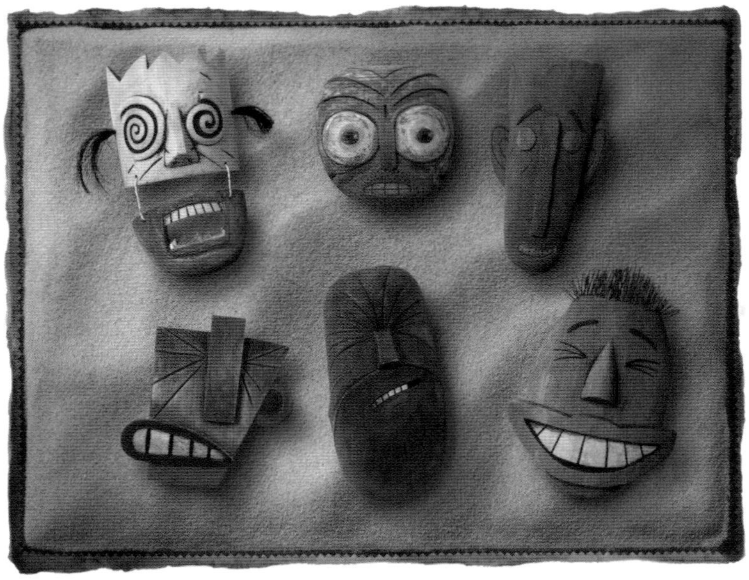

Finished wood masks painted by Kuper, clockwise from top left: *Lost Passport*, *Too Much Coffee*, *Just New in Town*, *Toothache*, *Constipation*, *Beached* (which Kuper carved upon return out of Balsa Foam).

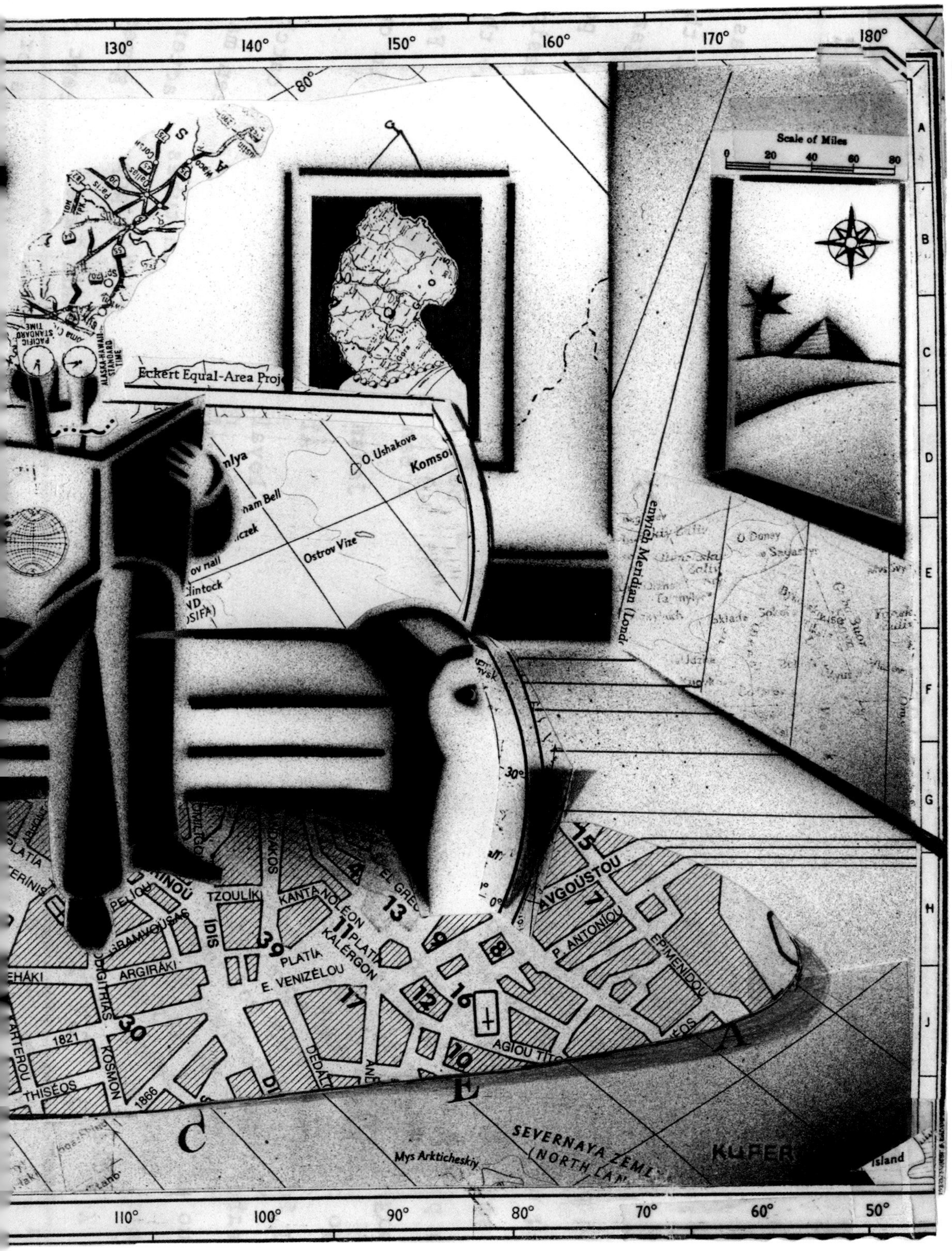

130°
140°
150°
160°
170°
180°
Scale of Miles
Eckert Equal-Area Proj
O. Ushakova
Ostrov Vize
AVGOUSTOU
PLATÍA
E. VENIZÉLOU
KALÉRGON
ARGIRÁKI
THISÉOS
KOSMON
SEVERNAYA ZEML
(NORTH LAN
Mys Arkticheskiy
KUPER
110°
100°
90°
80°
70°
60°
50°

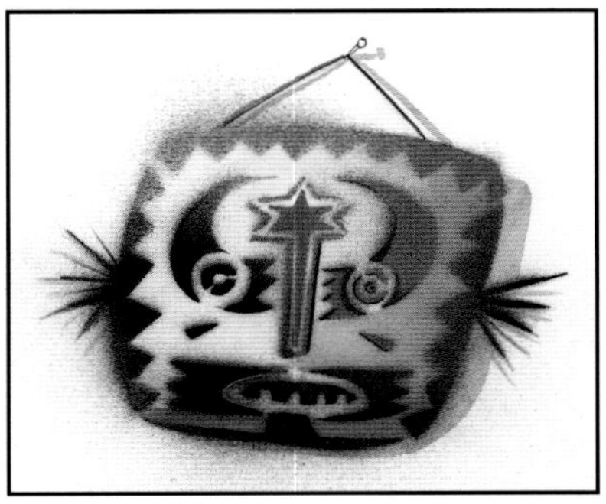

Late Night Car Alarm

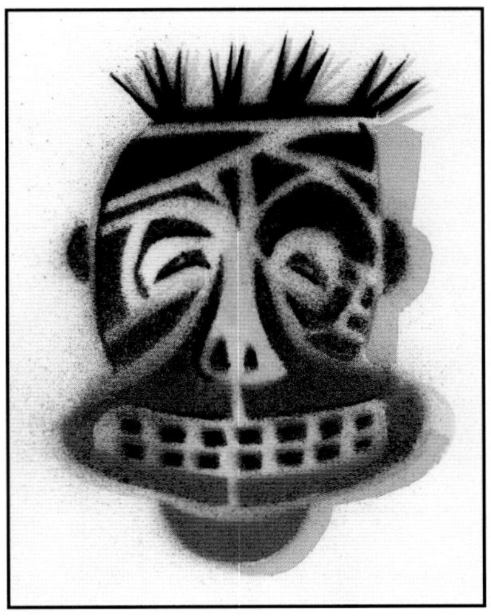

T.G.I.F.

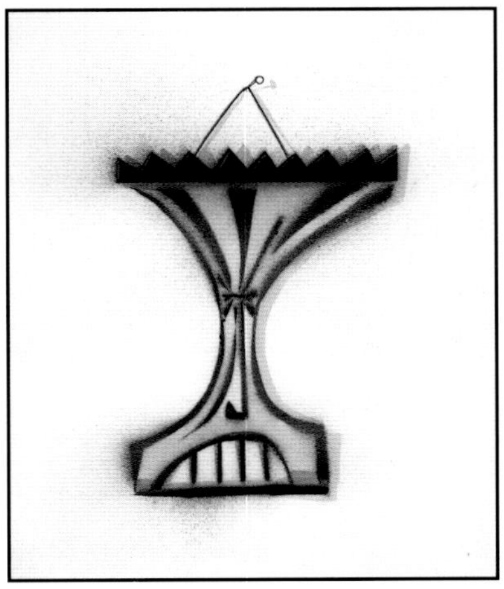

Rush Hour

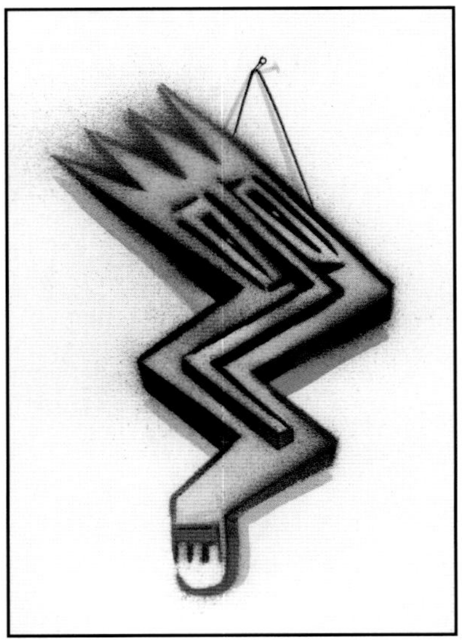

Crazed Cab Ride

1
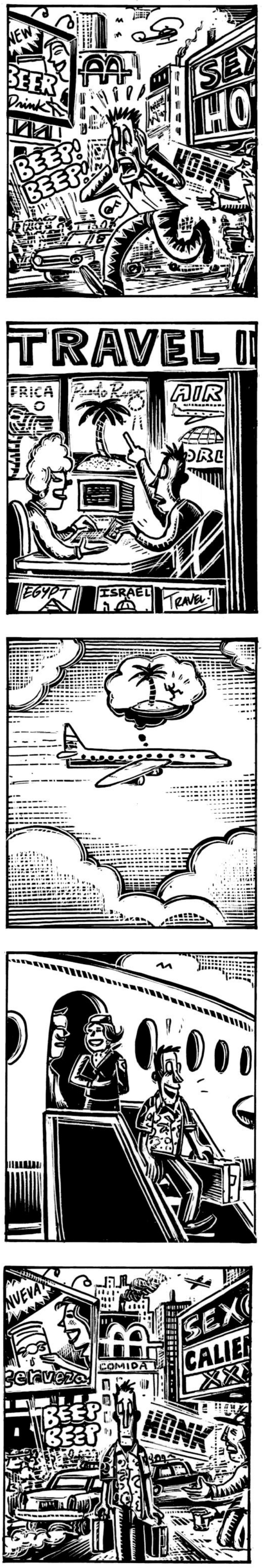
NEW
BEER
Drink
BEEP! BEEP!
HONK
TRAVEL
AIR
EGYPT
ISRAEL
TRAVEL
NUEVA
cerveza
COMIDA
BEEP BEEP
HONK

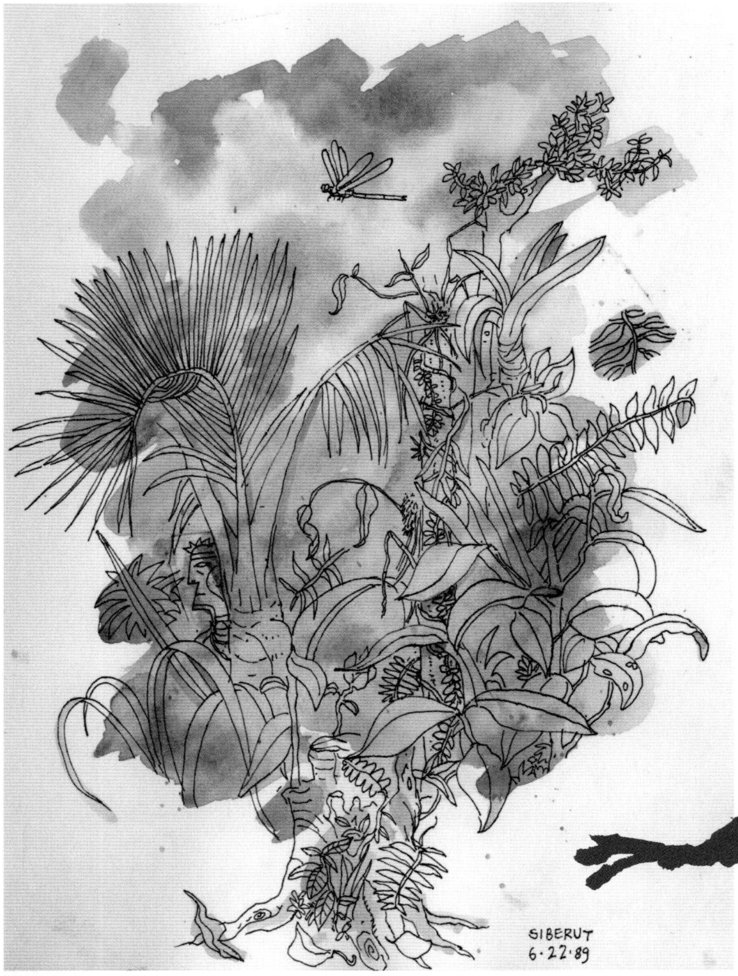
SIBERUT
6·22·89
2

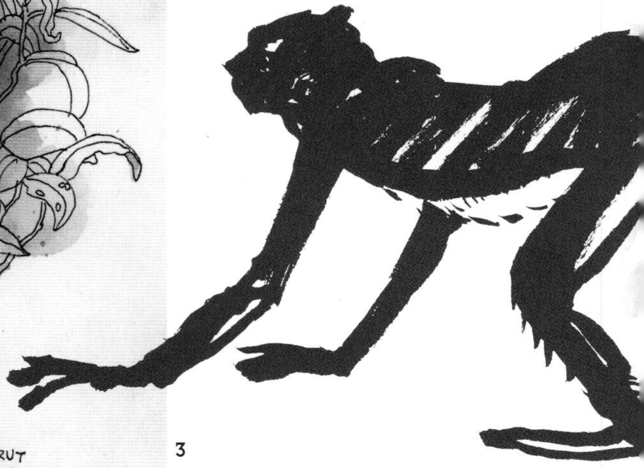
3

1. *Eye of the Beholder*, 1999.

2. Siberut, Indonesia, 1989.

3. Belize, 1992.

4. Guatemala, 1992.

5. Guatemala, 1992.

6. Hungary, 1990.

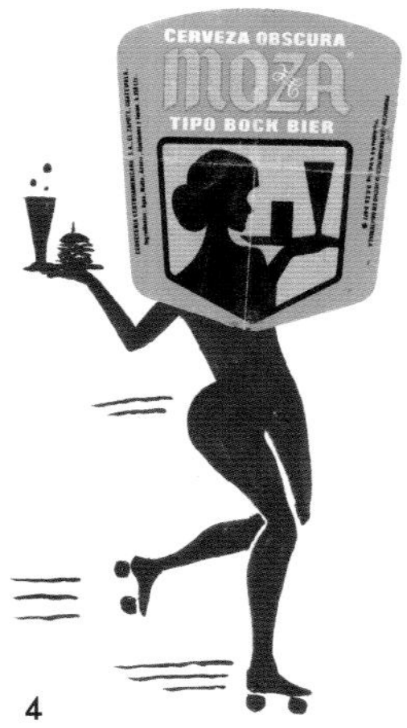
CERVEZA OBSCURA
MOZA
TIPO BOCK BIER
4

5
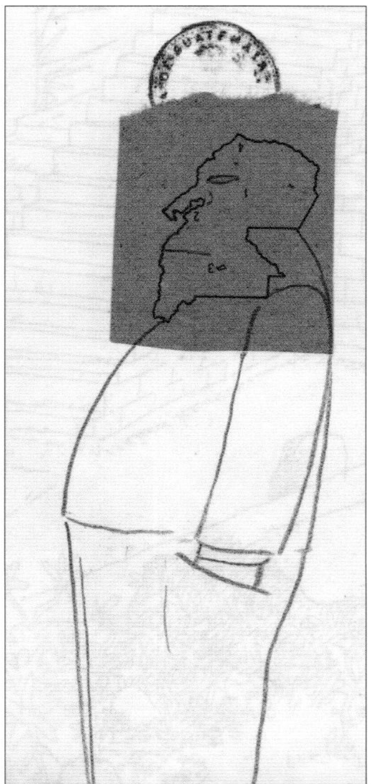

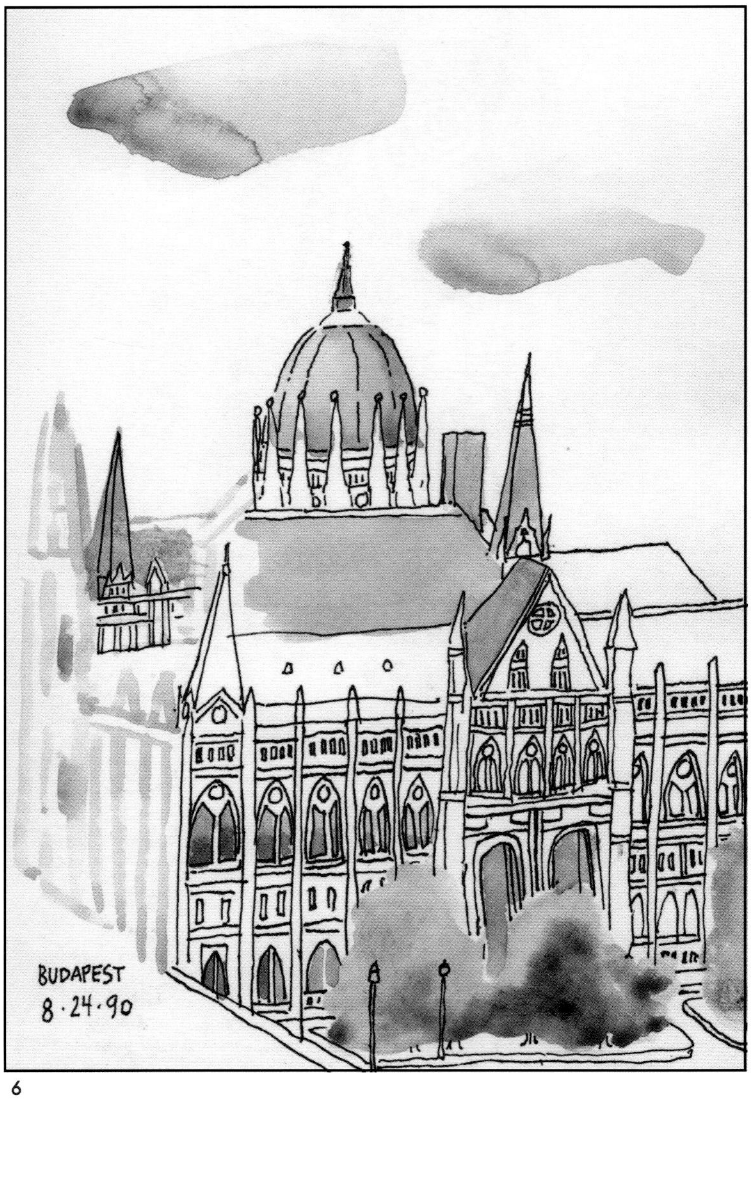
BUDAPEST
8·24·90
6

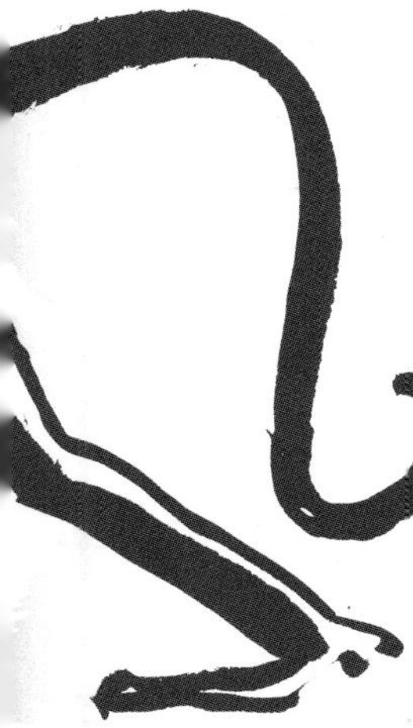

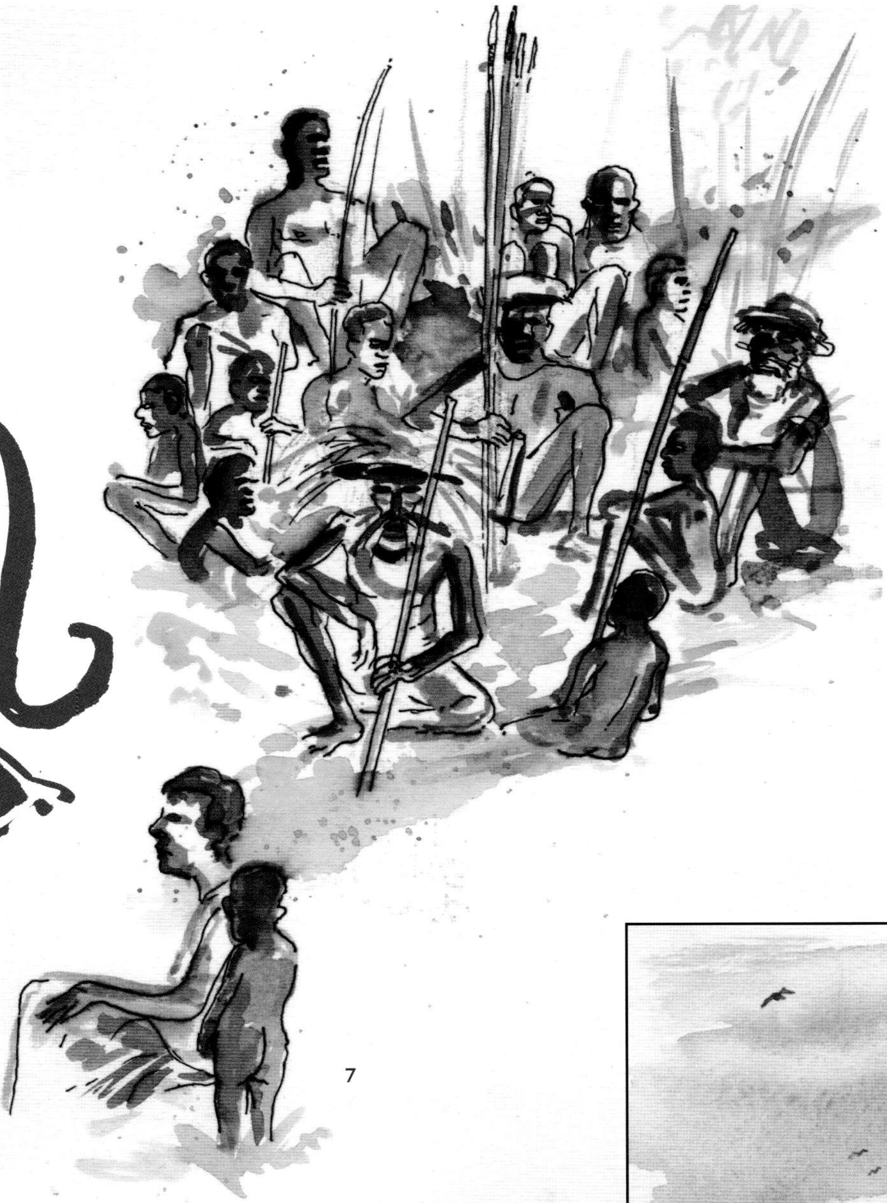

7

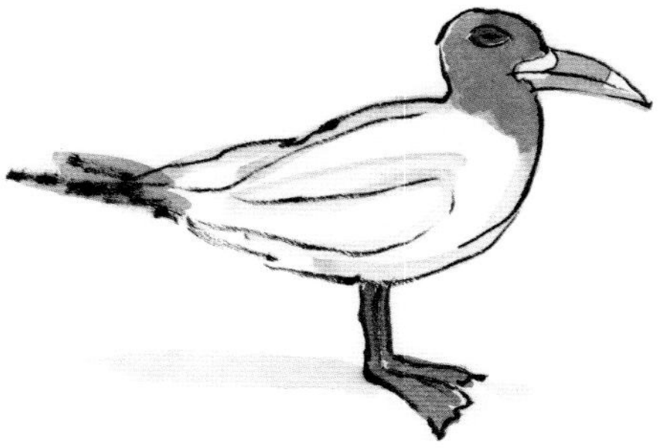

8

7. Irian Jaya, Indonesia, 1995.

8. Galapagos, Ecuador, 1993.

9. Galapagos, Ecuador, 1993.

10. Irian Jaya, Indonesia, 1993.

11. Bali, Indonesia, 1995.

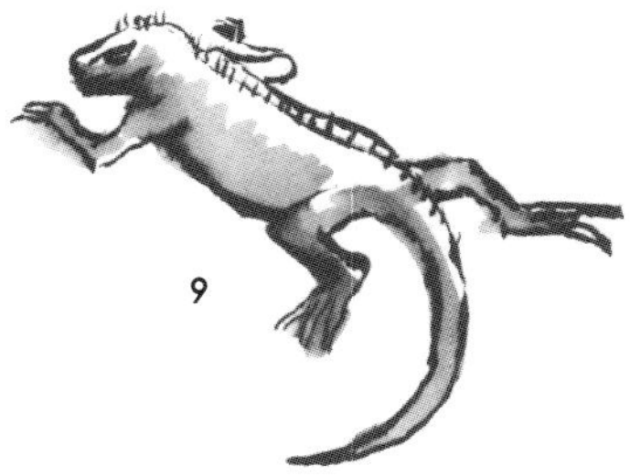

9

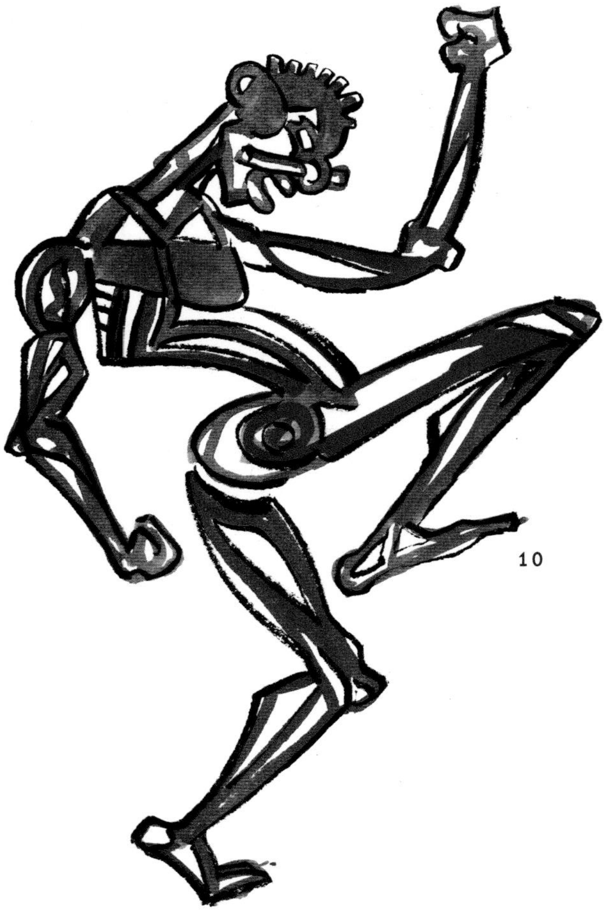

10

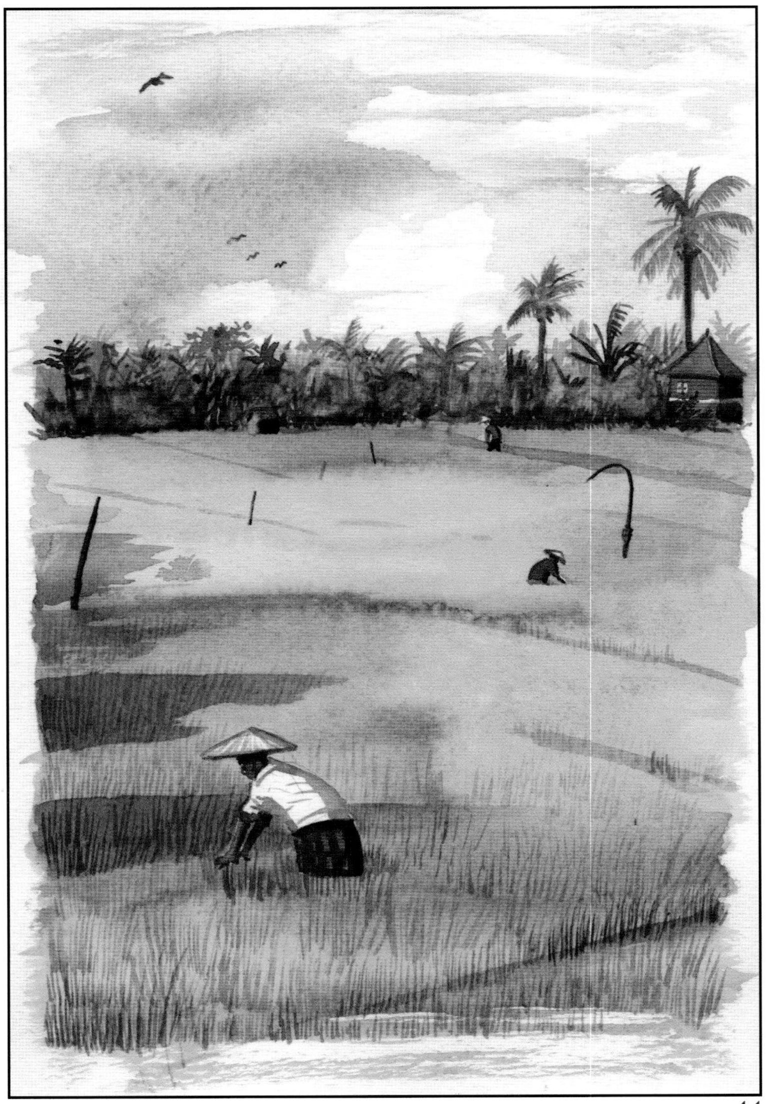

11

THE PROJECTS

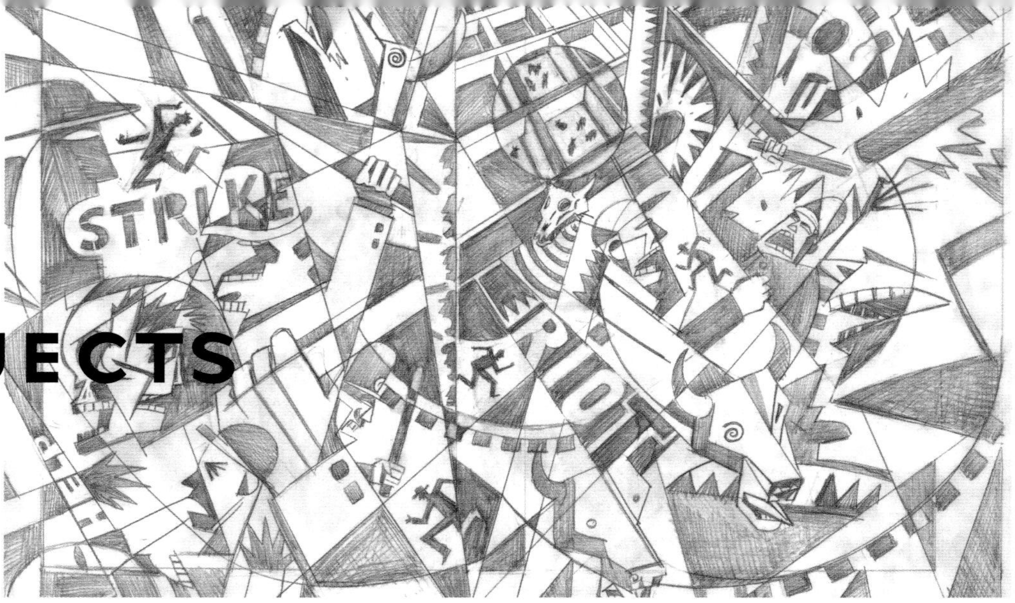
STRIKE
RIOT
HELP

1

1. Pencil drawing, for Riot scene, 1991.

2. Cover, *The Jungle* First Publishing, 1991.

3. Page 14, *The Jungle* First Publishing, 1991.

4. Page 41, *The Jungle* First Publishing, 1991.

5. Riot Scene, *The Jungle* First Publishing, 1991.

In 1990, I was given the opportunity to apply my stencil approach to comics, adapting Upton Sinclair's 1906 book, *The Jungle*. Up to that point I had not done full-color comics beyond a page or two, much less a graphic novel, but when I heard that Classics Illustrated was being revived, I contacted the editorial director, Wade Roberts, and expressed my interest in contributing to the line. One restriction was that the book would have to be in the public domain, which eliminated my first choice, *The Grapes of Wrath*. I then suggested *The Jungle*, recalling the powerful impact it had had on me as a teenager. Among other influences, its depiction of the horrible conditions in Chicago's meat packing factories converted me to a vegetarian for a number of years. I also felt the stencil style I employed would not only suit the subject, but would help to blur the line between my graphic approach with illustration and my comics work.

With the help of another writer, Emily Russell (who happens to be my sister-in-law), I broke the four hundred-page book down to forty-five pages. It is very nearly impossible to do justice to any novel in those confines, but I'd like to think the spirit of *The Jungle* is captured in this adaptation.

An ironic footnote: as I sent the last pages to the publisher, I discovered that virtually everyone I had been working with had been fired. The company, First Publishing, was shortly driven to bankruptcy by mismanagement, and I had to retain a lawyer to be paid my page rate. I never received any royalties, and *The Jungle*, a tale of worker's oppression, became the last book the company ever published.

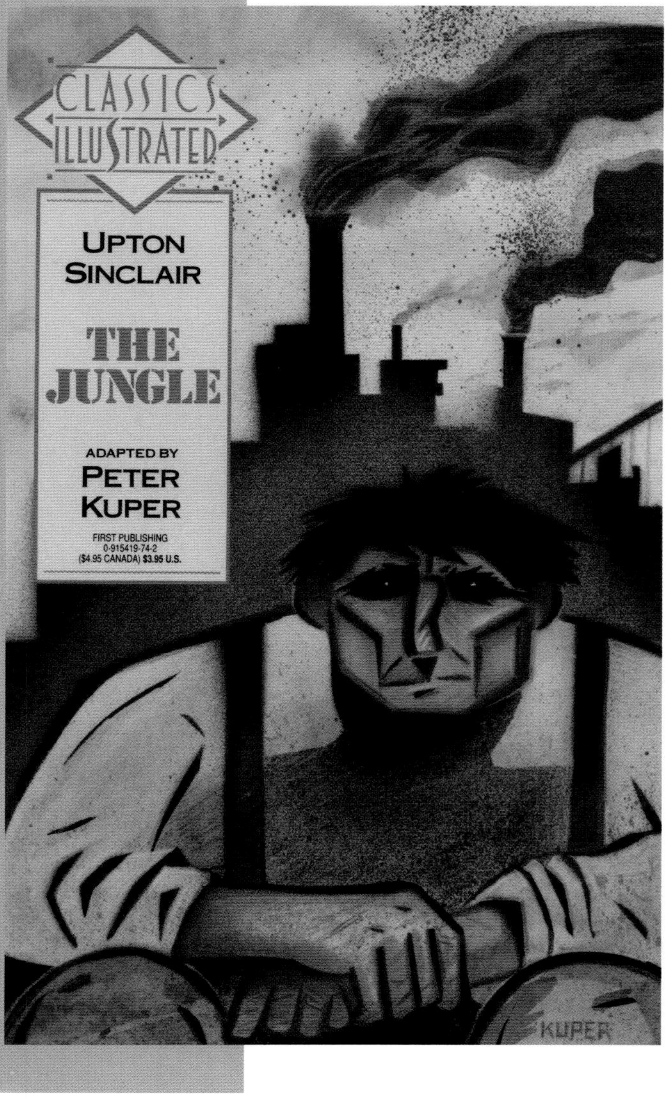
CLASSICS ILLUSTRATED
UPTON SINCLAIR
THE JUNGLE
ADAPTED BY
PETER KUPER
FIRST PUBLISHING
0-915419-74-2
($4.95 CANADA) $3.95 U.S.
KUPER

2

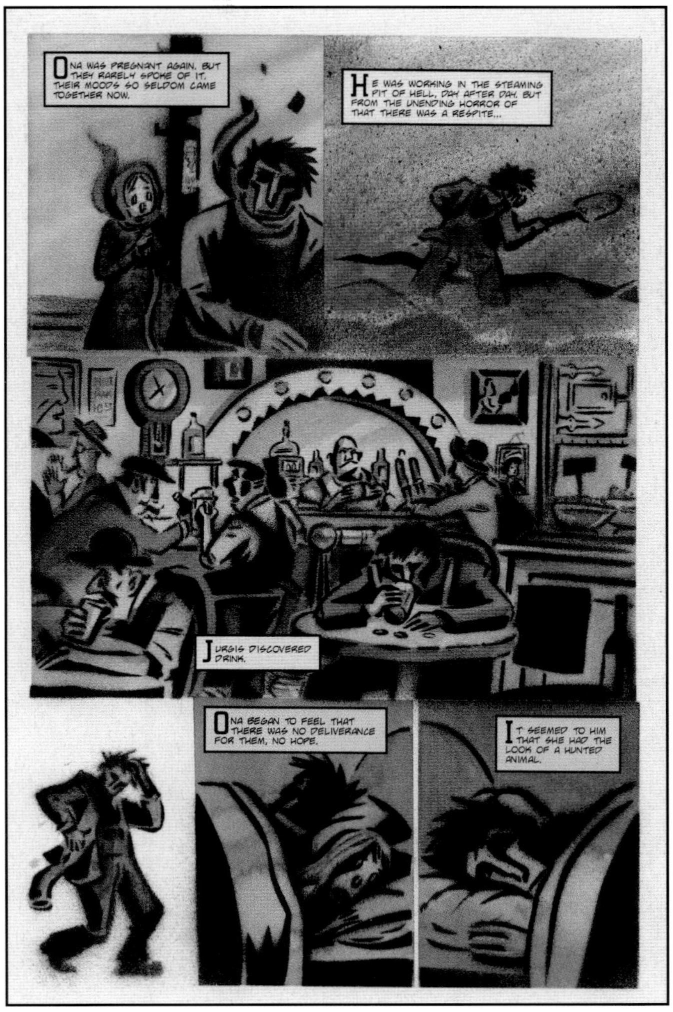
ONA WAS PREGNANT AGAIN, BUT THEY RARELY SPOKE OF IT. THEIR MOODS SO SELDOM CAME TOGETHER NOW.
HE WAS WORKING IN THE STEAMING PIT OF HELL, DAY AFTER DAY, BUT FROM THE UNENDING HORROR OF THAT THERE WAS A RESPITE...
JURGIS DISCOVERED DRINK.
ONA BEGAN TO FEEL THAT THERE WAS NO DELIVERANCE FOR THEM, NO HOPE.
IT SEEMED TO HIM THAT SHE HAD THE LOOK OF A HUNTED ANIMAL.

3

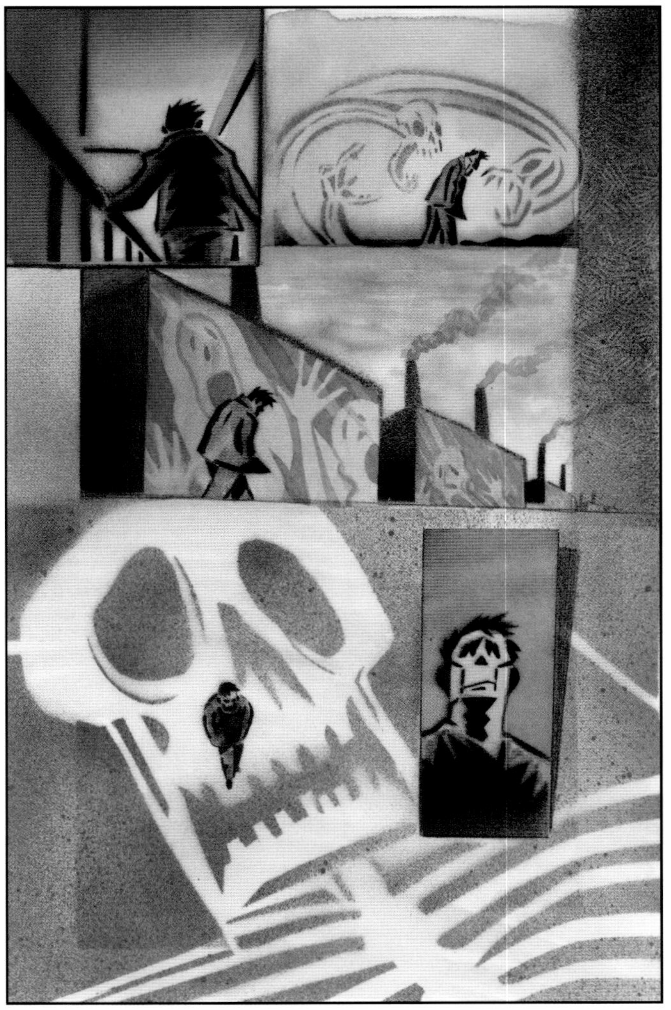

4

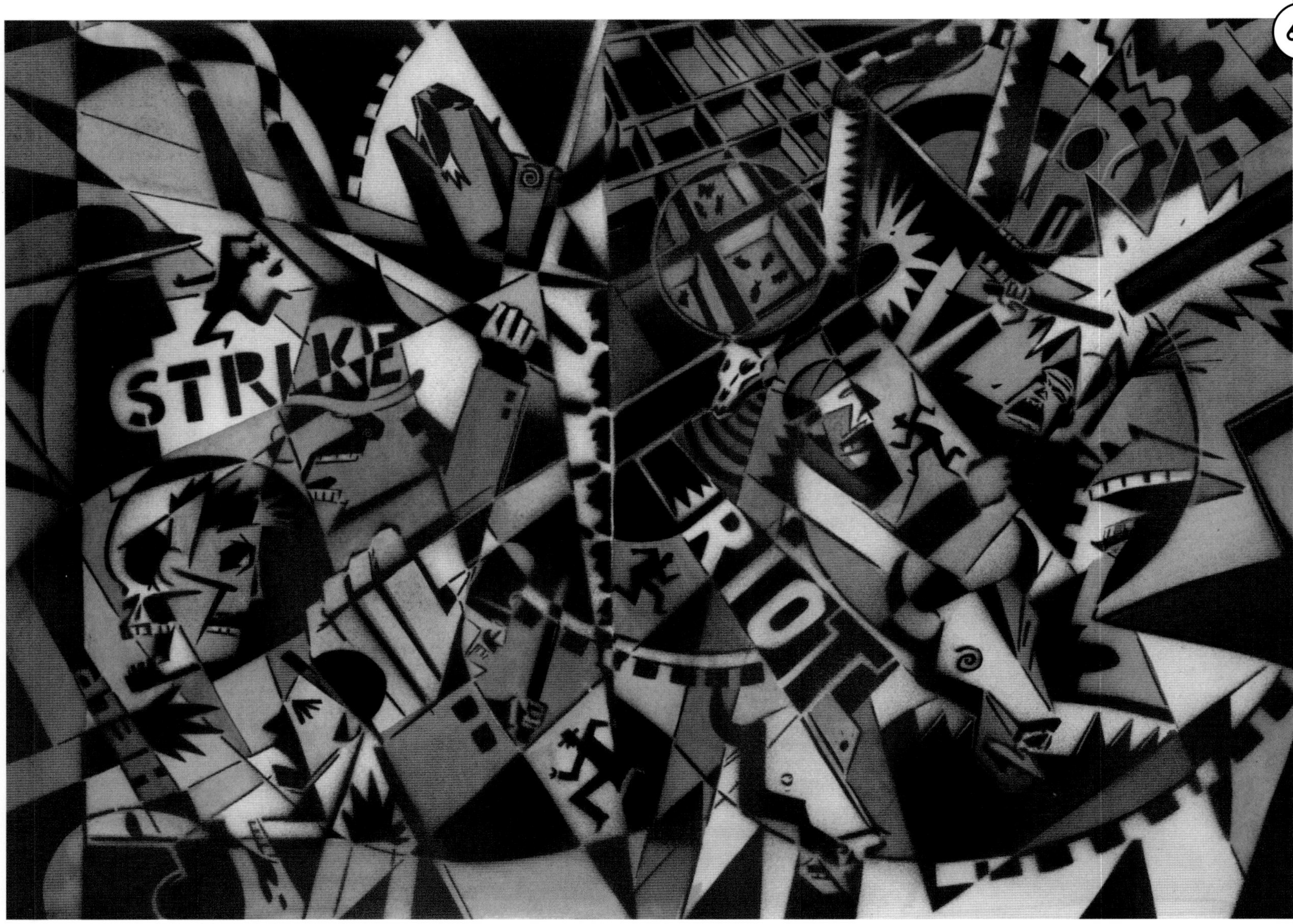
STRIKE
RIOT

5

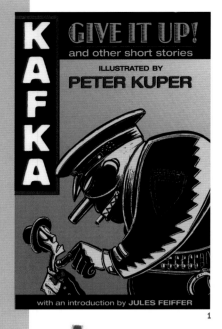

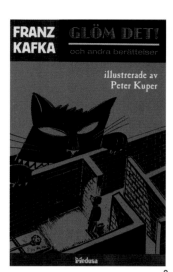

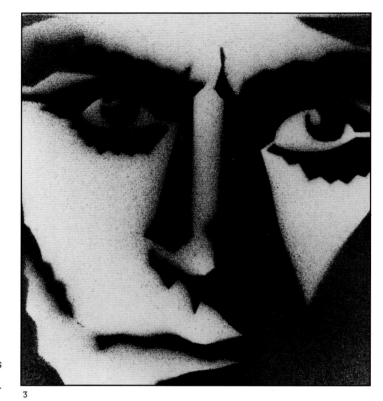

KAFKA
GIVE IT UP!
and other short stories
ILLUSTRATED BY
PETER KUPER
with an introduction by JULES FEIFFER

1

FRANZ KAFKA
GLÖM DET!
och andra berättelser
illustrerade av
Peter Kuper
Medusa

2

3

Like many people, my first exposure to Franz Kafka's writing was his famous story "The Metamorphosis." Happily, thanks to a friend of mine who enjoyed reading Kafka aloud over beers, I came to appreciate the hilarious, albeit dark, sense of humor in much of his work.

In 1988, I tried my hand at adapting Kafka to comics, beginning with "A Fratricide." I used scratchboard, a chalk-covered paper that can be inked and scratched, giving a woodcut-like effect, which immediately felt like the appropriate medium to convey the angst-ridden comedy in his work. Over the next eight years, I periodically drew other stories in the same style, including "The Vulture," "The Bridge," and "Give it Up!" The last one becoming the title of the collection when it was published in 1995.

I found that Kafka's stories, with their ordinary characters being placed in extraordinary situations, not only lent themselves to the form of comics, but were so evocative that the strips seemed to draw themselves, as well as allow me to experiment with extreme visual configurations. In addition, because many of Franz Kafka's short stories were sometimes no more than a few paragraphs, I was generally able to use his text without editing it in any way. However, there were a couple of stories I tackled, including "A Hunger Artist," that did require some adapting. Fortunately, Kafka was kind enough not to scream at my audacity.

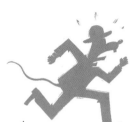

4

1. Cover, *Give it Up!*, published by NBM, 1995.
2. Swedish Edition, published by Medusa, 1997.
3. Kafka portrait, Unpublished, 1994.
4. Mouse from "A Little Fable," 1993.
5. *Give it Up!* adaptation, 1993.

Opposite page: Poster for Oporto, Portugal Comic Convention, 1993.

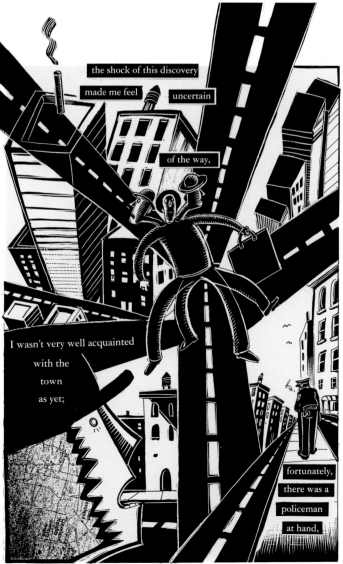

the shock of this discovery
made me feel
uncertain
of the way,
I wasn't very well acquainted
with the
town
as yet;
fortunately,
there was a
policeman
at hand,

5

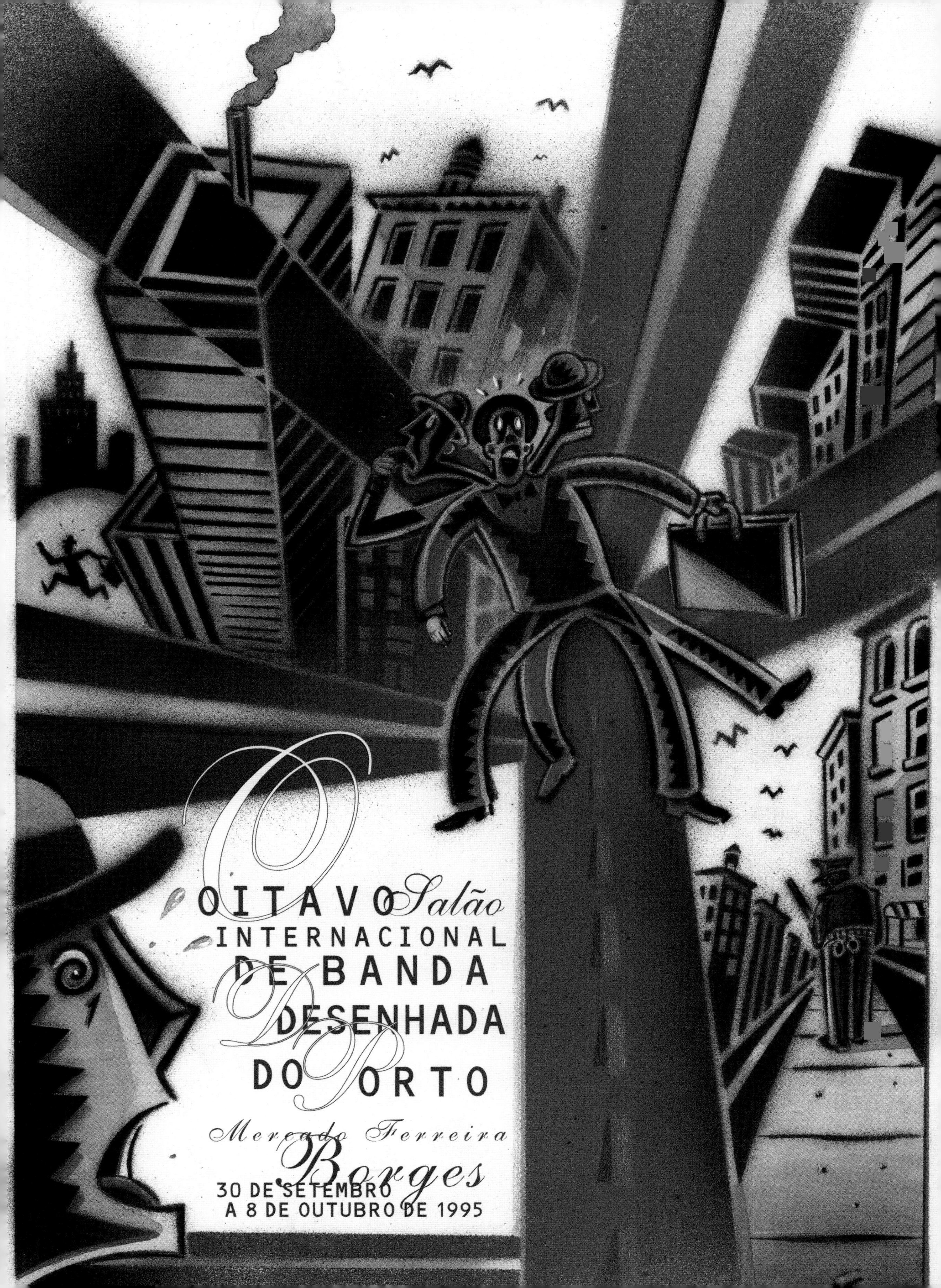

O
OITAVO Salão
INTERNACIONAL
DE BANDA
DESENHADA
DO PORTO
Mercado Ferreira
Borges
30 DE SETEMBRO
A 8 DE OUTUBRO DE 1995

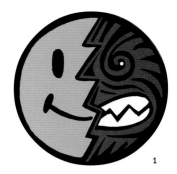

1

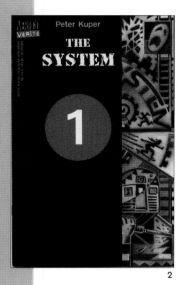

When editor Lou Stathis first approached me about creating something for DC Comics, the publisher of *Batman* and *Superman*, I wondered what I might produce that would even remotely fit into that world. After all, up to that point, most of my cartooning had been for small underground comix. Lou explained, however, that DC's new Vertigo Vérité imprint intended to reach an entirely different audience.

VERTIGO VÉRITÉ
Peter Kuper
THE SYSTEM
1

2

5

Well, given the nudge, my mind landed on an idea that had been rattling around in my head for about eight years. It was triggered by a subway ride I'd taken. Spacing out, with my eyes passing over my fellow passengers, I started wondering about who they all were. Was this trip all we had in common, or might our lives crisscross, and later, affect one another in a larger way? This got me thinking about the theory that the flap of a butterfly's wings in China can cause a storm in Manhattan; that seemingly small actions can ripple into tidal waves.

VERTIGO VÉRITÉ
Peter Kuper
THE SYSTEM
2

3

I decided to tell this tale with no dialogue, and let the images speak for themselves. This eliminated language barriers and forced the reader to interact with the characters and connect the dots. It also removed a comic book convention, the word balloon, that causes so many non-comic book readers to view this medium as one indistinguishable genre.

In a certain way, I didn't have to write to cook up *The System*. Instead, I just took stories I'd read in the newspapers and put them in a pot together. One tablespoon of missing woman, a dash of police corruption, a cup of the bombing of the World Trade Center; all spiced up with some insider trading. Mix in a broth of corporate takeovers and political scandals, then boil together over a high flame for six months with some secret ingredients of my first hand experiences: the woman I saw singing in the subway, the homeless guys I've seen on a daily basis, a crack dealer on my block, and a strip club I once visited.

VERTIGO VÉRITÉ
Peter Kuper
O SISTEMA
100 Páginas
Do autor de
Spy vs. Spy
da revista MAD

4

It's notable, that in the few short years since I produced *The System*, most of the locales I referenced have been obliterated. Times Square is unrecognizable, Checker cabs are history, and sadly, so is my editor, Lou Stathis, who died from cancer mere months after the book's publication. All a reminder of just how fragile the system actually is.

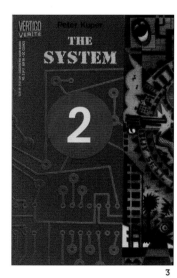

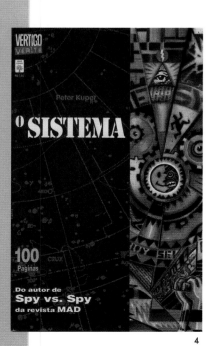

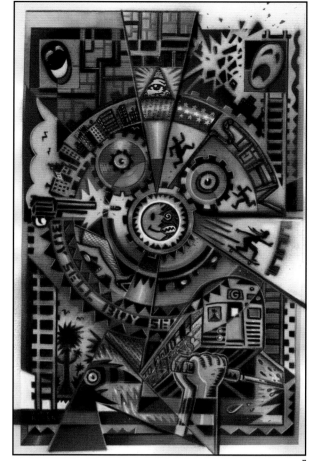

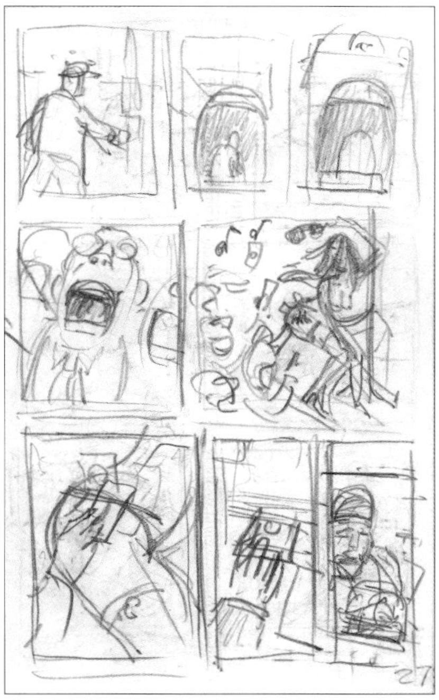
6

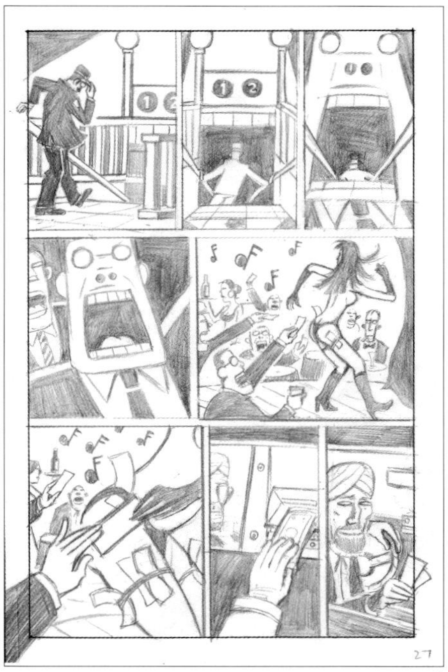
7

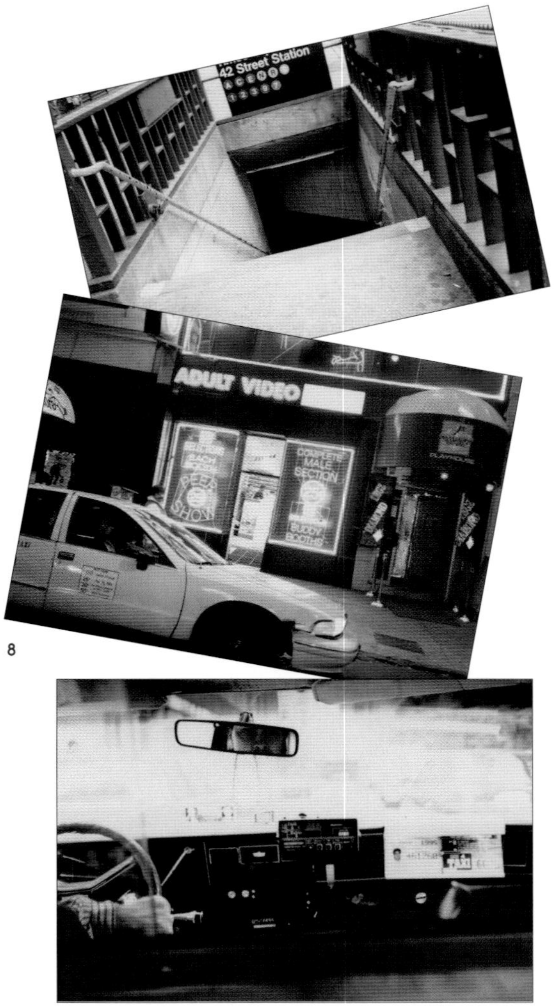
42 Street Station
ADULT VIDEO
COMPLETE MALE SECTION
8

1. *The System* button design, 1996.
2. *The System* #1 comic book, 1996.
3. *The System* #2 comic book, 1996.
4. *The System*, Brazilian edition, 1998.
5. Cover art for *The System* trade paperback, 1997.
6. Rough pencil sketch, 1995.
7. Finished pencil drawing, 1995.
8. Reference photos.
9. Finished art, page 27, 1996.
10. Finished art, page 28, 1996.

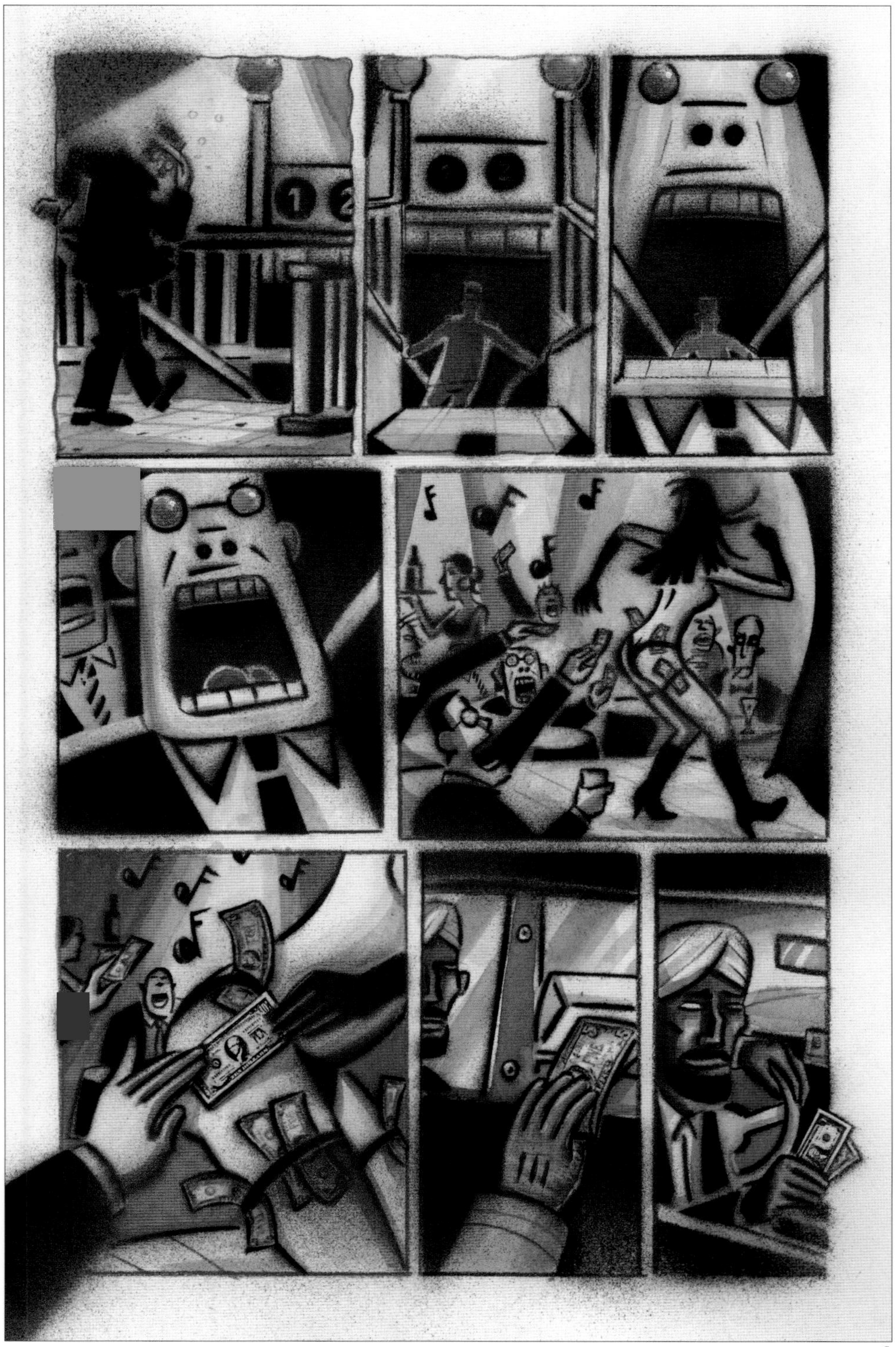
9

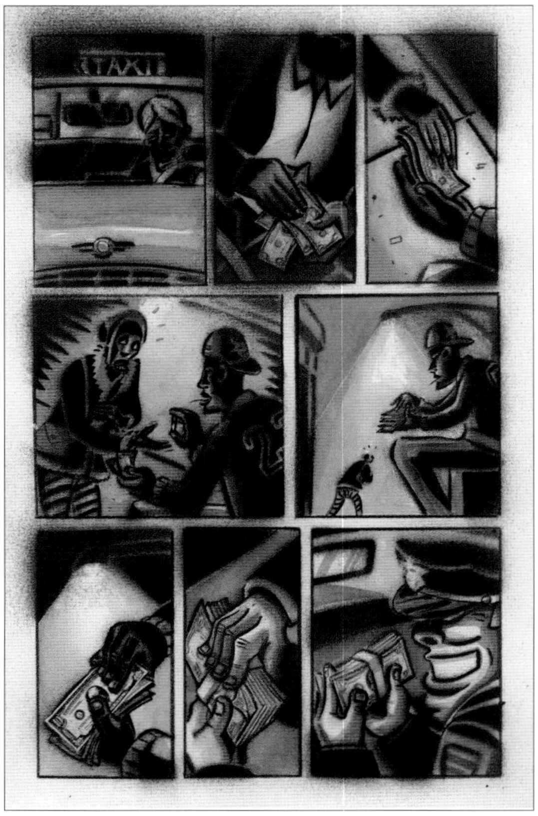
TAXI
10

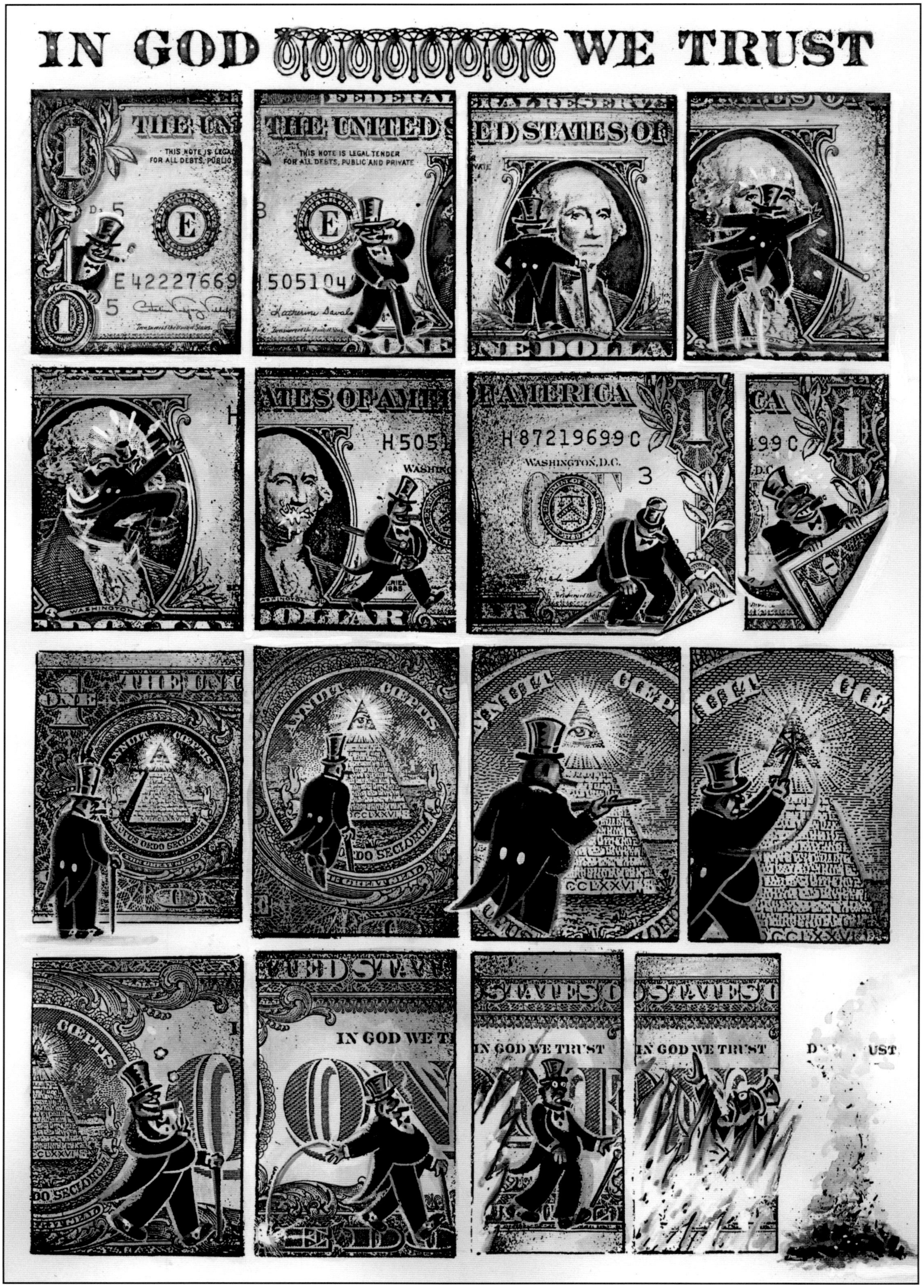
IN GOD WE TRUST

In God We Trust, Unpublished, 2000.

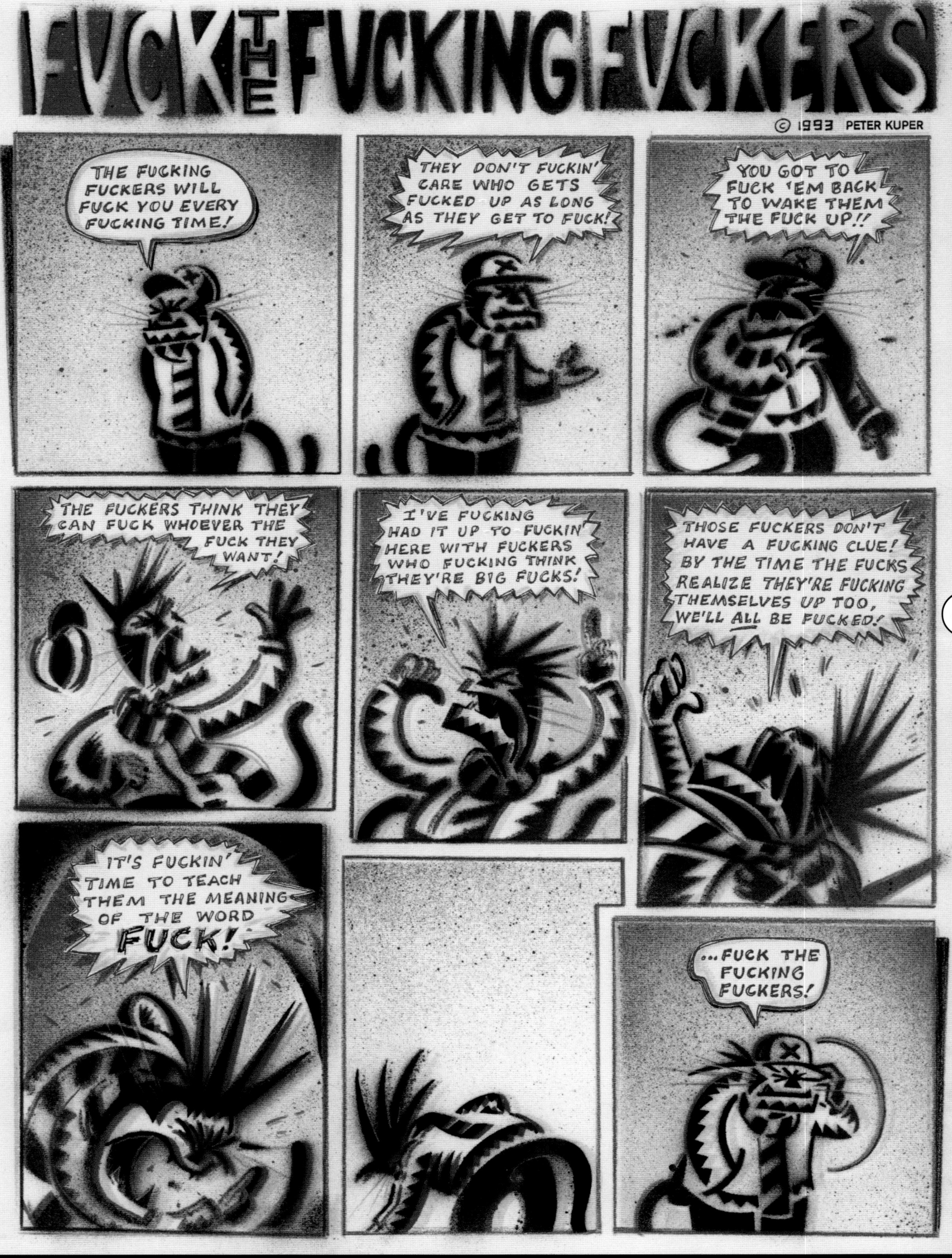
FUCK THE FUCKING FUCKERS
© 1993 PETER KUPER
THE FUCKING FUCKERS WILL FUCK YOU EVERY FUCKING TIME!
THEY DON'T FUCKIN' CARE WHO GETS FUCKED UP AS LONG AS THEY GET TO FUCK!
YOU GOT TO FUCK 'EM BACK TO WAKE THEM THE FUCK UP!!
THE FUCKERS THINK THEY CAN FUCK WHOEVER THE FUCK THEY WANT!
I'VE FUCKING HAD IT UP TO FUCKIN' HERE WITH FUCKERS WHO FUCKING THINK THEY'RE BIG FUCKS!
THOSE FUCKERS DON'T HAVE A FUCKING CLUE! BY THE TIME THE FUCKS REALIZE THEY'RE FUCKING THEMSELVES UP TOO, WE'LL ALL BE FUCKED!
IT'S FUCKIN' TIME TO TEACH THEM THE MEANING OF THE WORD FUCK!
...FUCK THE FUCKING FUCKERS!

Fuck the Fucking Fuckers, Unpublished, commissioned by *Details*, 1993.

ILLUMINATED MANUSCRIPTS

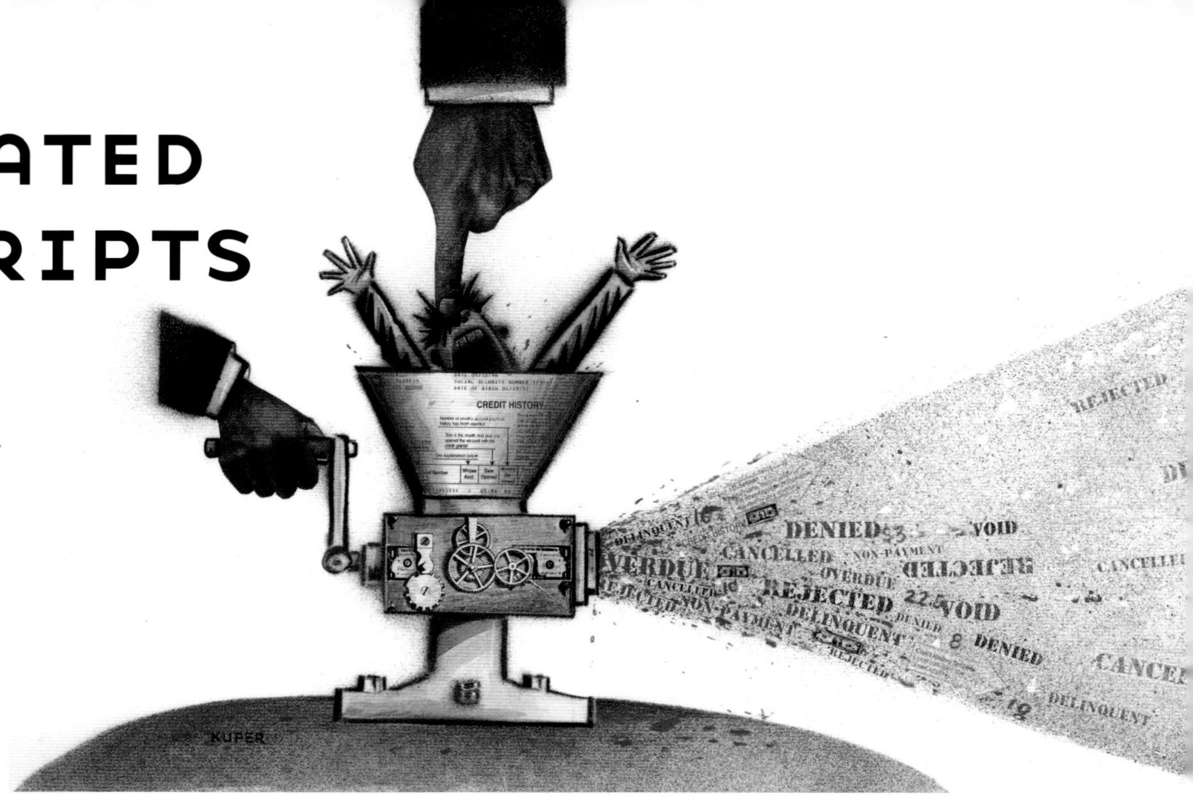

CREDIT HISTORY
DENIED
VOID
REJECTED
CANCELLED
OVERDUE
NON-PAYMENT
DELINQUENT
KUPER

1

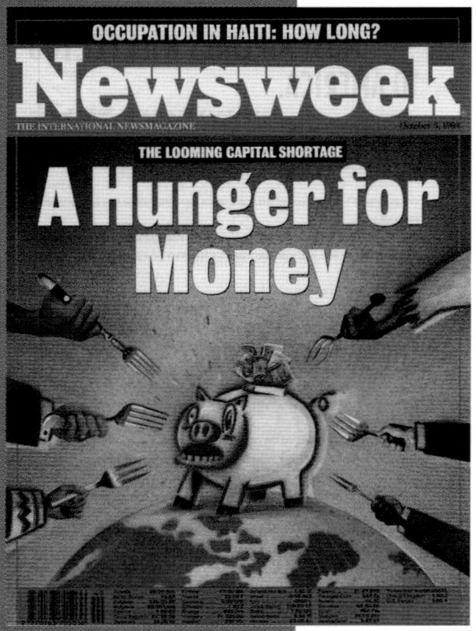

OCCUPATION IN HAITI: HOW LONG?
Newsweek
THE INTERNATIONAL NEWSMAGAZINE
THE LOOMING CAPITAL SHORTAGE
A Hunger for Money

2

As much as I love working on larger projects, there is nothing to compare with the immediate gratification of producing a drawing one day, that millions will see in print the next.

Although I've always hated test taking, many of my illustration assignments are just that. There is usually a ridiculously short deadline, a fickle editor, and the confines of a defined space to fill. What differentiates the two is possibility. With conceptual illustration there is no one right choice, but thousands of correct answers.

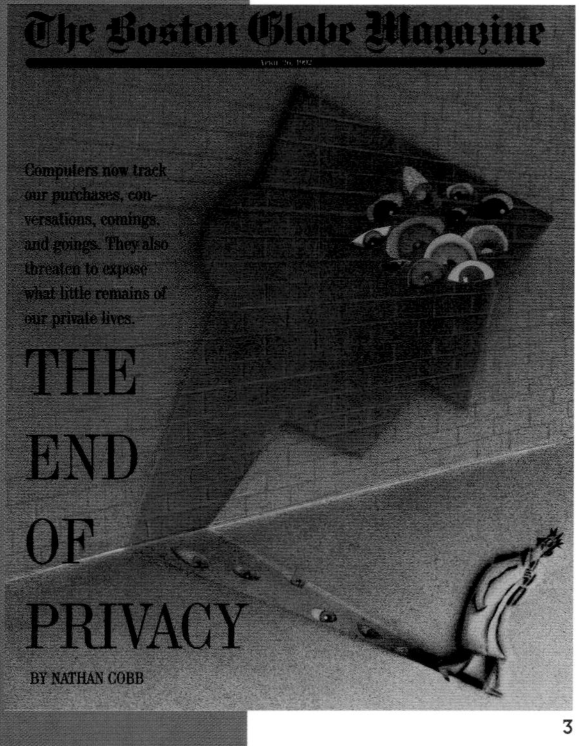

The Boston Globe Magazine
Computers now track our purchases, conversations, comings and goings. They also threaten to expose what little remains of our private lives.
THE END OF PRIVACY
BY NATHAN COBB

3

For me, the greatest challenge has been to define exactly what I want to accomplish within the framework of the illustration field, then maintain consistency throughout my work so that art directors only call when the assignments are appropriate.

After several years of attempting to compartmentalize my more political work from jobs that mostly called upon style alone, my brain was ready to explode. I found it impossible to juggle purely commercial assignments with those that were close to my heart, so I began turning down work that had no room for content.

Thanks to that decision, the calls to illustrate widgets have evaporated. Although I've vastly narrowed my job options, I've vanquished the nagging feeling that I'm just fiddling while Rome burns.

5

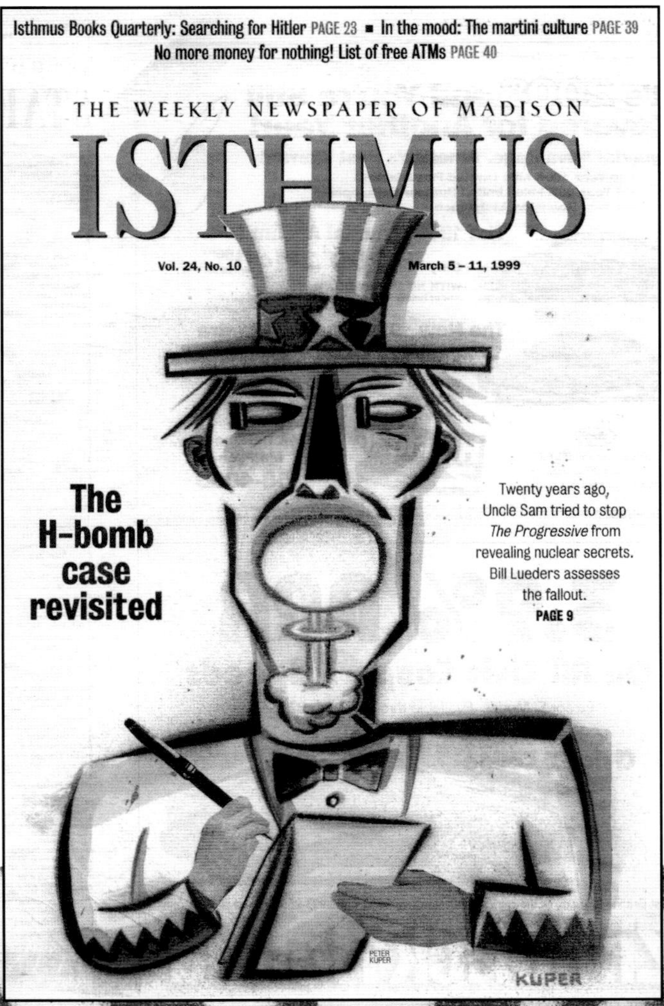
Isthmus Books Quarterly: Searching for Hitler PAGE 23 ■ In the mood: The martini culture PAGE 39
No more money for nothing! List of free ATMs PAGE 40
THE WEEKLY NEWSPAPER OF MADISON
ISTHMUS
Vol. 24, No. 10
March 5 – 11, 1999
The H-bomb case revisited
Twenty years ago, Uncle Sam tried to stop The Progressive from revealing nuclear secrets. Bill Lueders assesses the fallout.
PAGE 9
PETER KUPER
KUPER

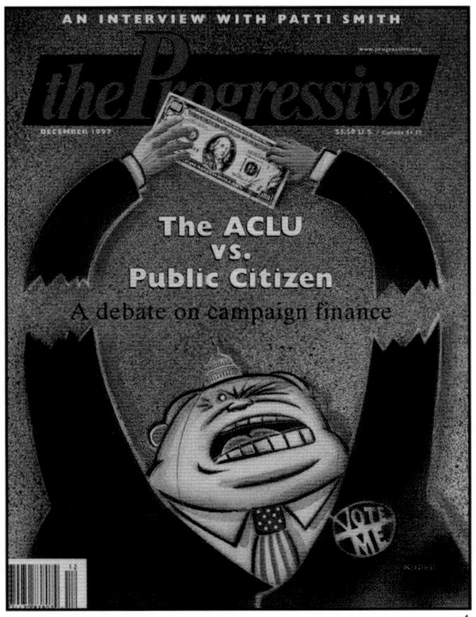
AN INTERVIEW WITH PATTI SMITH
the Progressive
DECEMBER 1997
The ACLU vs. Public Citizen
A debate on campaign finance
VOTE ME

4

1. Illustration for *Smart Money* , 1996.
2. Cover, *Newsweek*, 1995.
3. Cover, *Boston Globe Magazine*, 1995.
4. Cover, the *Progressive*, 1998.
5. Cover, *Isthmus*, 1999.
6. *Hate Radio*, Unpublished, commissioned by *Entertainment Weekly*, 1997.

6

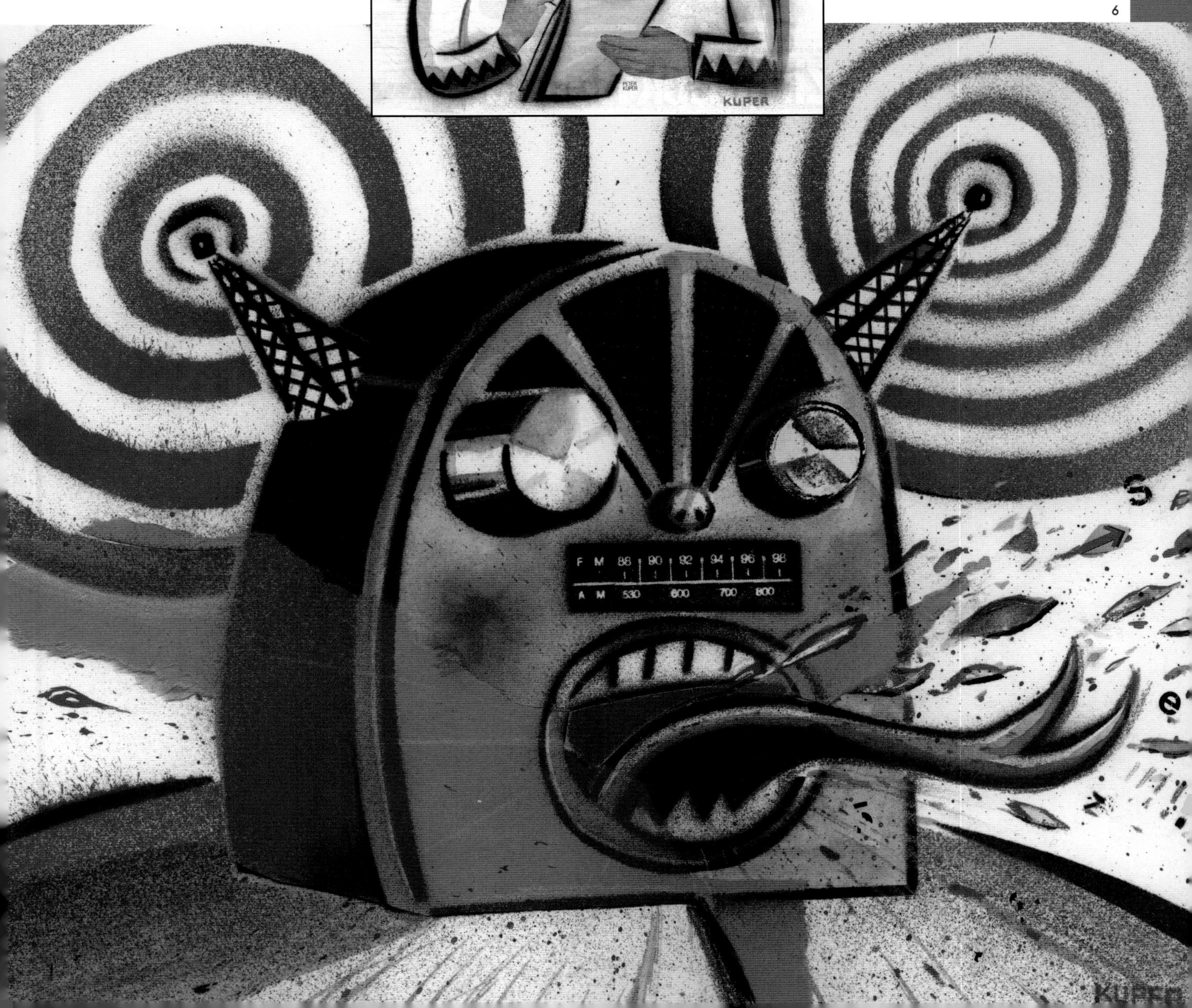
F M 88 90 92 94 96 98
A M 530 600 700 800

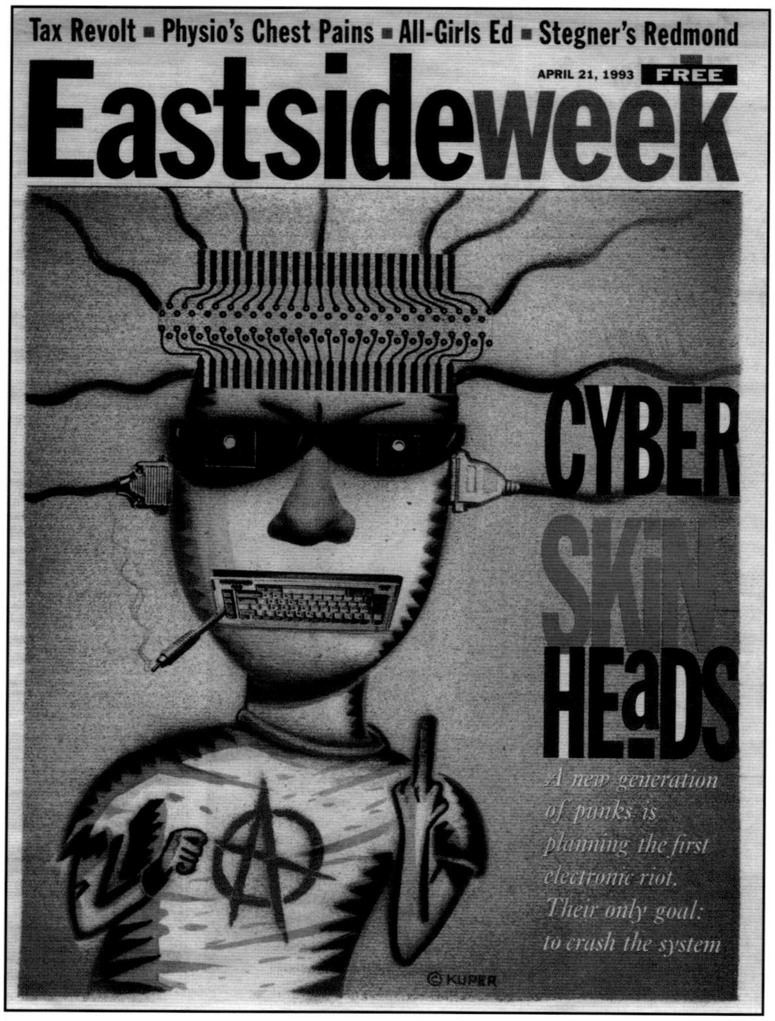
Tax Revolt ▪ Physio's Chest Pains ▪ All-Girls Ed ▪ Stegner's Redmond
APRIL 21, 1993
FREE
Eastsideweek
CYBER
SKIN
HEaDS
A new generation of punks is planning the first electronic riot. Their only goal: to crash the system
© KUPER

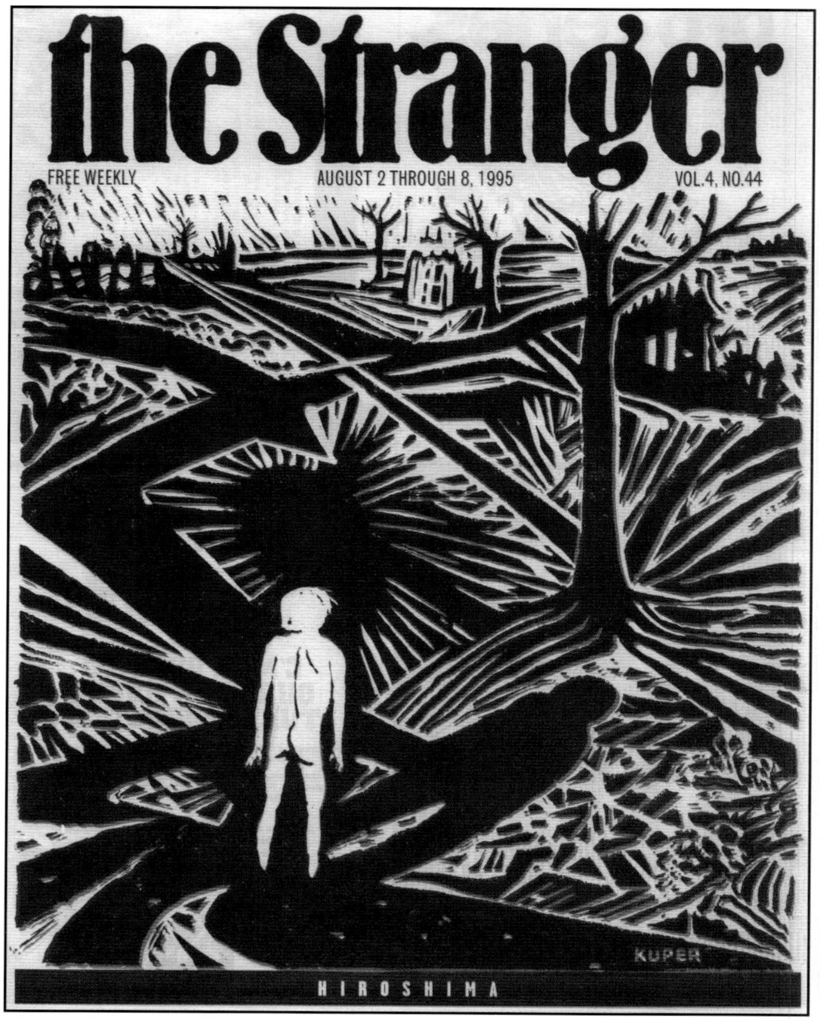
the Stranger
FREE WEEKLY
AUGUST 2 THROUGH 8, 1995
VOL.4, NO.44
KUPER
HIROSHIMA

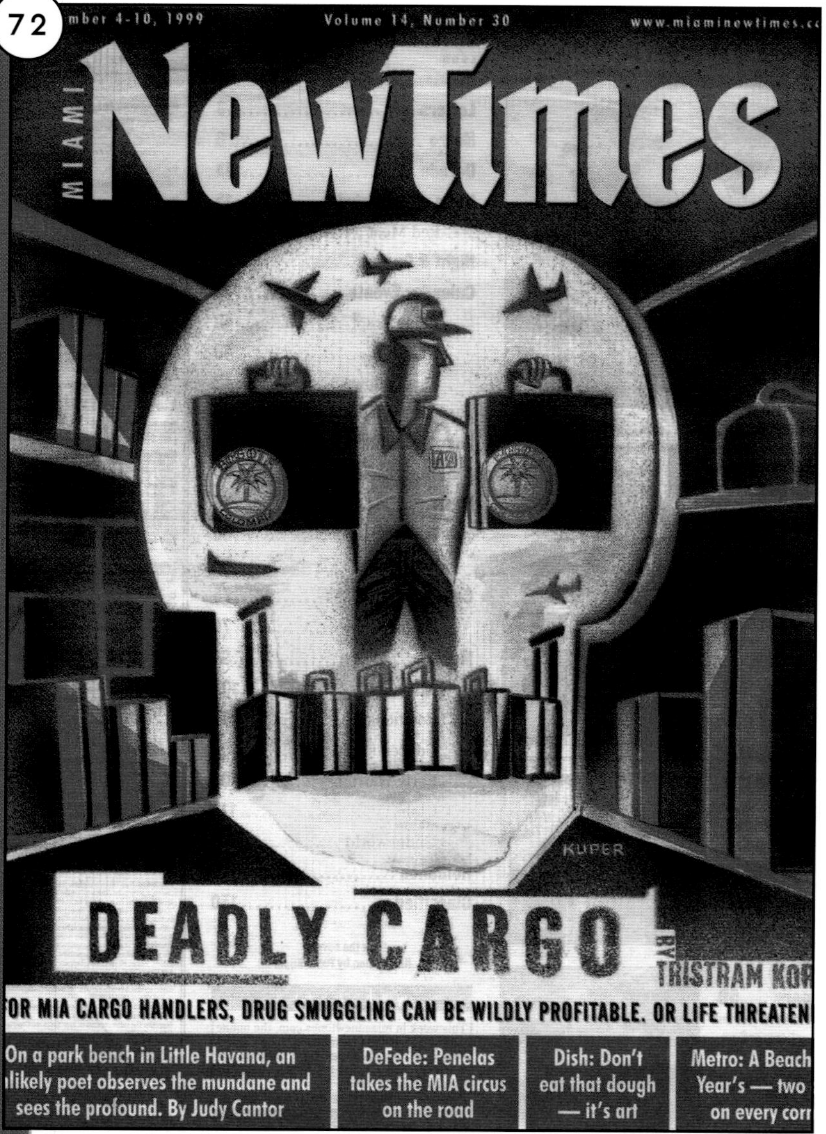
mber 4-10, 1999
Volume 14, Number 30
www.miaminewtimes.c
MIAMI
NewTimes
KUPER
DEADLY CARGO
BY TRISTRAM KOR
FOR MIA CARGO HANDLERS, DRUG SMUGGLING CAN BE WILDLY PROFITABLE. OR LIFE THREATEN
On a park bench in Little Havana, an likely poet observes the mundane and sees the profound. By Judy Cantor
DeFede: Penelas takes the MIA circus on the road
Dish: Don't eat that dough — it's art
Metro: A Beach Year's — two on every corr

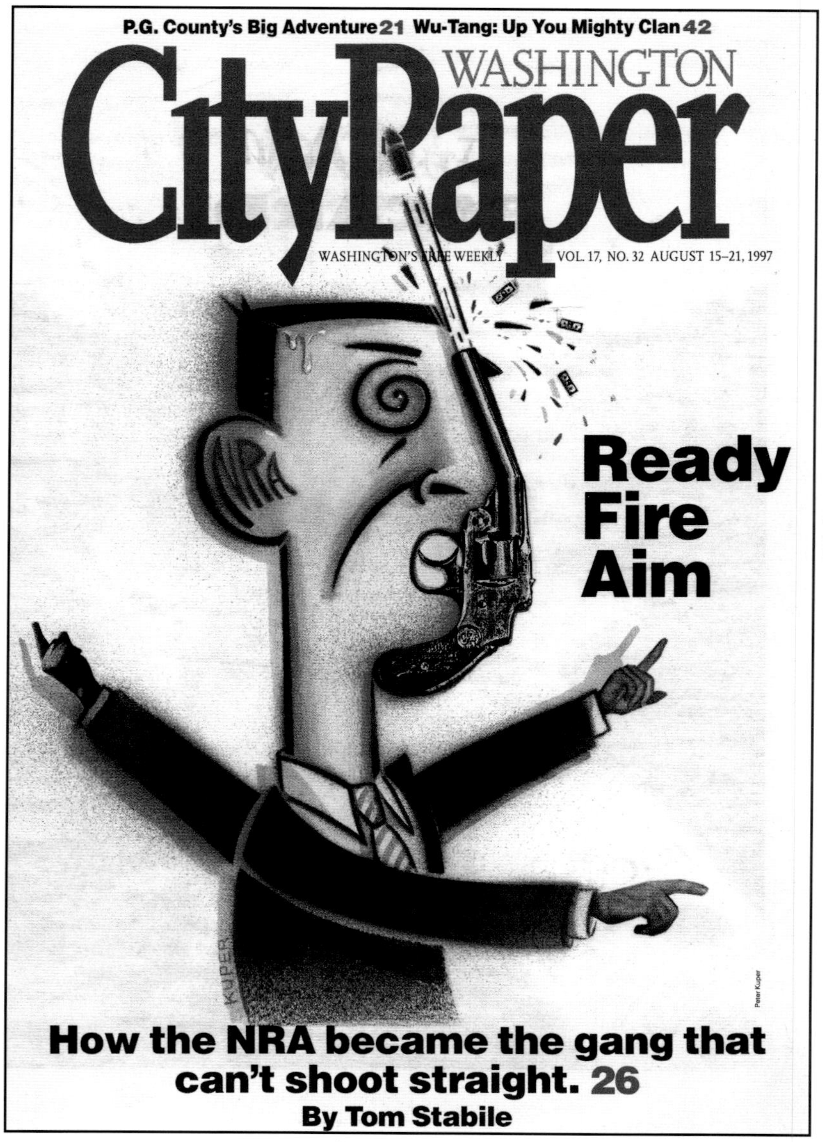
P.G. County's Big Adventure 21 Wu-Tang: Up You Mighty Clan 42
WASHINGTON
City Paper
WASHINGTON'S FREE WEEKLY
VOL. 17, NO. 32 AUGUST 15–21, 1997
NRA
Ready
Fire
Aim
KUPER
How the NRA became the gang that can't shoot straight. 26
By Tom Stabile

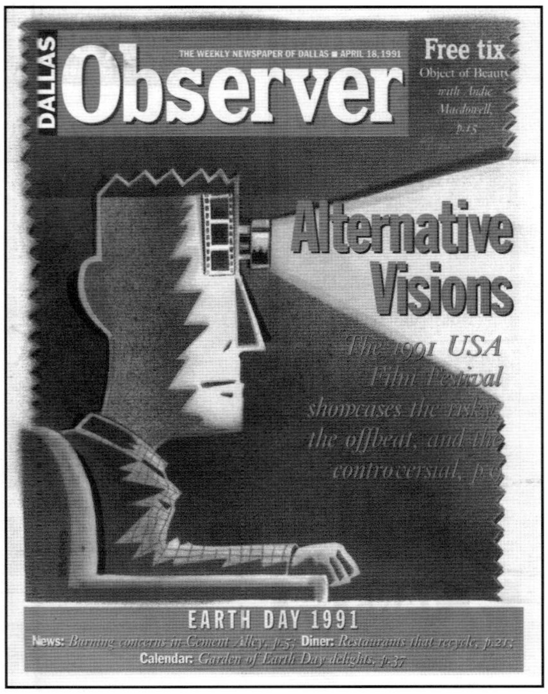
DALLAS
Observer
THE WEEKLY NEWSPAPER OF DALLAS ■ APRIL 18, 1991
Free tix
Alternative Visions
The 1991 USA Film Festival showcases the risky, the offbeat, and the controversial
EARTH DAY 1991
News:
Diner:
Calendar:

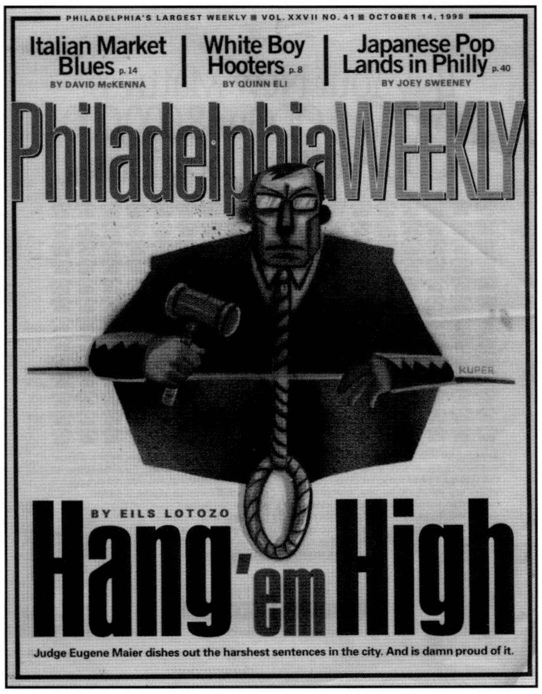
PHILADELPHIA'S LARGEST WEEKLY ■ VOL. XXVII NO. 41 ■ OCTOBER 14, 1998
Italian Market Blues p. 14
BY DAVID McKENNA
White Boy Hooters p. 8
BY QUINN ELI
Japanese Pop Lands in Philly p. 40
BY JOEY SWEENEY
PhiladelphiaWEEKLY
BY EILS LOTOZO
Hang 'em High
Judge Eugene Maier dishes out the harshest sentences in the city. And is damn proud of it.
KUPER

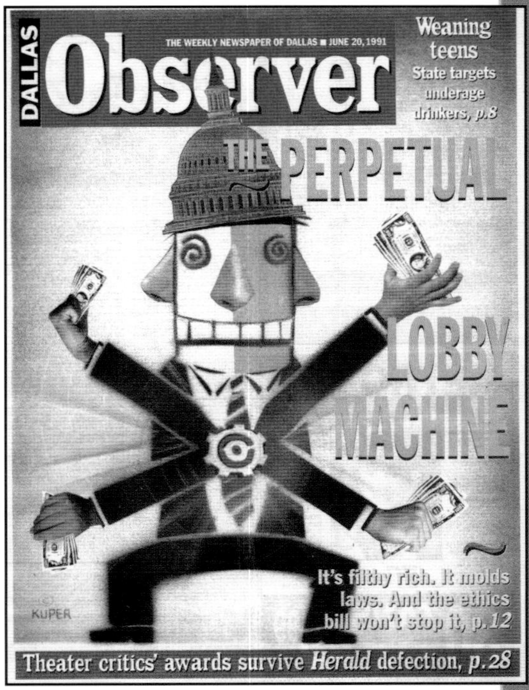
DALLAS
Observer
THE WEEKLY NEWSPAPER OF DALLAS ■ JUNE 20, 1991
Weaning teens
State targets underage drinkers, p.8
THE PERPETUAL LOBBY MACHINE
It's filthy rich. It molds laws. And the ethics bill won't stop it, p.12
KUPER
Theater critics' awards survive Herald defection, p.28

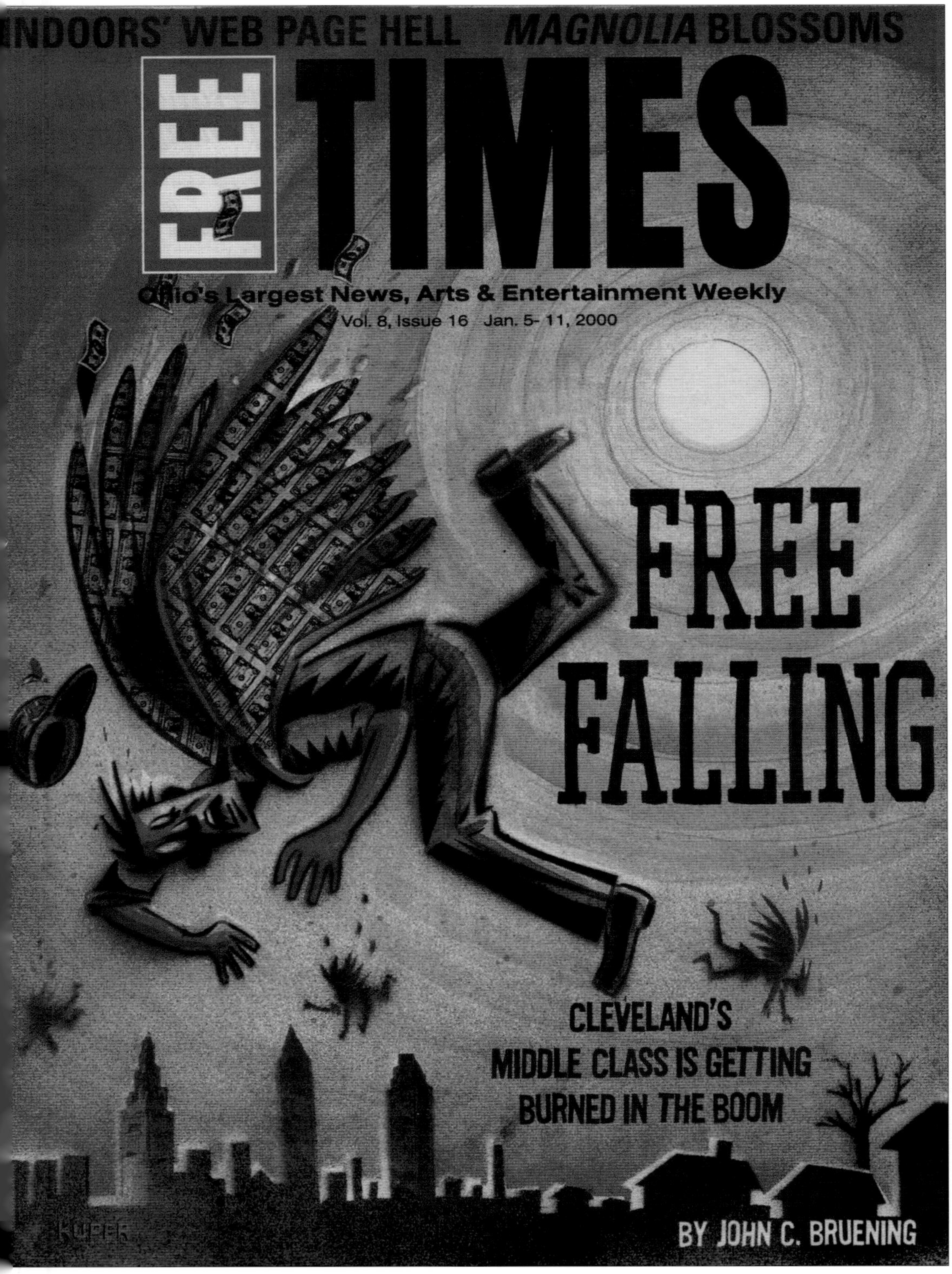
INDOORS' WEB PAGE HELL
MAGNOLIA BLOSSOMS
FREE TIMES
Ohio's Largest News, Arts & Entertainment Weekly
Vol. 8, Issue 16 Jan. 5- 11, 2000
FREE FALLING
CLEVELAND'S MIDDLE CLASS IS GETTING BURNED IN THE BOOM
BY JOHN C. BRUENING

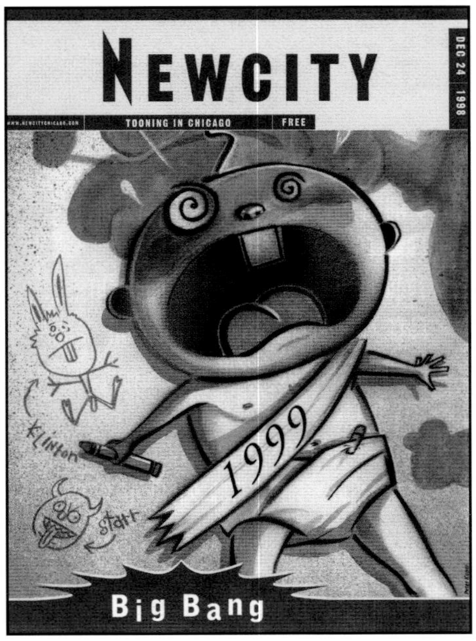
NEWCITY
DEC 24 1998
TOONING IN CHICAGO
FREE
1999
Big Bang

Covers from various alternative newspapers, 1991-2000.

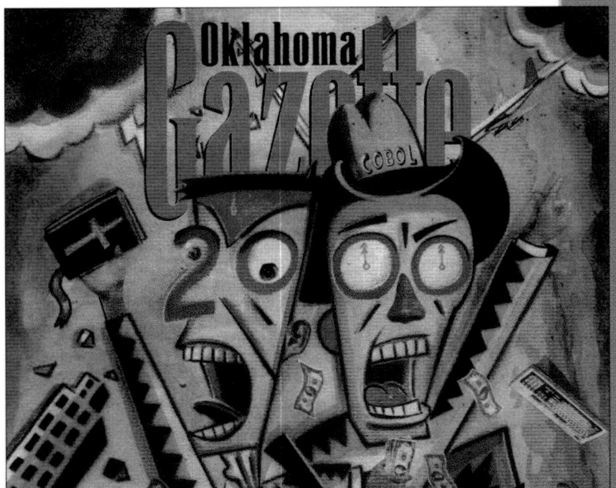
Oklahoma Gazette
COBOL
Y2K
Y2K as metaphor
What the millennium bug really tells us about the new carelessness
by Jay Porter Pg. 25
KUPER

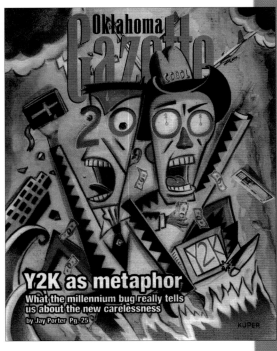

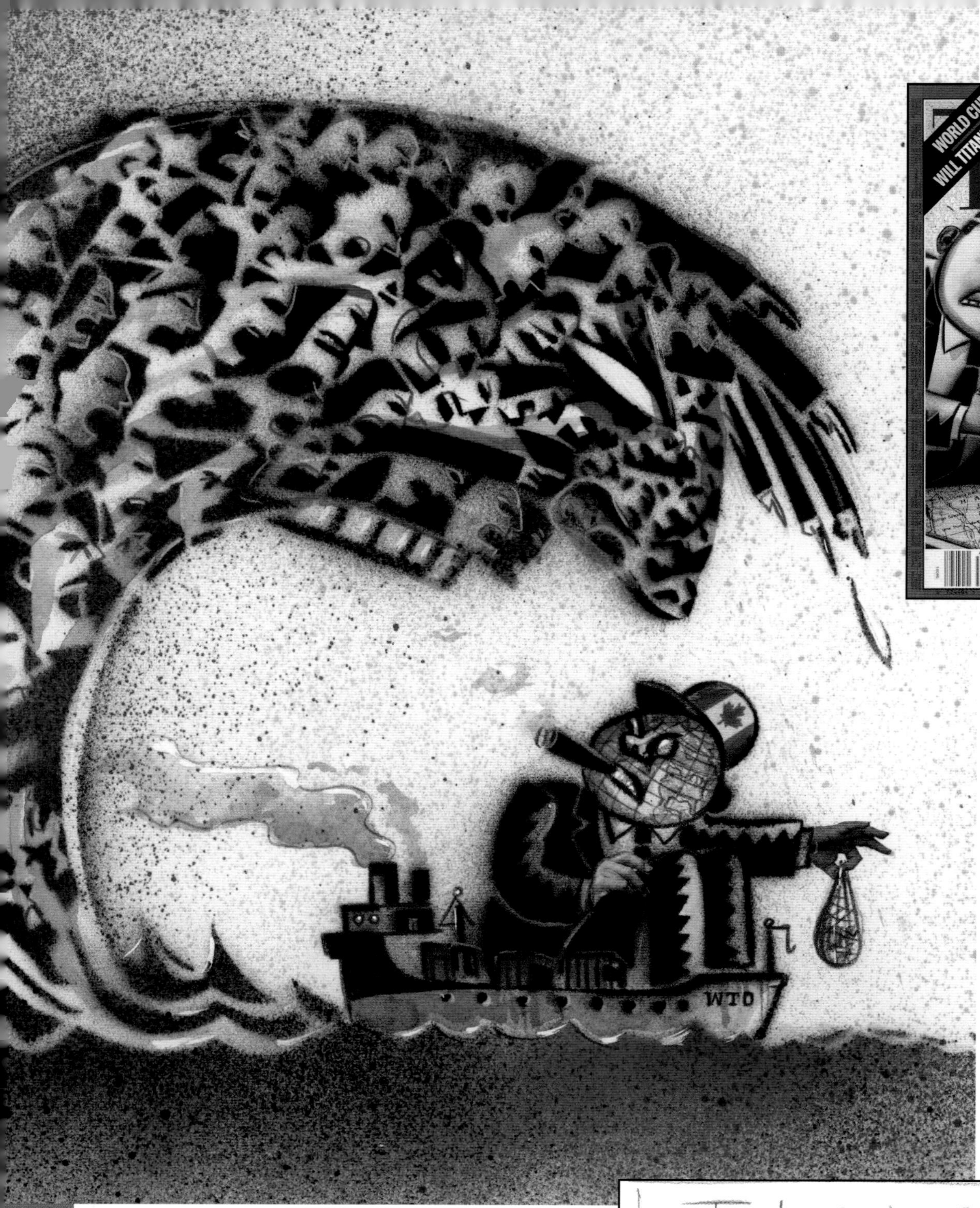
WTO

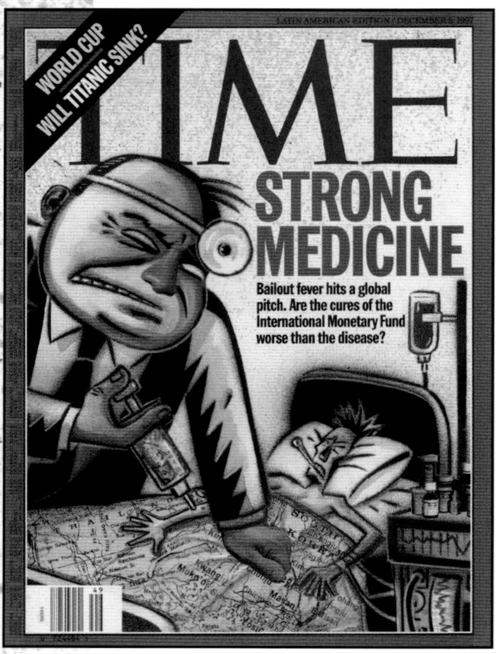
WORLD CUP
WILL TITANIC SINK?
TIME
STRONG
MEDICINE
Bailout fever hits a global pitch. Are the cures of the International Monetary Fund worse than the disease?

1

Left: *WTO Summit Protest*, published in *Time*, Canadian edition, 2000.

Right: Unpublished cover, commissioned by *Business Week*, 1994.

1. *Strong Medicine*, Time cover, Latin Edition, 1998.

2. *Scary Markets*, Time cover, Canadian Edition, 2000.

3. *Attica Settlement*, the *New York Times* Opinion Page, 1999.

Anatomy of a *Time* cover

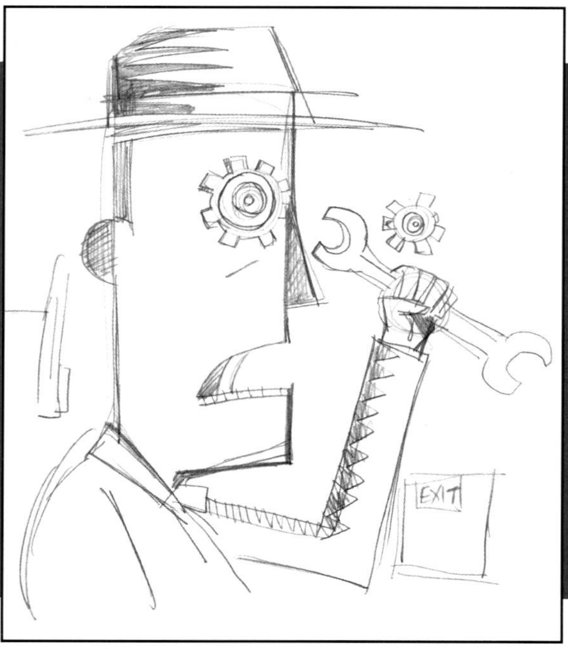
EXIT

Friday, November 11th, 1993, 12:06 p.m.: Art director calls and describes cover subject; I sketch this during our conversation...

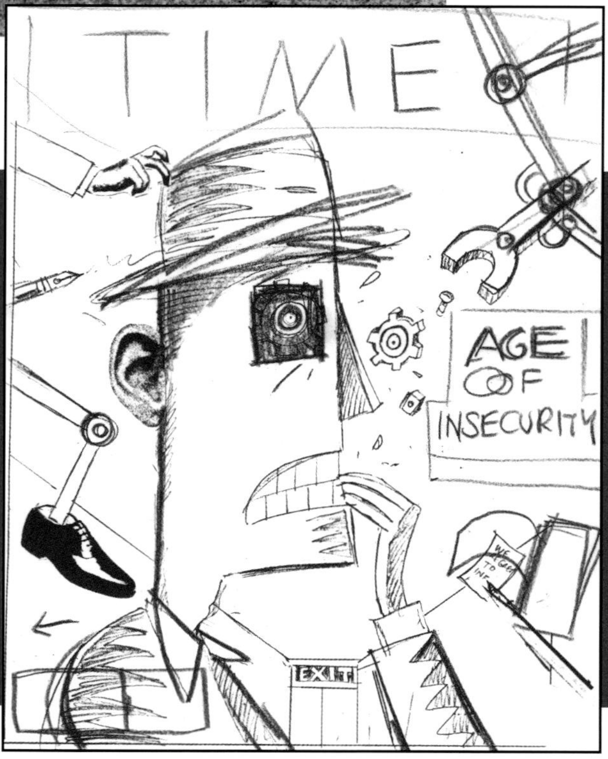
TIME
AGE OF INSECURITY
EXIT

1:16 p.m.: I fax a tighter version of my sketch...

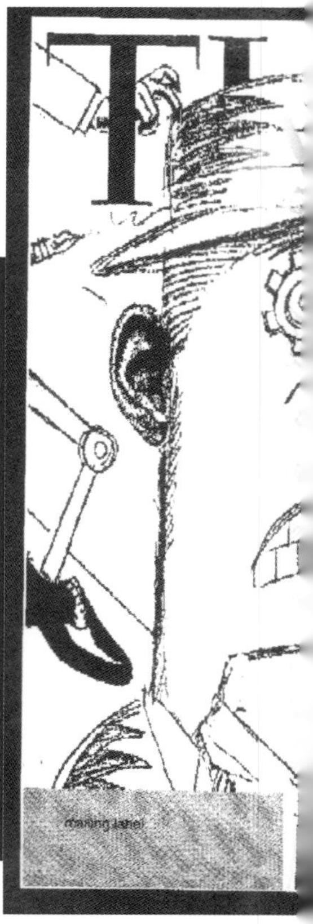

2:33 p.m.: Sketch approved, faxed back with type added...

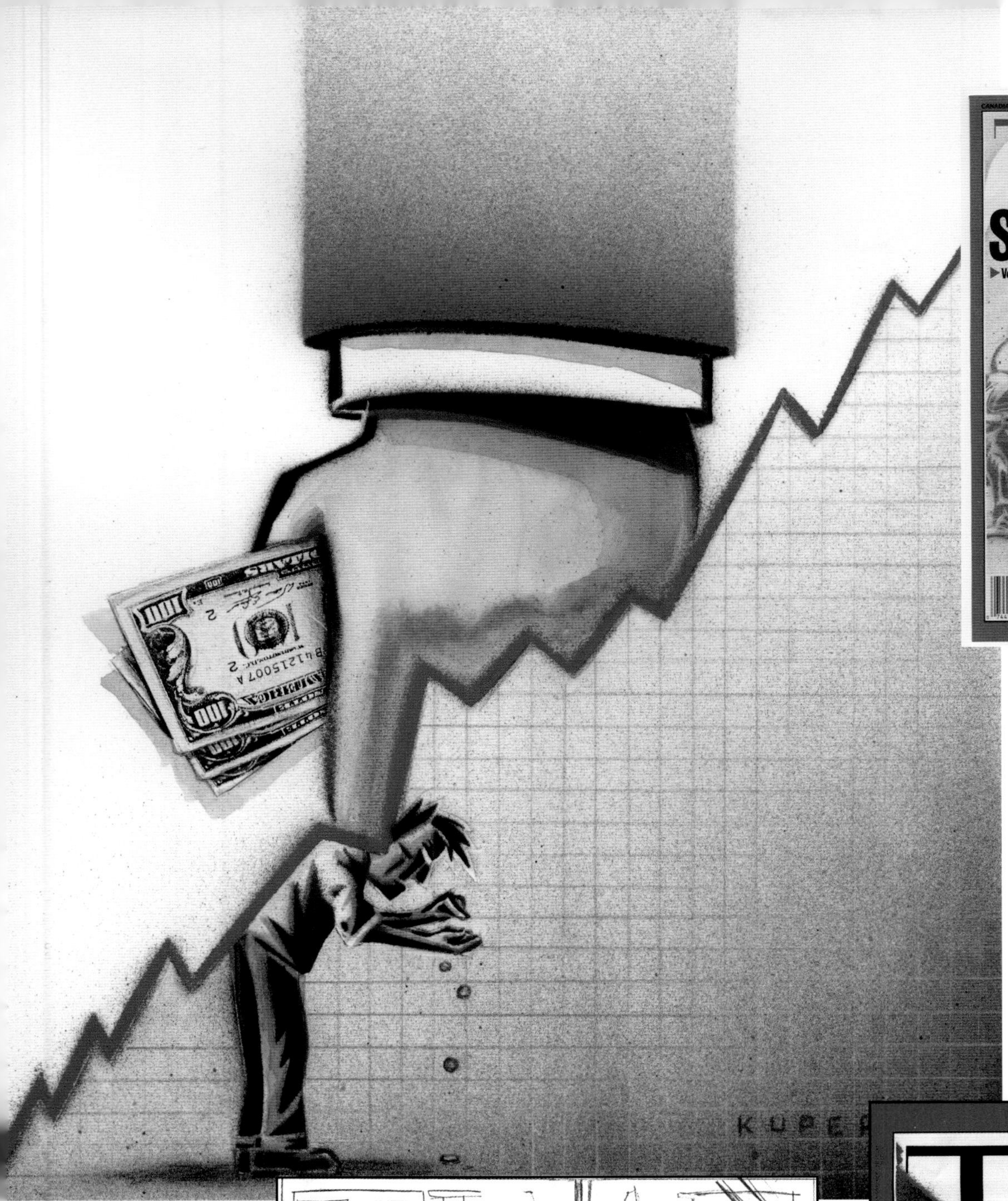
KUPER

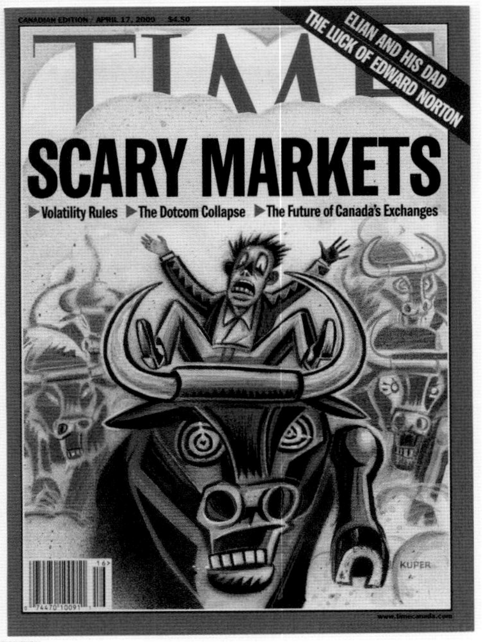
CANADIAN EDITION · APRIL 17, 2000 $4.50
TIME
ELIAN AND HIS DAD
THE LUCK OF EDWARD NORTON
SCARY MARKETS
▶Volatility Rules ▶The Dotcom Collapse ▶The Future of Canada's Exchanges
KUPER

2

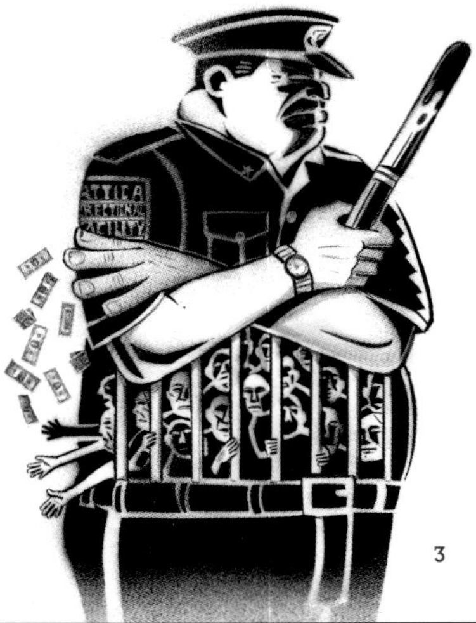

3

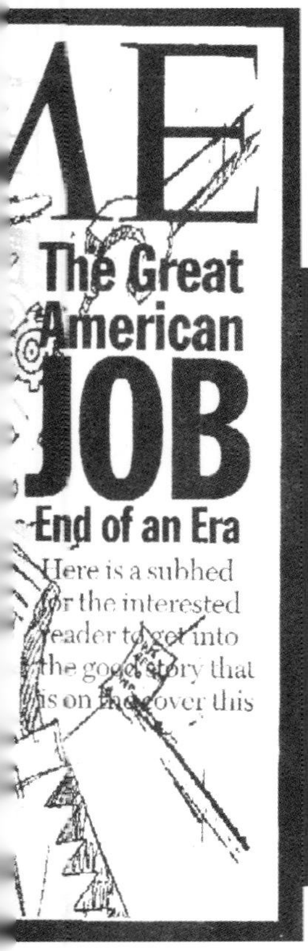
ME
The Great
American
JOB
End of an Era
Here is a subhed
for the interested
reader to get into
the good story that
is on the cover this

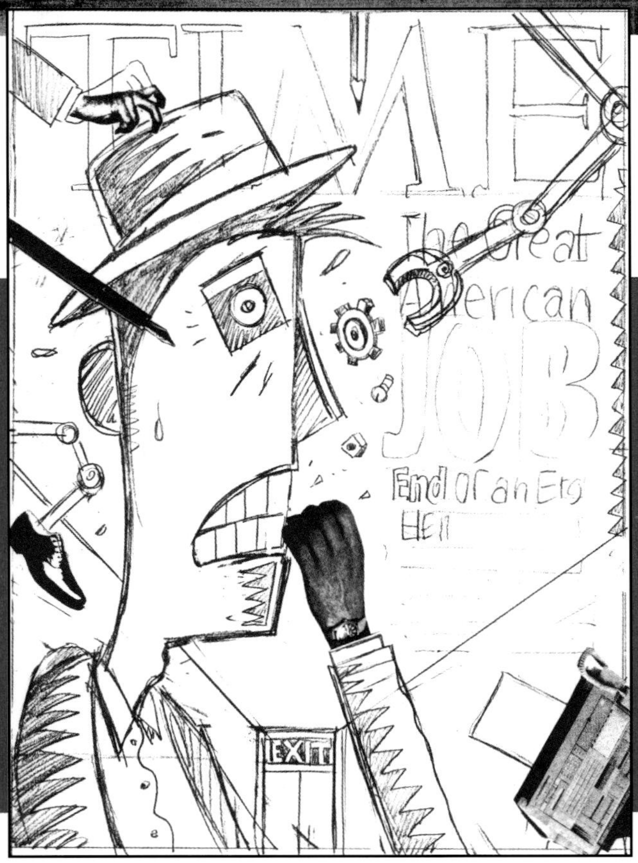
TIME
The Great
American
JOB
End of an Era
EXIT

3:46 p.m.: Finished pencil drawing with collage elements, ready to be cut as stencil...

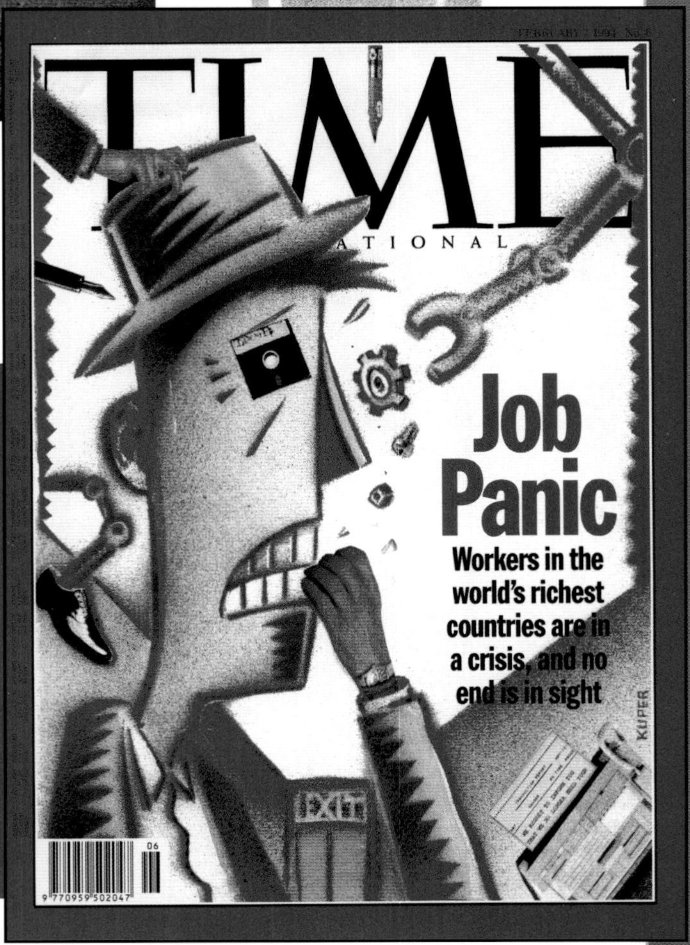
TIME
ATIONAL
Job
Panic
Workers in the
world's richest
countries are in
a crisis, and no
end is in sight
EXIT
KUPER

7:04 p.m.: I deliver finished art. Editors decide to use different design and above cover runs months later...

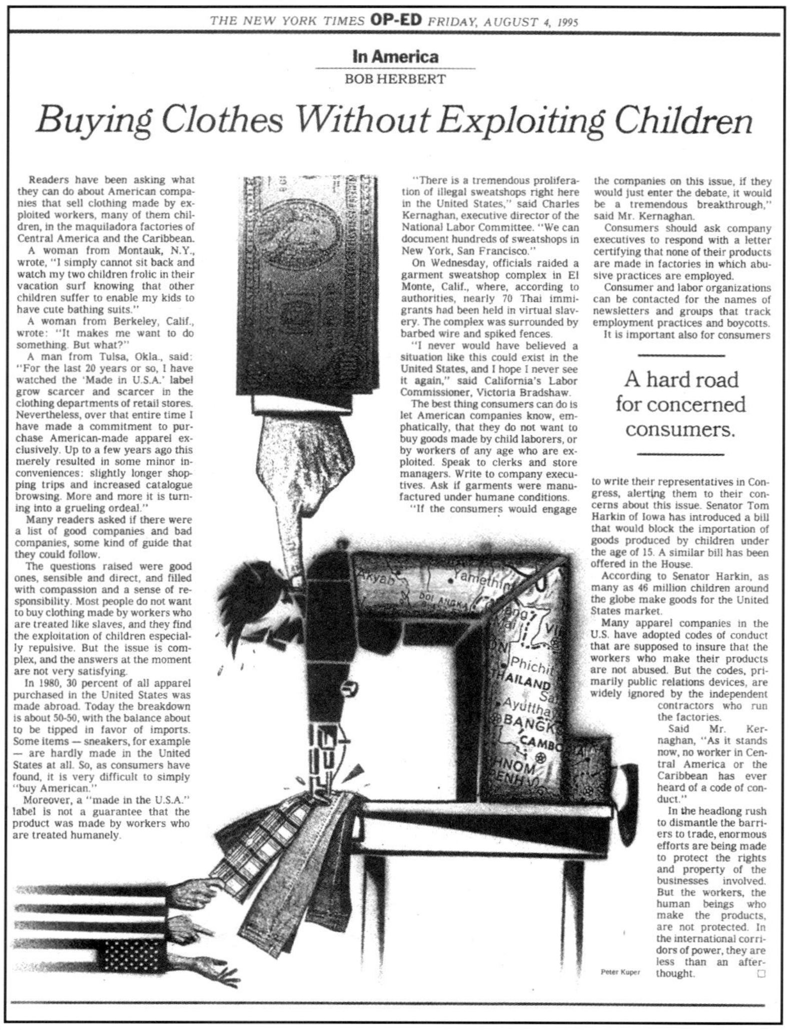

THE NEW YORK TIMES **OP-ED** FRIDAY, AUGUST 4, 1995

In America

BOB HERBERT

Buying Clothes Without Exploiting Children

Readers have been asking what they can do about American companies that sell clothing made by exploited workers, many of them children, in the maquiladora factories of Central America and the Caribbean.

A woman from Montauk, N.Y., wrote, "I simply cannot sit back and watch my two children frolic in their vacation surf knowing that other children suffer to enable my kids to have cute bathing suits."

A woman from Berkeley, Calif., wrote: "It makes me want to do something. But what?"

A man from Tulsa, Okla., said: "For the last 20 years or so, I have watched the 'Made in U.S.A.' label grow scarcer and scarcer in the clothing departments of retail stores. Nevertheless, over that entire time I have made a commitment to purchase American-made apparel exclusively. Up to a few years ago this merely resulted in some minor inconveniences: slightly longer shopping trips and increased catalogue browsing. More and more it is turning into a grueling ordeal."

Many readers asked if there were a list of good companies and bad companies, some kind of guide that they could follow.

The questions raised were good ones, sensible and direct, and filled with compassion and a sense of responsibility. Most people do not want to buy clothing made by workers who are treated like slaves, and they find the exploitation of children especially repulsive. But the issue is complex, and the answers at the moment are not very satisfying.

In 1980, 30 percent of all apparel purchased in the United States was made abroad. Today the breakdown is about 50-50, with the balance about to be tipped in favor of imports. Some items — sneakers, for example — are hardly made in the United States at all. So, as consumers have found, it is very difficult to simply "buy American."

Moreover, a "made in the U.S.A." label is not a guarantee that the product was made by workers who are treated humanely.

"There is a tremendous proliferation of illegal sweatshops right here in the United States," said Charles Kernaghan, executive director of the National Labor Committee. "We can document hundreds of sweatshops in New York, San Francisco."

On Wednesday, officials raided a garment sweatshop complex in El Monte, Calif., where, according to authorities, nearly 70 Thai immigrants had been held in virtual slavery. The complex was surrounded by barbed wire and spiked fences.

"I never would have believed a situation like this could exist in the United States, and I hope I never see it again," said California's Labor Commissioner, Victoria Bradshaw.

The best thing consumers can do is let American companies know, emphatically, that they do not want to buy goods made by child laborers, or by workers of any age who are exploited. Speak to clerks and store managers. Write to company executives. Ask if garments were manufactured under humane conditions.

"If the consumers would engage the companies on this issue, if they would just enter the debate, it would be a tremendous breakthrough," said Mr. Kernaghan.

Consumers should ask company executives to respond with a letter certifying that none of their products are made in factories in which abusive practices are employed.

Consumer and labor organizations can be contacted for the names of newsletters and groups that track employment practices and boycotts.

It is important also for consumers

A hard road for concerned consumers.

to write their representatives in Congress, alerting them to their concerns about this issue. Senator Tom Harkin of Iowa has introduced a bill that would block the importation of goods produced by children under the age of 15. A similar bill has been offered in the House.

According to Senator Harkin, as many as 46 million children around the globe make goods for the United States market.

Many apparel companies in the U.S. have adopted codes of conduct that are supposed to insure that the workers who make their products are not abused. But the codes, primarily public relations devices, are widely ignored by the independent contractors who run the factories.

Said Mr. Kernaghan, "As it stands now, no worker in Central America or the Caribbean has ever heard of a code of conduct."

In the headlong rush to dismantle the barriers to trade, enormous efforts are being made to protect the rights and property of the businesses involved. But the workers, the human beings who make the products, are not protected. In the international corridors of power, they are less than an afterthought. □

Peter Kuper

1

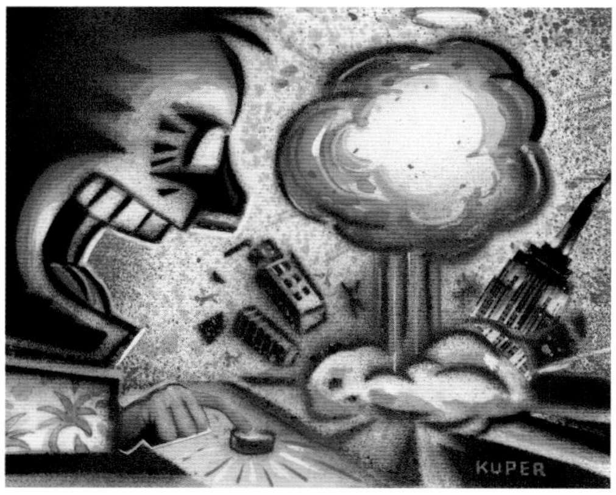
KUPER

2

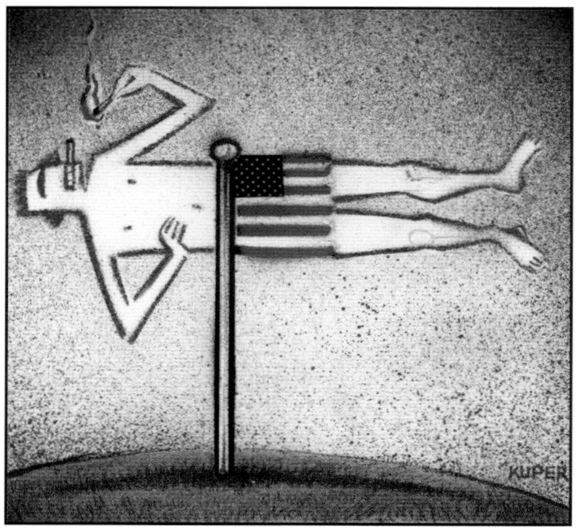
KUPER

3

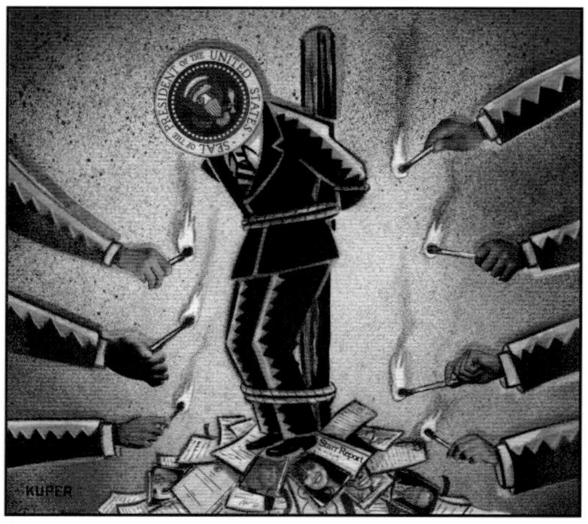
KUPER

4

1. *Sweatshop Worker*, published on the *New York Times* Opinion Page, 1997.
2. *Hollywood vs New York*, published in the *New Yorker*, 1994.
3. *Flag Burning*, published in *Time*, 1998.
4. *Presidential Sex Scandal* published in *New York Magazine*, 1999.
5. *Tabloid Journalism,* Unpublished, 1994.

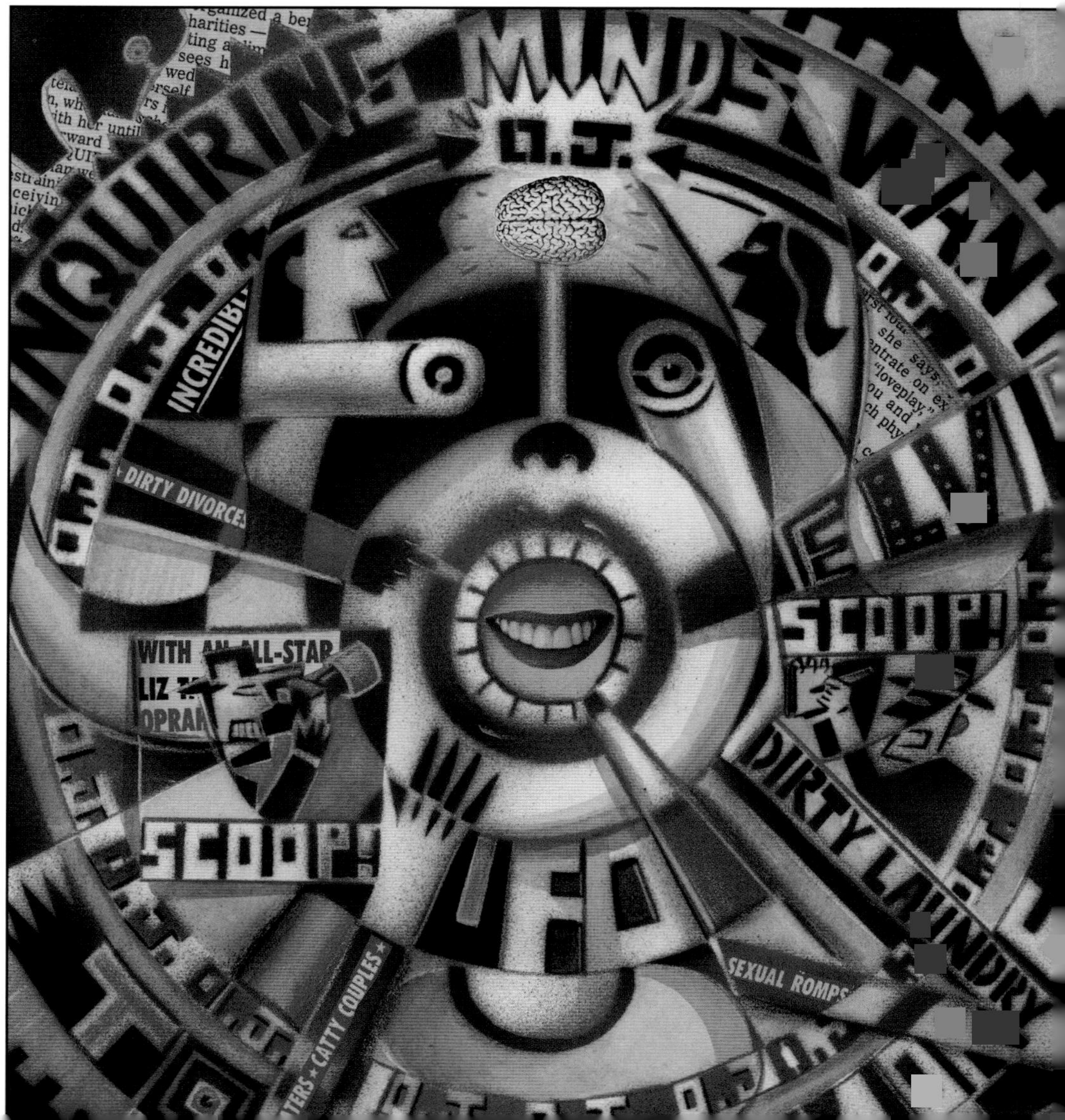
INQUIRING MINDS
O.J.
INCREDIBLE
DIRTY DIVORCE
SCOOP!
SCOOP!
DIRTY LAUNDRY
UFO
SEXUAL ROMPS
CATTY COUPLES
WITH AN ALL-STAR

5

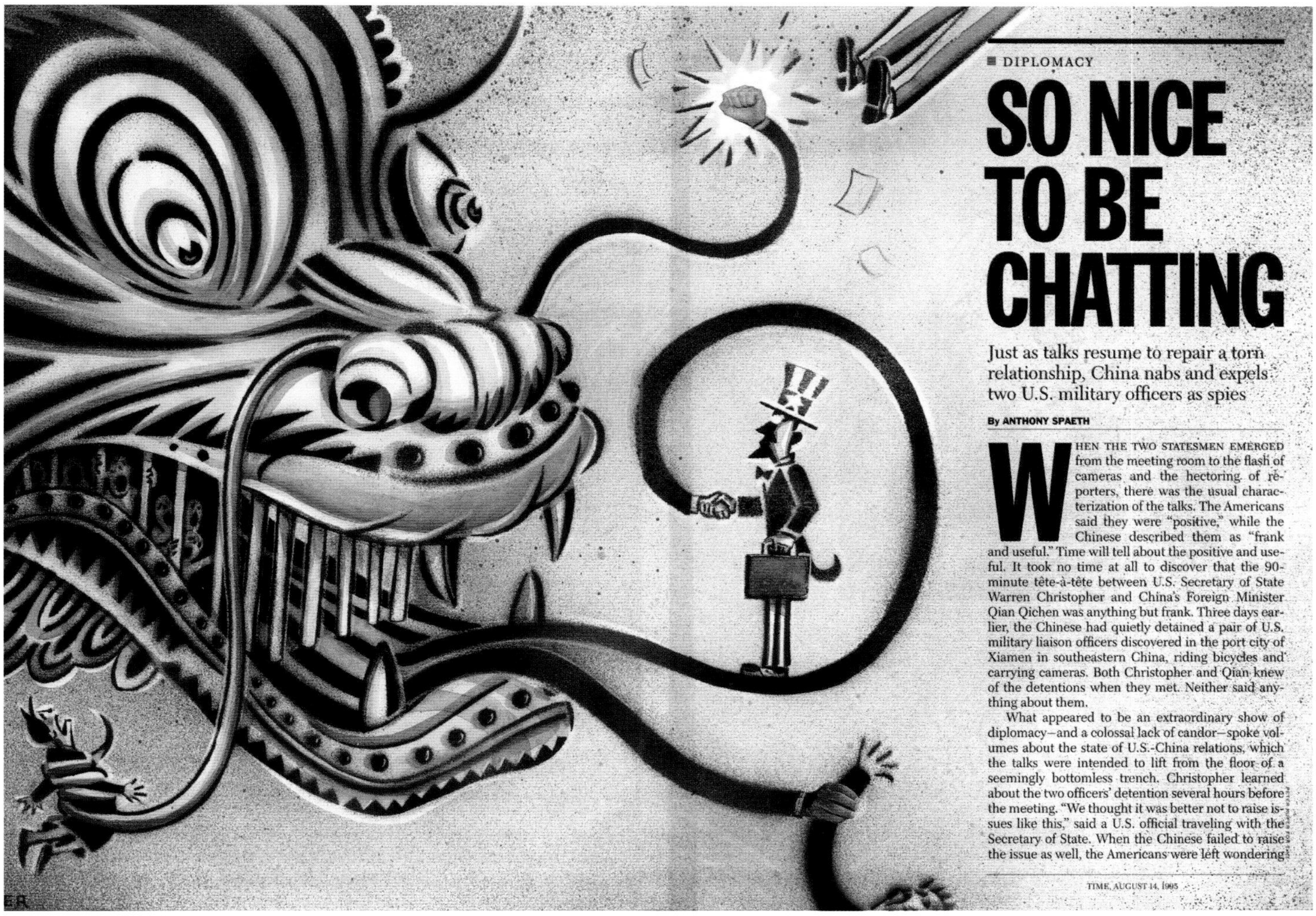

DIPLOMACY

SO NICE TO BE CHATTING

Just as talks resume to repair a torn relationship, China nabs and expels two U.S. military officers as spies

By ANTHONY SPAETH

WHEN THE TWO STATESMEN EMERGED from the meeting room to the flash of cameras and the hectoring of reporters, there was the usual characterization of the talks. The Americans said they were "positive," while the Chinese described them as "frank and useful." Time will tell about the positive and useful. It took no time at all to discover that the 90-minute tête-à-tête between U.S. Secretary of State Warren Christopher and China's Foreign Minister Qian Qichen was anything but frank. Three days earlier, the Chinese had quietly detained a pair of U.S. military liaison officers discovered in the port city of Xiamen in southeastern China, riding bicycles and carrying cameras. Both Christopher and Qian knew of the detentions when they met. Neither said anything about them.

What appeared to be an extraordinary show of diplomacy—and a colossal lack of candor—spoke volumes about the state of U.S.-China relations, which the talks were intended to lift from the floor of a seemingly bottomless trench. Christopher learned about the two officers' detention several hours before the meeting. "We thought it was better not to raise issues like this," said a U.S. official traveling with the Secretary of State. When the Chinese failed to raise the issue as well, the Americans were left wondering

TIME, AUGUST 14, 1995

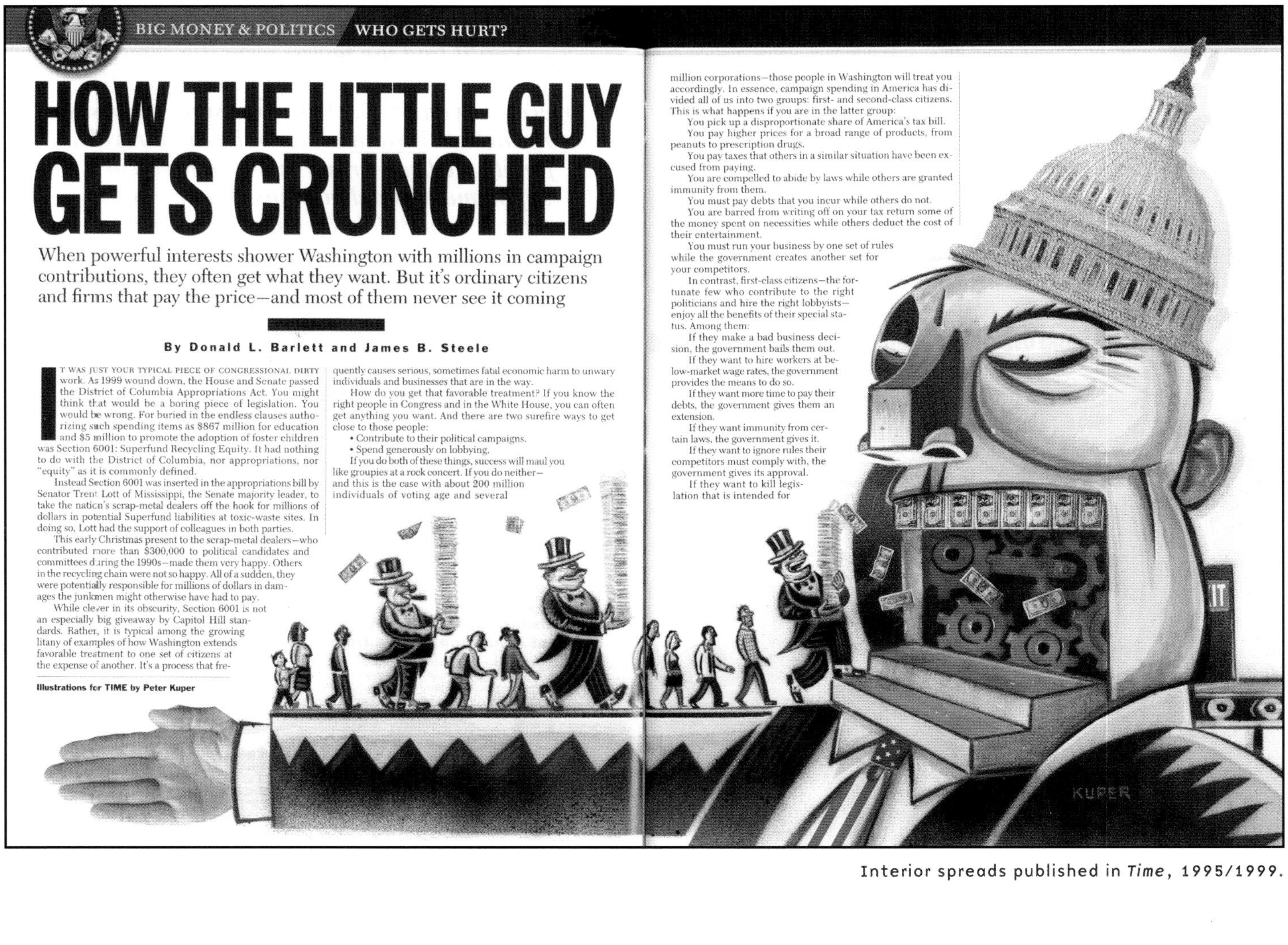

BIG MONEY & POLITICS | WHO GETS HURT?

HOW THE LITTLE GUY GETS CRUNCHED

When powerful interests shower Washington with millions in campaign contributions, they often get what they want. But it's ordinary citizens and firms that pay the price—and most of them never see it coming

By Donald L. Barlett and James B. Steele

IT WAS JUST YOUR TYPICAL PIECE OF CONGRESSIONAL DIRTY work. As 1999 wound down, the House and Senate passed the District of Columbia Appropriations Act. You might think that would be a boring piece of legislation. You would be wrong. For buried in the endless clauses authorizing such spending items as $867 million for education and $5 million to promote the adoption of foster children was Section 6001: Superfund Recycling Equity. It had nothing to do with the District of Columbia, nor appropriations, nor "equity" as it is commonly defined.

Instead Section 6001 was inserted in the appropriations bill by Senator Trent Lott of Mississippi, the Senate majority leader, to take the nation's scrap-metal dealers off the hook for millions of dollars in potential Superfund liabilities at toxic-waste sites. In doing so, Lott had the support of colleagues in both parties.

This early Christmas present to the scrap-metal dealers—who contributed more than $300,000 to political candidates and committees during the 1990s—made them very happy. Others in the recycling chain were not so happy. All of a sudden, they were potentially responsible for millions of dollars in damages the junkmen might otherwise have had to pay.

While clever in its obscurity, Section 6001 is not an especially big giveaway by Capitol Hill standards. Rather, it is typical among the growing litany of examples of how Washington extends favorable treatment to one set of citizens at the expense of another. It's a process that frequently causes serious, sometimes fatal economic harm to unwary individuals and businesses that are in the way.

How do you get that favorable treatment? If you know the right people in Congress and in the White House, you can often get anything you want. And there are two surefire ways to get close to those people:

- Contribute to their political campaigns.
- Spend generously on lobbying.

If you do both of these things, success will maul you like groupies at a rock concert. If you do neither—and this is the case with about 200 million individuals of voting age and several million corporations—those people in Washington will treat you accordingly. In essence, campaign spending in America has divided all of us into two groups: first- and second-class citizens. This is what happens if you are in the latter group:

You pick up a disproportionate share of America's tax bill.

You pay higher prices for a broad range of products, from peanuts to prescription drugs.

You pay taxes that others in a similar situation have been excused from paying.

You are compelled to abide by laws while others are granted immunity from them.

You must pay debts that you incur while others do not.

You are barred from writing off on your tax return some of the money spent on necessities while others deduct the cost of their entertainment.

You must run your business by one set of rules while the government creates another set for your competitors.

In contrast, first-class citizens—the fortunate few who contribute to the right politicians and hire the right lobbyists—enjoy all the benefits of their special status. Among them:

If they make a bad business decision, the government bails them out.

If they want to hire workers at below-market wage rates, the government provides the means to do so.

If they want more time to pay their debts, the government gives them an extension.

If they want immunity from certain laws, the government gives it.

If they want to ignore rules their competitors must comply with, the government gives its approval.

If they want to kill legislation that is intended for

Illustrations for TIME by Peter Kuper

KUPER

Interior spreads published in *Time*, 1995/1999.

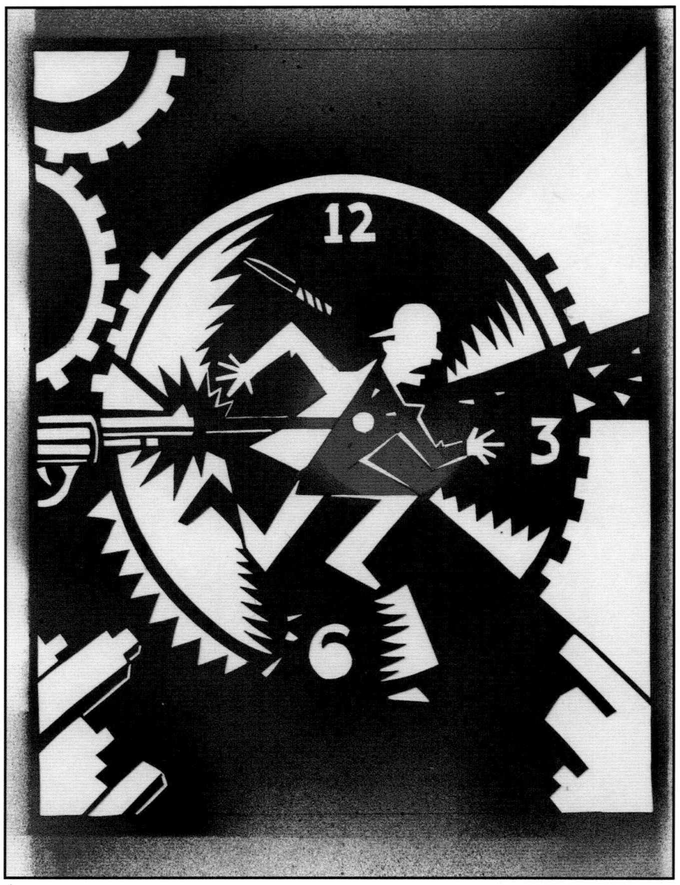
12
3
6

1

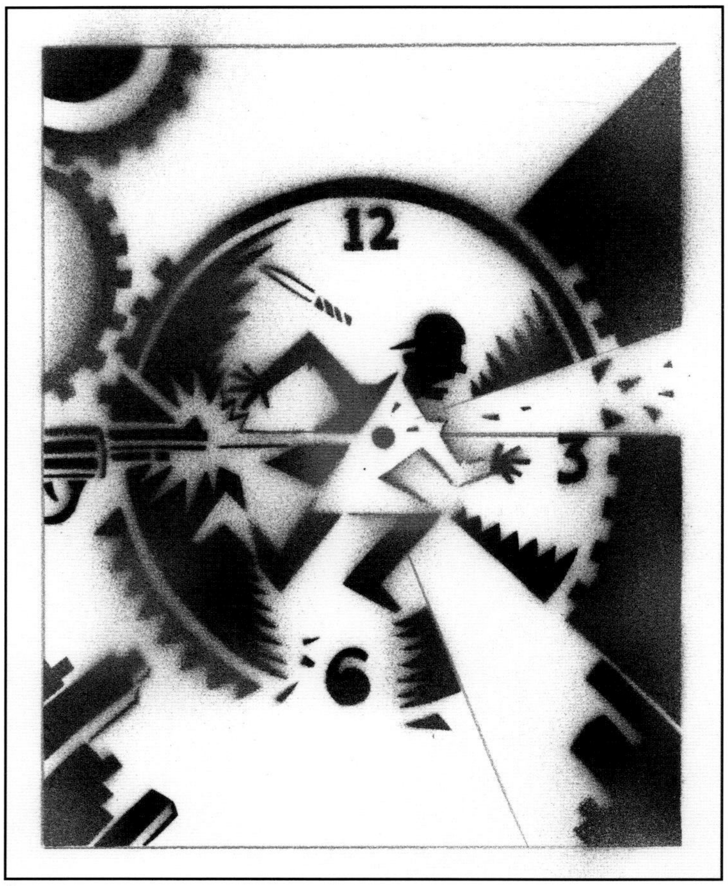
12
3
6

2

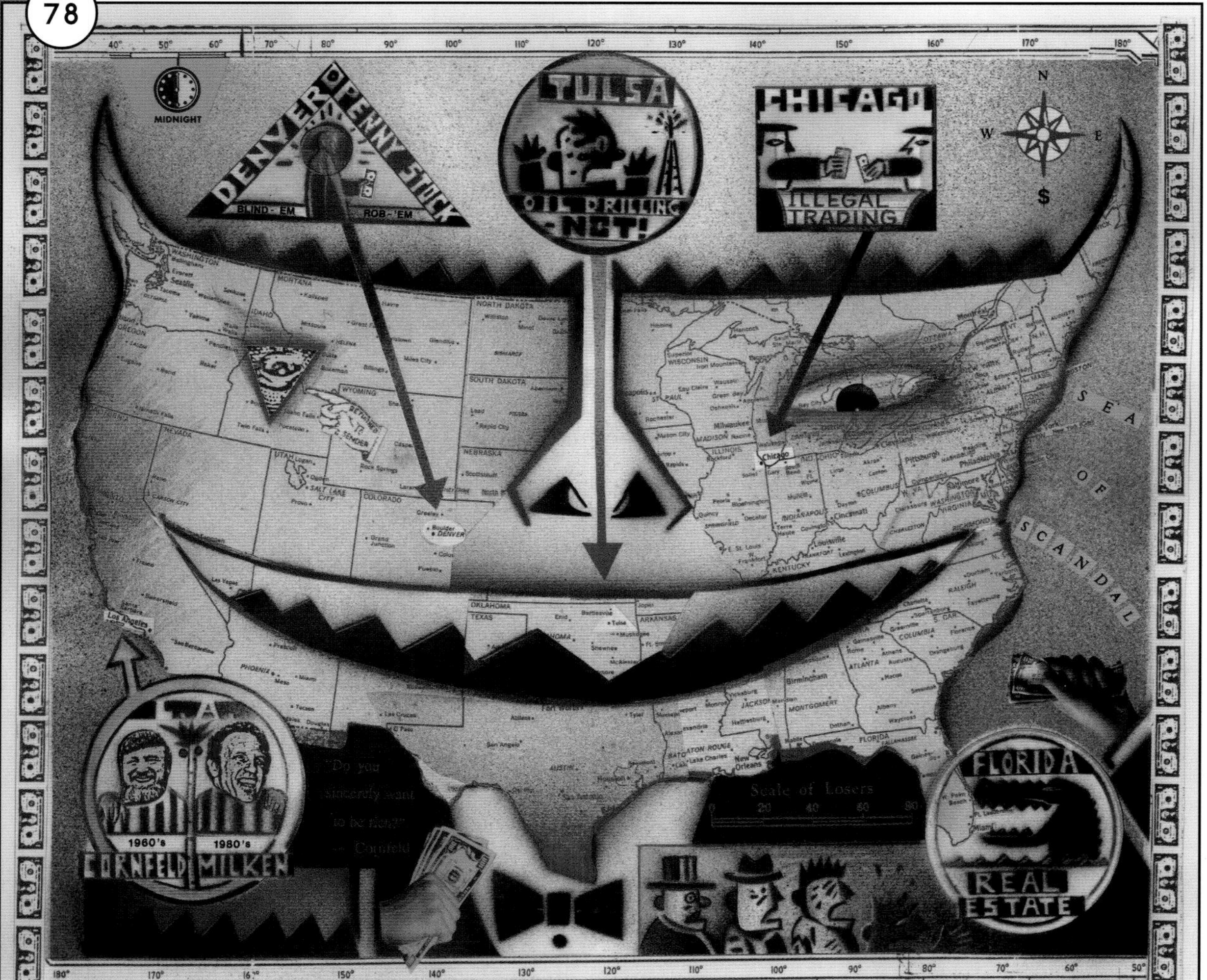
MIDNIGHT
DENVER
PENNY STOCK
BLIND-EM
ROB-EM
TULSA
OIL DRILLING
NOT!
CHICAGO
ILLEGAL TRADING
SEA OF SCANDAL
L.A.
1960's
1980's
CORNFELD
MILKEN
Scale of Losers
FLORIDA
REAL ESTATE

4

1. *Village Voice* cover, stencil cut from copy paper.

2. Sprayed with red and black enamel paint on watercolor paper.

Opposite page: Finished cover art with watercolor, colored pencil and collage added.

3. Final Cover, published in the *Village Voice*, 1997.

4. *Scandal Map*, published in *Worth*, 1994.

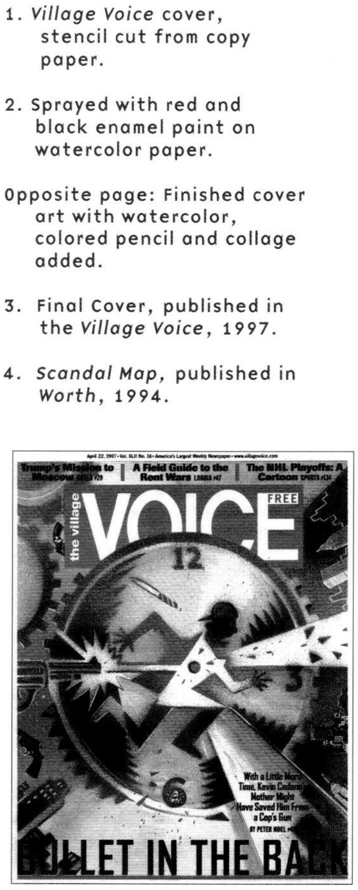
A Field Guide to the Rent Wars
The NHL Playoffs: A Cartoon
the village
VOICE
FREE
12

3

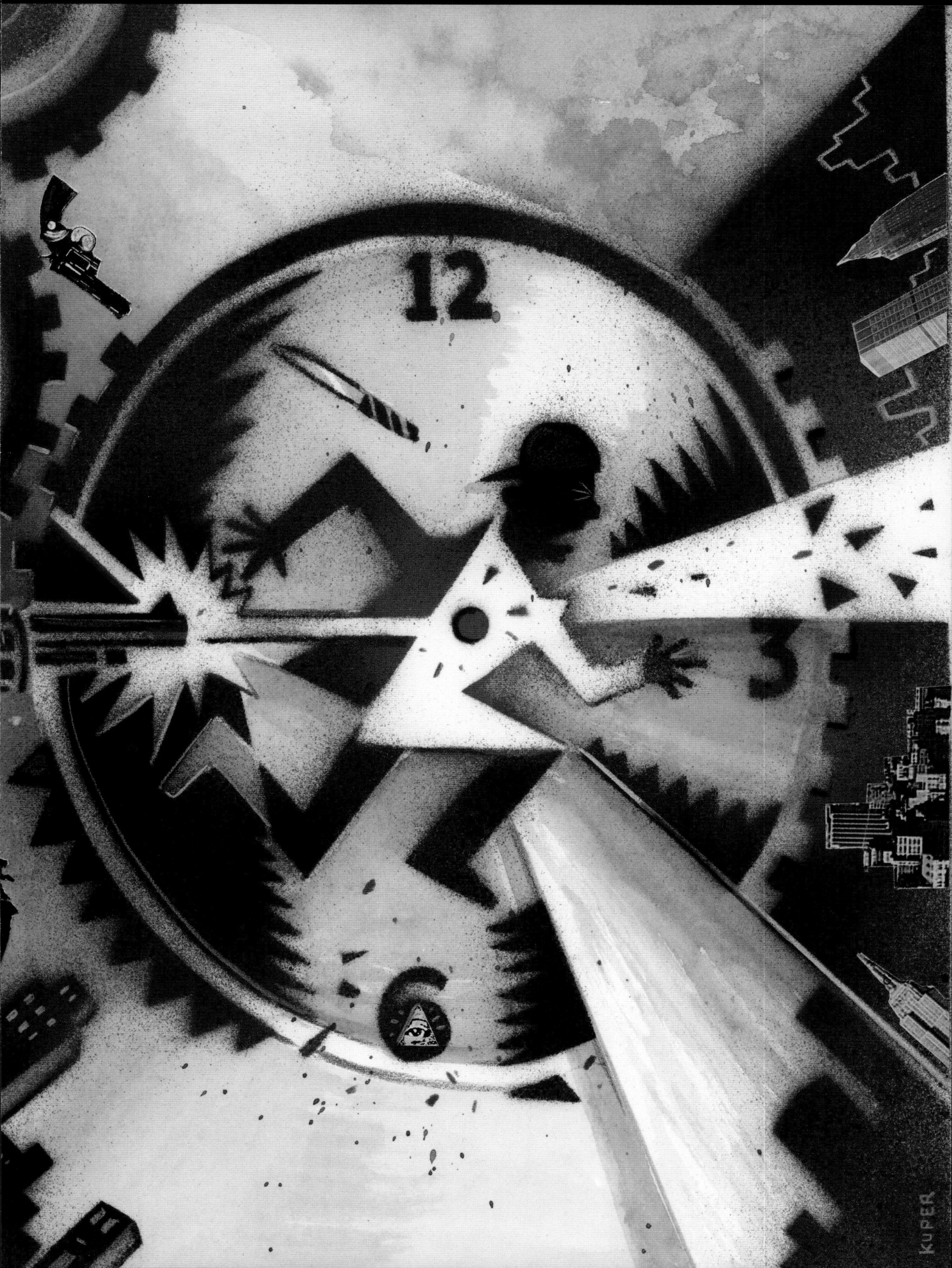
12
3
6
KUPER

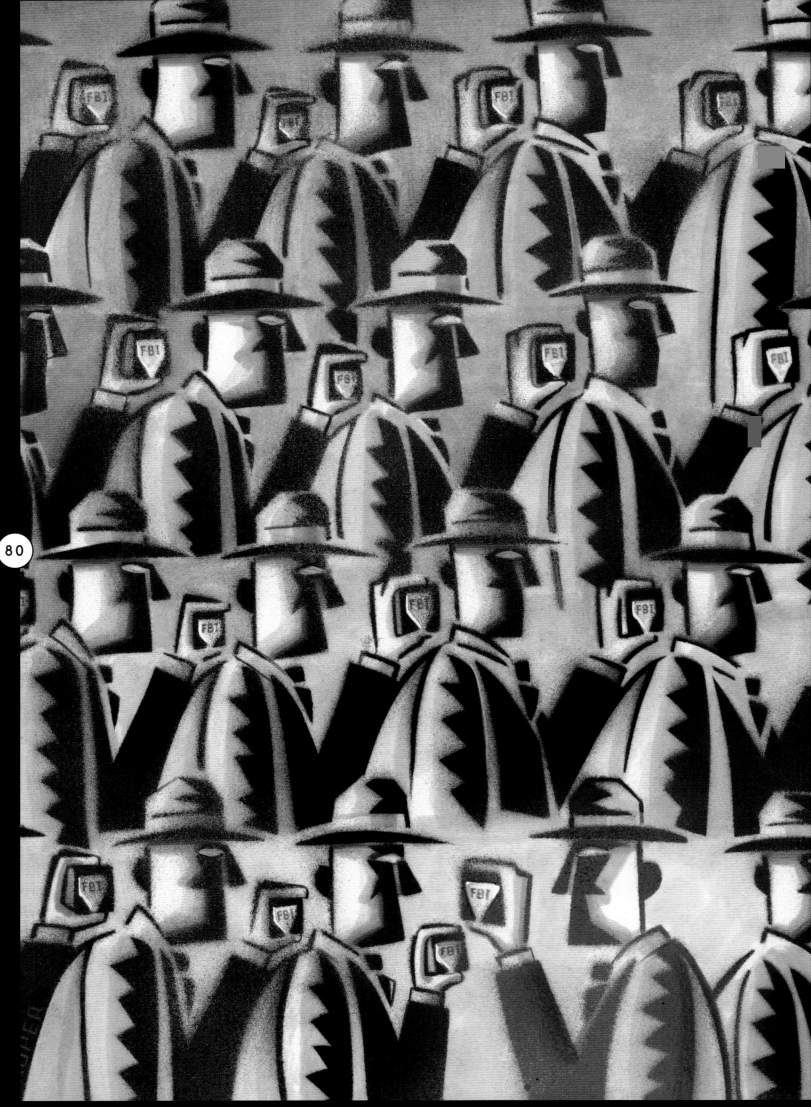

Illustration on gays in the FBI, published in *Out Magazine*, 1997.

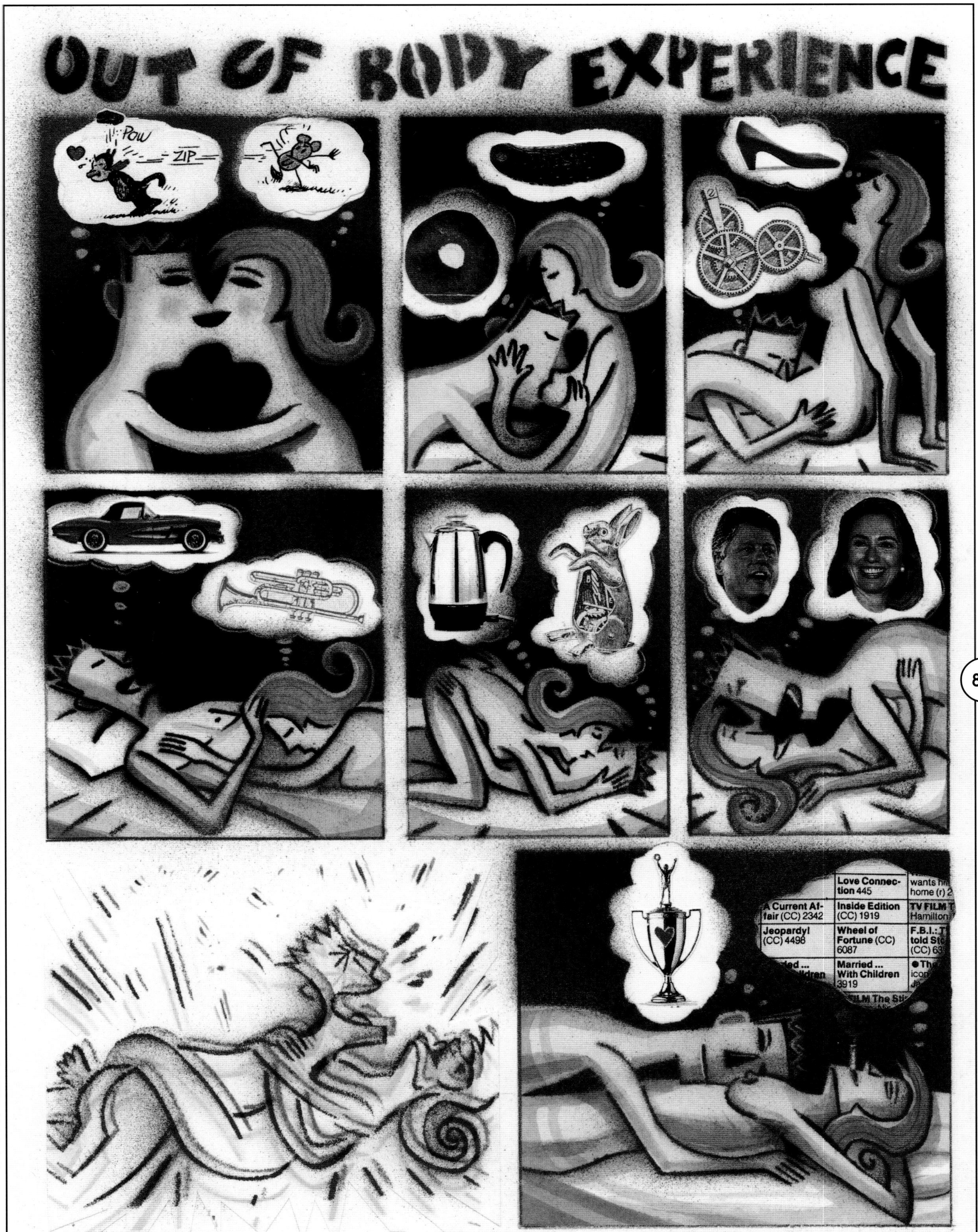
OUT OF BODY EXPERIENCE
POW
ZIP
Love Connection 445
Inside Edition (CC) 1919
A Current Affair (CC) 2342
Jeopardy! (CC) 4498
Wheel of Fortune (CC) 6087
Married ... With Children 3919
© PETER KUPER 1993

Out of Body Experience, published in *Details*, 1993.
This piece resulted in complaints from advertisers and the loss of some distribution in the South, causing the editors to drop my next contribution, *Fuck the Fucking Fuckers* (see page 69).

STRIPPED: AUTOBIO COMICS

2

$2.50 ($2.95 CANADA)
PETER KUPERS
FANTAGRAPHICS BOOKS
NUMBER 5
MATURE READERS ONLY
Bleeding HEART
I LOVE YOU WITH ALL OF MY HEART AND SOUL!
THE COMIC THAT DOESN'T KNOW WHEN TO QUIT!

1

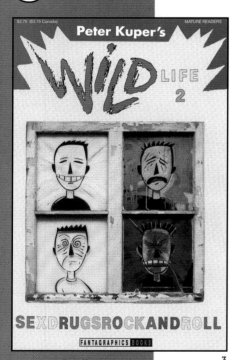

There is a certain cathartic quality to putting personal experiences down on paper. In the process of remembering past situations, one's subconscious often presents surprises with what it dredges up. God is in the details (or is that the Devil?), and certain conversations and images will make all the difference in the world as to how genuine a story rings.

Although I start with an overall idea of the tale I want to tell, I try to let the events talk back to me along the way. Often I don't know if the anecdote has a greater point to convey, or even where the story necessarily ends, until I arrive there along with the characters.

Even though autobiographical work can be nerve-racking to produce, as it compels you to relive embarrassing events, ultimately it's the most rewarding. The more I will myself to dig into uncomfortable personal territory, the greater the odds I will uncover that elusive treasure, truth.

STRIPPED
SEX
SHE SAID
YOU SAID
IF ONLY I'D...
WORKAHOLISM
HAPPINESS
Hatred of most politicians
fear of global destruction
an unauthorized autobiography

4

$2.75 ($3.75 Canada)
MATURE READERS
Peter Kuper's
WILD LIFE 2
SEXDRUGSROCKANDROLL
FANTAGRAPHICS BOOKS

3

5

1. Cover, *Bleeding Heart* #5, Fantagraphics Books, 1993.
2. Panel from "Exorcise," *Blab!* #9, 1997.
3. Cover, *Wildlife* #2, Fantagraphics Books, 1994.
4. Cover, *Stripped*, Fantagraphics Books, 1995.
5. "Wormboy" model sheet for animation project, 1999.

First ♥ Love

IT WAS NEW YEAR'S EVE THE FIRST TIME I FELL IN LOVE --
I'M NOT TALKIN' ABOUT SOME PUPPY – WANNA – WEAR – MY – RING – BABY SHIT –
THIS WAS THE BIG TIME, HEART-THUMPIN', *BIG, BOOM, BAM*,
KNOCK-DOWN, GOOSE-BUMPIN', STOP-IN-THE-NAME-OF *LOVE!*

Although I had known Leslie in junior high school, her family had moved away and I hadn't seen her since she had developed breasts...

...SO YOU'RE JUST VISITING?

YEP

WHAT ARE YOU THINKIN' ABOUT?

...ER-- NUTIN'.

...FINE, GET BACK TO ME WHEN YOU FEEL LIKE BEING HONEST!

BUT I...

...O.K. -- YOU WANT THE TRUTH...

I-I FIND YOU INCREDIBLY ATTRACTIVE AND I WOULD L-LOVE TO SLEEP WITH YOU... ≥GULP≤

≥SMOOCH≤

THERE IS A GOD!

83

My parents were out of town, so we were able to be together just like adults!

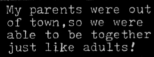

TEE-HEE ≥SMOOCH≤

MY MOM'S CAR.

SWERVE!

I was still pretty geeky, but fortunately Leslie was fairly versed in the art of love...

DON'T JUST SHOVE YOUR TONGUE IN MY MOUTH... MOVE IT GENTLY IN RHYTHM WITH MINE...

MMM LIKE THIS?

PERFECT!

It was like a magical chemical reaction between our molecular blah-blah-blah...

I FEEL SO HAPPY AND COMFORTABLE WITH YOU!

IT'S ALL PART OF MY MASTER PLAN OF LOVE!

LESS GEEKY ALREADY!

Unfortunately, when Christmas vacation ended, Leslie returned home. Then we had to face the torturous process of having a long-distance relationship...

I MISS YOU SO MUCH!

*WARNING DON'T TRY THIS AT HOME!

© PETER KUPER 1993

Our relationship never came to any definitive end, time and space just made it slowly fade...

HEART-STRINGS

Last time I heard, she had gotten married... (so have I)

It's been over a decade since I've seen Leslie, but to this day she still will show up in my dreams...

MY HUSBAND AND I JUST DIVORCED.

DREAMT LAST WEEK!

I-I WISH I COULD HELP...

You never forget your first love.

First Love, published in *Details*, 1993.

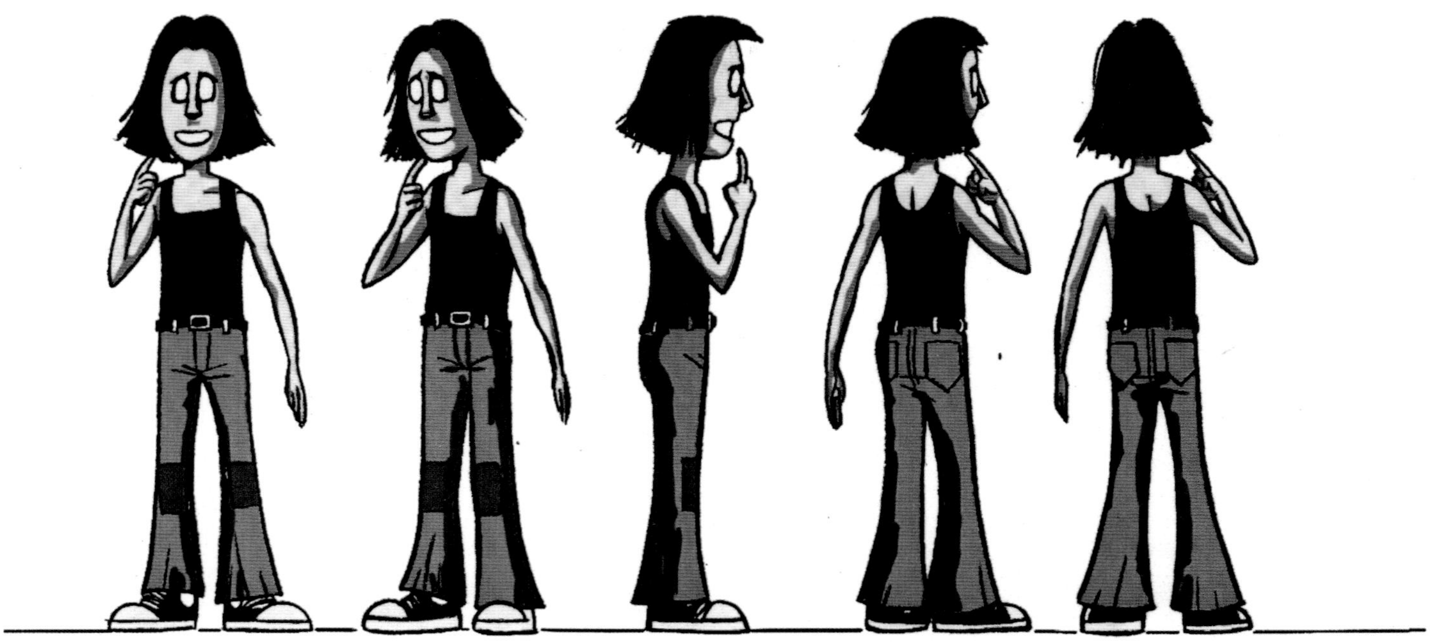

1

I've had a couple of forays into Hollywood where my comics were optioned for development into animated television shows. It was incredibly exciting to see my concepts rendered by storyboard artists, hear actors (like Marisa Tomei, Billy West, Wallace Langham and Laraine Newman) speak dialogue I had written, and work with directors as they brought my characters to life. Unfortunately, in getting the shows on the air, I encountered too many insurmountable hurdles.

Happily, to produce my work, I don't require big studios, agents, or contracts, just a pen and ink. Then again, the lure of animation with its tremendous possibilities and the huge audience television can provide is always intriguing. But, as anyone who's been there can tell you, those waters are teeming with Tinseltown sharks.

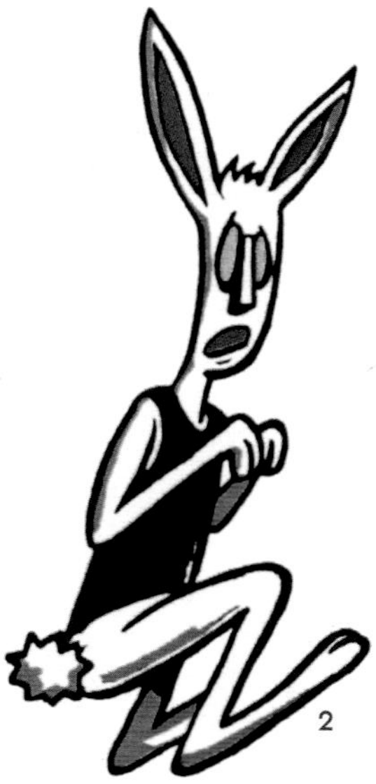

2

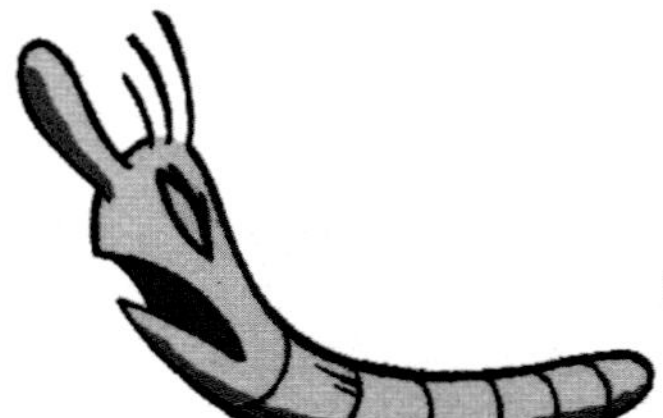

3

1. *Younger Self* animation model sheet, 1997.
2. *Bunnyboy* model sheet, 1997.
3. *Wormboy* model sheet, 1997.
4. *Dream Studio*, painted by HBO Animation background artist based on Kuper's pencil sketch, 1997.
5. *Older Self* model sheet, 1997.

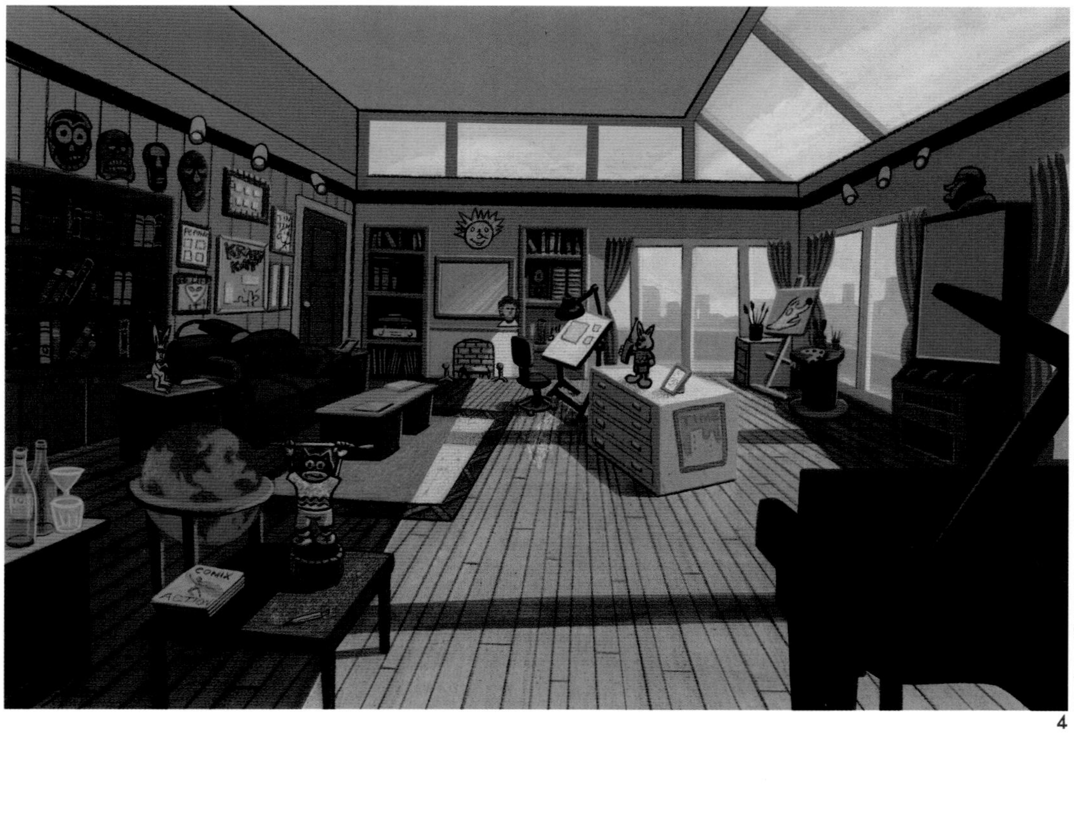

4

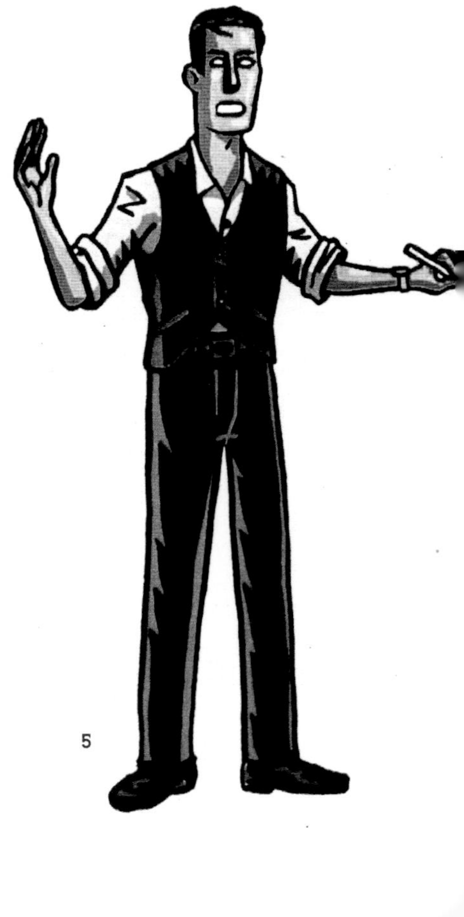

5

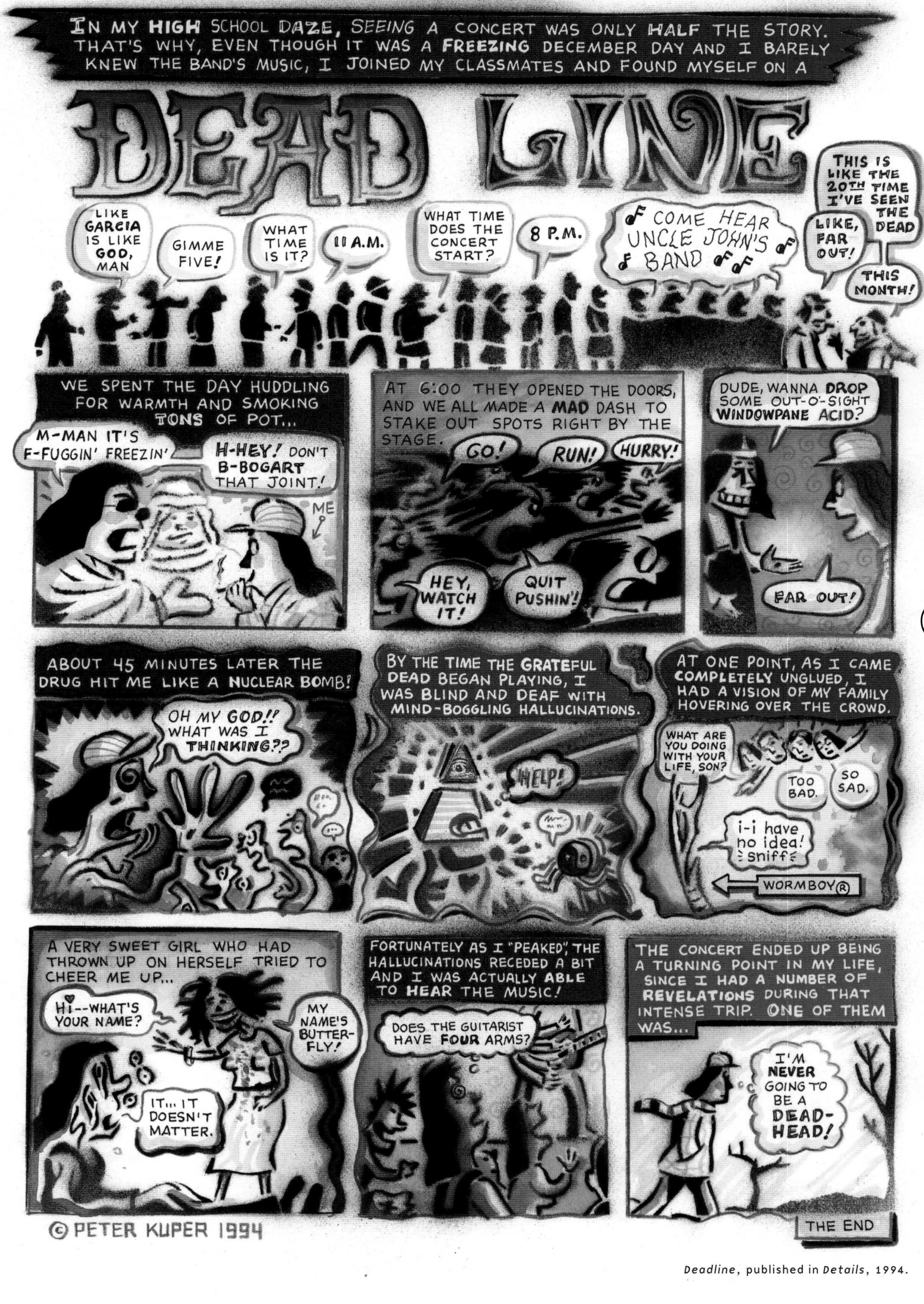

IN MY HIGH SCHOOL DAZE, SEEING A CONCERT WAS ONLY HALF THE STORY. THAT'S WHY, EVEN THOUGH IT WAS A FREEZING DECEMBER DAY AND I BARELY KNEW THE BAND'S MUSIC, I JOINED MY CLASSMATES AND FOUND MYSELF ON A
DEAD LINE
LIKE GARCIA IS LIKE GOD, MAN
GIMME FIVE!
WHAT TIME IS IT?
11 A.M.
WHAT TIME DOES THE CONCERT START?
8 P.M.
COME HEAR UNCLE JOHN'S BAND
LIKE, FAR OUT!
THIS IS LIKE THE 20TH TIME I'VE SEEN THE DEAD
THIS MONTH!
WE SPENT THE DAY HUDDLING FOR WARMTH AND SMOKING TONS OF POT...
M-MAN IT'S F-FUGGIN' FREEZIN'
H-HEY! DON'T B-BOGART THAT JOINT!
ME
AT 6:00 THEY OPENED THE DOORS, AND WE ALL MADE A MAD DASH TO STAKE OUT SPOTS RIGHT BY THE STAGE.
GO!
RUN!
HURRY!
HEY, WATCH IT!
QUIT PUSHIN'!
DUDE, WANNA DROP SOME OUT-O'-SIGHT WINDOWPANE ACID?
FAR OUT!
ABOUT 45 MINUTES LATER THE DRUG HIT ME LIKE A NUCLEAR BOMB!
OH MY GOD!! WHAT WAS I THINKING??
BY THE TIME THE GRATEFUL DEAD BEGAN PLAYING, I WAS BLIND AND DEAF WITH MIND-BOGGLING HALLUCINATIONS.
HELP!
AT ONE POINT, AS I CAME COMPLETELY UNGLUED, I HAD A VISION OF MY FAMILY HOVERING OVER THE CROWD.
WHAT ARE YOU DOING WITH YOUR LIFE, SON?
TOO BAD.
SO SAD.
i-i have no idea! sniff
WORMBOY®
A VERY SWEET GIRL WHO HAD THROWN UP ON HERSELF TRIED TO CHEER ME UP...
HI--WHAT'S YOUR NAME?
MY NAME'S BUTTERFLY!
IT... IT DOESN'T MATTER.
FORTUNATELY AS I "PEAKED", THE HALLUCINATIONS RECEDED A BIT AND I WAS ACTUALLY ABLE TO HEAR THE MUSIC!
DOES THE GUITARIST HAVE FOUR ARMS?
THE CONCERT ENDED UP BEING A TURNING POINT IN MY LIFE, SINCE I HAD A NUMBER OF REVELATIONS DURING THAT INTENSE TRIP. ONE OF THEM WAS...
I'M NEVER GOING TO BE A DEAD-HEAD!
THE END
© PETER KUPER 1994

Deadline, published in *Details*, 1994.

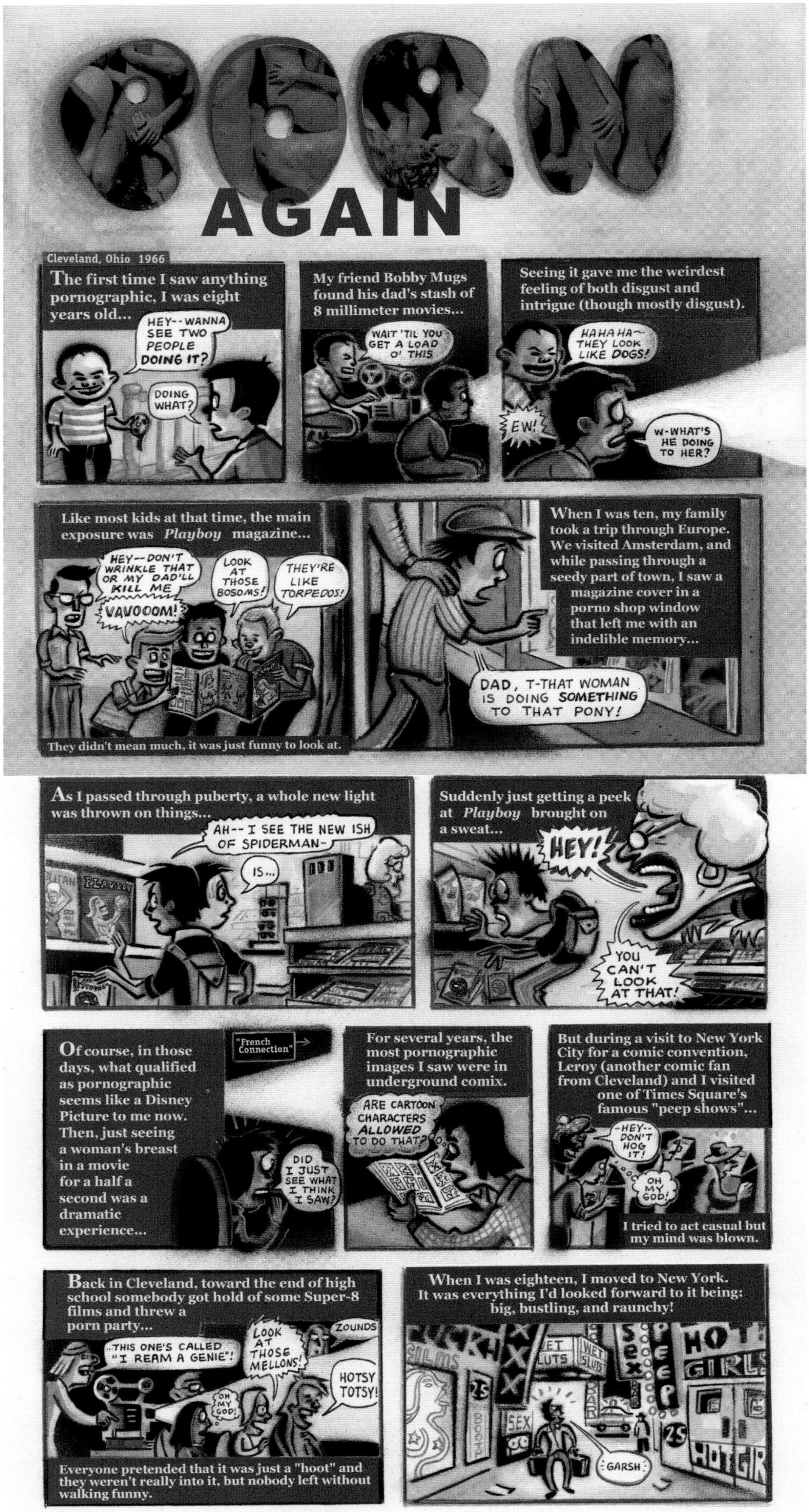
PORN
AGAIN
Cleveland, Ohio 1966
The first time I saw anything pornographic, I was eight years old...
HEY--WANNA SEE TWO PEOPLE DOING IT?
DOING WHAT?
My friend Bobby Mugs found his dad's stash of 8 millimeter movies...
WAIT 'TIL YOU GET A LOAD O' THIS
Seeing it gave me the weirdest feeling of both disgust and intrigue (though mostly disgust).
HAHAHA--THEY LOOK LIKE DOGS!
EW!
W-WHAT'S HE DOING TO HER?
Like most kids at that time, the main exposure was Playboy magazine...
HEY--DON'T WRINKLE THAT OR MY DAD'LL KILL ME
VAVOOOM!
LOOK AT THOSE BOSOMS!
THEY'RE LIKE TORPEDOS!
They didn't mean much, it was just funny to look at.
When I was ten, my family took a trip through Europe. We visited Amsterdam, and while passing through a seedy part of town, I saw a magazine cover in a porno shop window that left me with an indelible memory...
DAD, T-THAT WOMAN IS DOING SOMETHING TO THAT PONY!
As I passed through puberty, a whole new light was thrown on things...
AH-- I SEE THE NEW ISH OF SPIDERMAN-
IS...
Suddenly just getting a peek at Playboy brought on a sweat...
HEY!
YOU CAN'T LOOK AT THAT!
Of course, in those days, what qualified as pornographic seems like a Disney Picture to me now. Then, just seeing a woman's breast in a movie for a half a second was a dramatic experience...
"French Connection"
DID I JUST SEE WHAT I THINK I SAW?
For several years, the most pornographic images I saw were in underground comix.
ARE CARTOON CHARACTERS ALLOWED TO DO THAT?
But during a visit to New York City for a comic convention, Leroy (another comic fan from Cleveland) and I visited one of Times Square's famous "peep shows"...
HEY-- DON'T HOG IT!
OH MY GOD!
I tried to act casual but my mind was blown.
Back in Cleveland, toward the end of high school somebody got hold of some Super-8 films and threw a porn party...
..THIS ONE'S CALLED "I REAM A GENIE"!
LOOK AT THOSE MELLONS!
ZOUNDS
HOTSY TOTSY!
OH MY GOD!
Everyone pretended that it was just a "hoot" and they weren't really into it, but nobody left without walking funny.
When I was eighteen, I moved to New York. It was everything I'd looked forward to it being: big, bustling, and raunchy!
XXX
WET SLUTS
SEX
PEEP
HOT GIRLS
GARSH

Porn Again, published in the comics anthology *Blab!* #10, 1998.

My first few years living there were pretty lonely, and on occasion I'd furtively enter my local porn shop to view what was missing from my life...
I'M THE ONLY NORMAL ONE HERE.
PEEP 25
I'M THE ONLY NORMAL ONE HERE
I'M THE ONLY NORMAL ONE HERE.
I'M THE ONLY NORMAL ONE HERE
I'M THE ONLY NORMAL ONE HERE.
"Clockwork Orgasm"
ACTS OF LOVE
In the early 1980's, I took care of a neighbor's apartment who had a "Betamax" player and a fantastic collection of films...
...STAR WHORES, 2001 A SPACE ORGASM, PLANET OF THE ASS...
I LOVE SCIENCE FICTION!
After a weekend of watching videos I had used up the thrill, and for at least 24 hours didn't even want to *think* about sex...
I'M SURE VANESSA DEL RIO IS A VERY NICE PERSON AND COULD ACT IN LEGITIMATE FILMS IF SHE SO DESIRED.
I had also broken a few personal records and developed some sort of carpal-tunnel wrist problems.
During one apartment-sit weekend, a girl I was dating visited. At her suggestion we watched some porn, but it was awkward...
...SO YOU ENJOY SEEING THESE CLOSE-UPS OF PEOPLE'S GENITALS?
...WELL, YEAH.
AHHH!
EW GROSS, HE CAME IN HER HAIR. YUCK!
On a few other occasions I saw porno flicks with women friends...
THIS IS HILARIOUS!
YEAH, HAHA
OH MY GOD!
HA HA HA HA
Like in college seeing "Fiona on Fire"...
And "Debbie does Dallas" (part of which was filmed at my art school), but it was always awkward.
LOOK-- IT'S THE LIBRARY!
HUH? OH YEAH
GROSS- HE CAME IN HER FACE!
OH MY GOD
Generally speaking, most of the women I've known were never much interested in porn. Of course, this may have something to do with the fact that most of it is geared toward male's fantasies and our basic animal urges...
IF RON JEREMY CAN SCORE, SO CAN I!
Today
...FRANKLY, (WHEN I DISCOUNT THE NAGGING FEELING THAT I'M JUST ANOTHER PERVERT) I REALLY ENJOY PORNOGRAPHY...
"Hannah Does Her Sisters"
IT CUTS THROUGH THE INTELLECTUAL VENEER THAT DISCONNECTS US FROM OUR TRUE ANIMAL NATURE...
I FIND NOTHING OBSCENE ABOUT TWO (OR MORE) CONSENTING ADULTS ENGAGING IN SEXUAL ACTS ON FILM...
YOU WANT OBSCENE, WATCH THE NIGHTLY NEWS!
CLIK
NICE RATIONALIZING!
YA LITTLE PUD POUNDER!
WHAT THE—
SMEK!
DO YOU HAVE ANY IDEA HOW UNCOMFORTABLE IT IS KEEPING YOUR LEGS IN THE AIR WHILE SOME SWEATY TOAD BANGS AWAY FOR YOUR VIEWING PLEASURE??
N-NO
HEY—NO ONE'S MAKING YOU DO IT, AND I'VE READ THAT THE WOMEN MAKE MORE THAN THE MEN...
HMPH!
HAVE YOU EVER HAD TO WASH CUM OUT OF YOUR HAIR OR SAT UNDER A HOT LIGHT WITH A COCK IN YOUR ASS??
WELL NO I--
TRY IT THE NEXT TIME YOU WANT TO GET IN TOUCH WITH YOUR "TRUE ANIMAL NATURE"!
CARTOON BOY.
CLIK!
OHH YES AHH, RIGHT THERE.
END

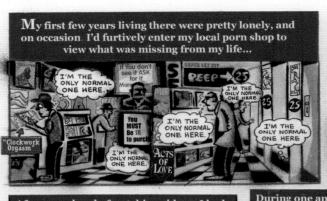

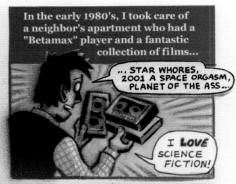

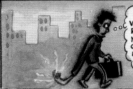

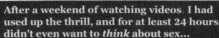

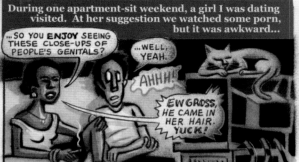

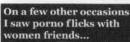

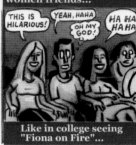

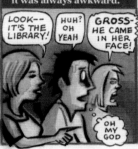

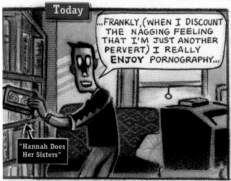

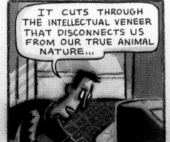

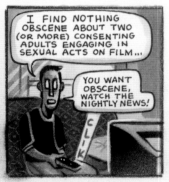

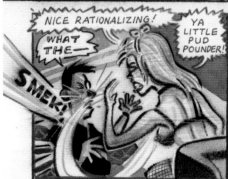

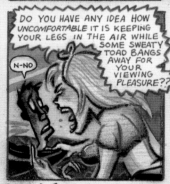

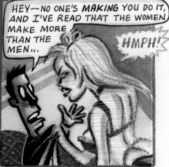

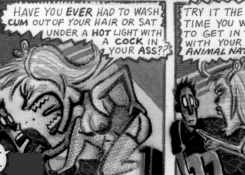

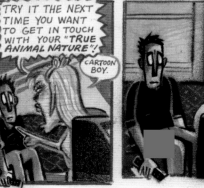

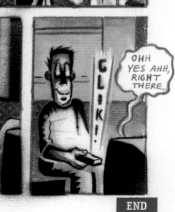

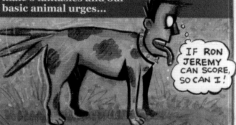

CROSSING LINES

EYE OF THE BEHOLDER

1

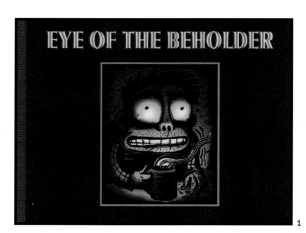

1. Cover, *Eye of the Beholder*, published by NBM, 2000.
2. First "Eye of the Beholder" strip published in the *New York Times* City Section, 1993.
3. Illustration, published on the Opinion Page of the *New York Times*, 1997.
4. *Eye of the Beholder,* syndicated, 1998.

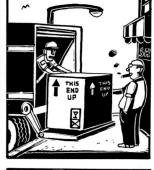

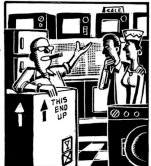

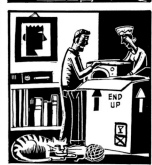

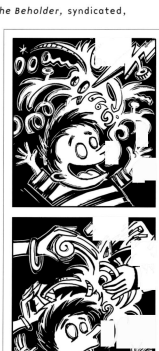

It's ironic that comics enjoy a readership of all ages across the globe, while here in America, where the medium originated, they're still struggling to be recognized for their possible application beyond Spider-Man and Dilbert.

For years I didn't share the fact that I drew comics with my illustration clients. On the rare occasions that I did, it invariably led to calls for me to mimic the "Superman" style.

Fortunately, in the 1990's, a number of art directors and editors who were hip to the possibilities of the form gained positions at major magazines. These days it is common to find comics in the *New Yorker*, *Time*, *Mother Jones* and the Opinion Pages of the *New York Times*.

It may take a new generation of readers before the United States catches up with the rest of the world, but there are signs we're finally on the verge. Today, there are more innovative artists producing fully realized masterworks of fiction, journalism and autobiography in comic form than in the medium's entire history. Perhaps the over used headline, "Bam! Pow! Zap! Comics aren't just for kids anymore!" will finally stop being news in America.

THIS END UP
THIS END UP
SALE
THIS END UP
END UP
END UP
THIS END UP

2

3

4

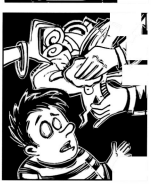

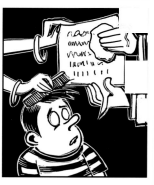

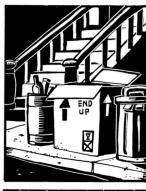

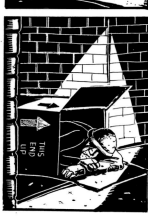

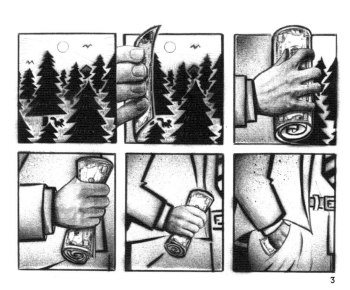

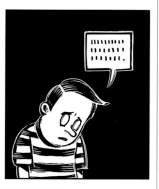

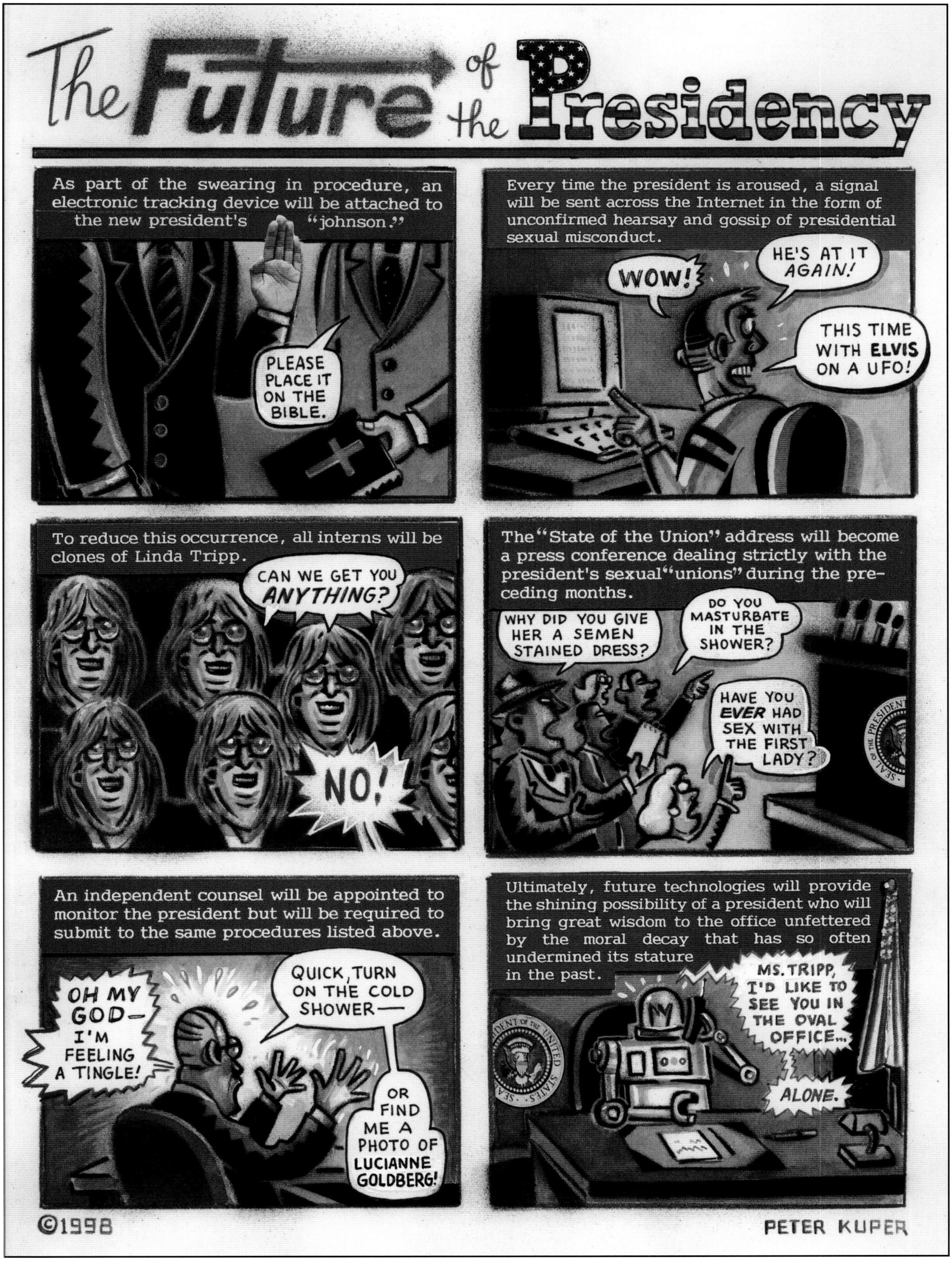

The Future of the Presidency
As part of the swearing in procedure, an electronic tracking device will be attached to the new president's "johnson."
PLEASE PLACE IT ON THE BIBLE.
Every time the president is aroused, a signal will be sent across the Internet in the form of unconfirmed hearsay and gossip of presidential sexual misconduct.
WOW!
HE'S AT IT AGAIN!
THIS TIME WITH ELVIS ON A UFO!
To reduce this occurrence, all interns will be clones of Linda Tripp.
CAN WE GET YOU ANYTHING?
NO!
The "State of the Union" address will become a press conference dealing strictly with the president's sexual "unions" during the preceding months.
WHY DID YOU GIVE HER A SEMEN STAINED DRESS?
DO YOU MASTURBATE IN THE SHOWER?
HAVE YOU EVER HAD SEX WITH THE FIRST LADY?
An independent counsel will be appointed to monitor the president but will be required to submit to the same procedures listed above.
OH MY GOD— I'M FEELING A TINGLE!
QUICK, TURN ON THE COLD SHOWER—
OR FIND ME A PHOTO OF LUCIANNE GOLDBERG!
Ultimately, future technologies will provide the shining possibility of a president who will bring great wisdom to the office unfettered by the moral decay that has so often undermined its stature in the past.
MS. TRIPP, I'D LIKE TO SEE YOU IN THE OVAL OFFICE...
ALONE.
©1998
PETER KUPER

89

The Future of the Presidency, published in *Mother Jones*, 1999.

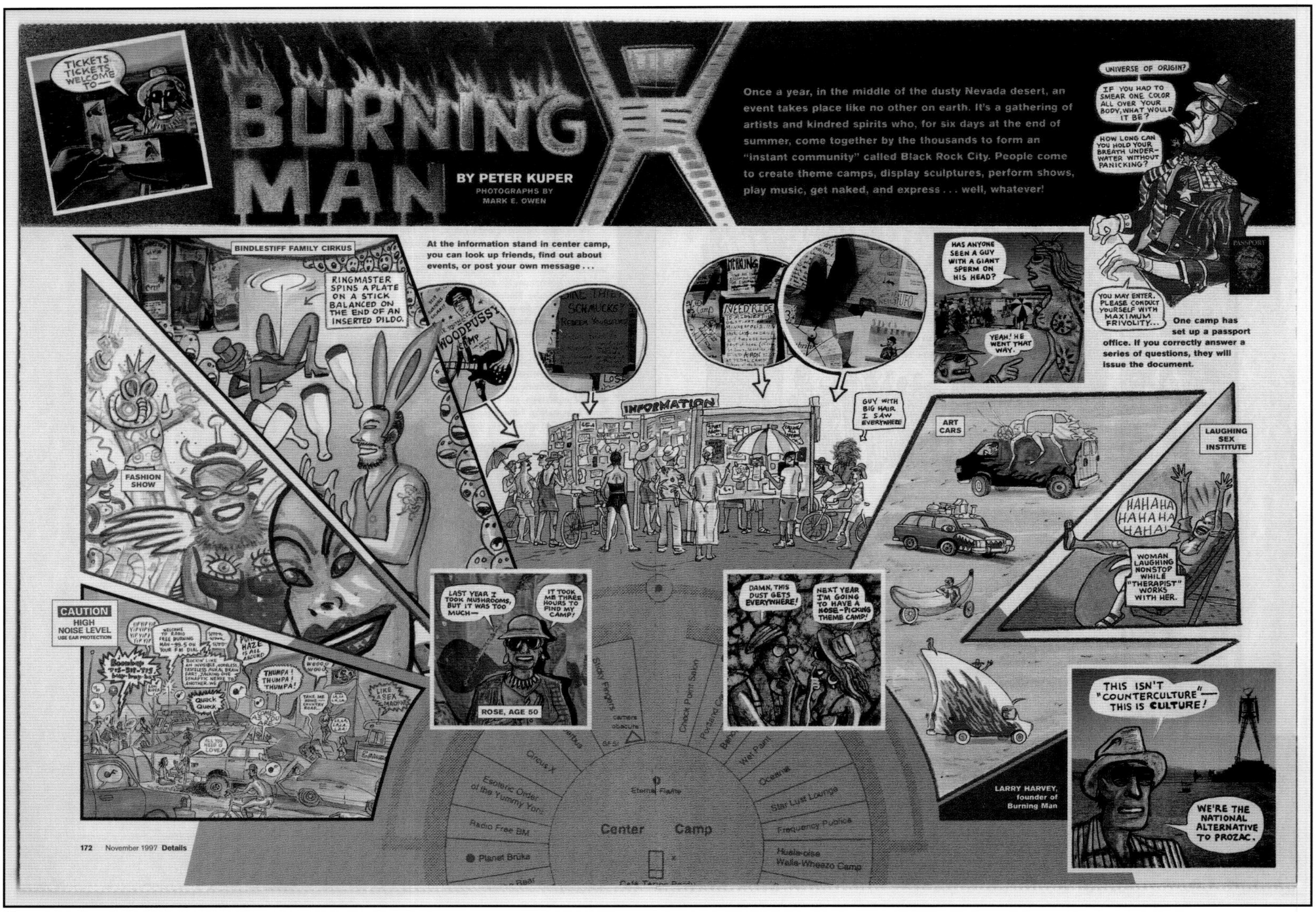
TICKETS, TICKETS, WELCOME TO—
BURNING MAN
BY PETER KUPER
PHOTOGRAPHS BY MARK E. OWEN
Once a year, in the middle of the dusty Nevada desert, an event takes place like no other on earth. It's a gathering of artists and kindred spirits who, for six days at the end of summer, come together by the thousands to form an "instant community" called Black Rock City. People come to create theme camps, display sculptures, perform shows, play music, get naked, and express . . . well, whatever!
UNIVERSE OF ORIGIN?
IF YOU HAD TO SMEAR ONE COLOR ALL OVER YOUR BODY, WHAT WOULD IT BE?
HOW LONG CAN YOU HOLD YOUR BREATH UNDER-WATER WITHOUT PANICKING?
YOU MAY ENTER. PLEASE CONDUCT YOURSELF WITH MAXIMUM FRIVOLITY...
One camp has set up a passport office. If you correctly answer a series of questions, they will issue the document.
BINDLESTIFF FAMILY CIRKUS
RINGMASTER SPINS A PLATE ON A STICK BALANCED ON THE END OF AN INSERTED DILDO.
FASHION SHOW
At the information stand in center camp, you can look up friends, find out about events, or post your own message . . .
INFORMATION
HAS ANYONE SEEN A GUY WITH A GIANT SPERM ON HIS HEAD?
YEAH! HE WENT THAT WAY.
GUY WITH BIG HAIR I SAW EVERYWHERE
ART CARS
LAUGHING SEX INSTITUTE
HAHAHA HAHAHA HAHA!
WOMAN LAUGHING NONSTOP WHILE "THERAPIST" WORKS WITH HER.
CAUTION HIGH NOISE LEVEL USE EAR PROTECTION
THUMPA! THUMPA! THUMPA!
LAST YEAR I TOOK MUSHROOMS, BUT IT WAS TOO MUCH—
IT TOOK ME THREE HOURS TO FIND MY CAMP!
ROSE, AGE 50
DAMN, THIS DUST GETS EVERYWHERE!
NEXT YEAR I'M GOING TO HAVE A NOSE-PICKING THEME CAMP!
THIS ISN'T "COUNTERCULTURE" — THIS IS CULTURE!
LARRY HARVEY, founder of Burning Man
WE'RE THE NATIONAL ALTERNATIVE TO PROZAC.
Center Camp
172 November 1997 Details

1

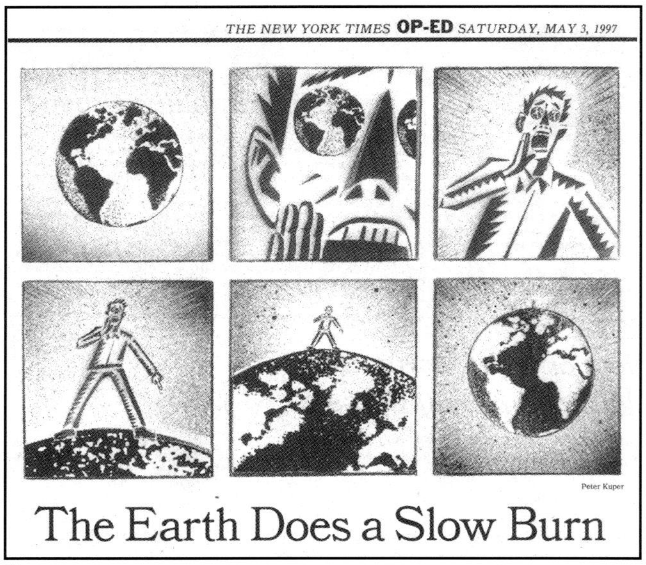
THE NEW YORK TIMES OP-ED SATURDAY, MAY 3, 1997
Peter Kuper
The Earth Does a Slow Burn

2

1. *Burning Man*, published in *Details*, 1997.
2. Illustration published on the Opinion Page of the *New York Times*, 1997.
3. *What If?*, published in the *New York Daily News*, 2000.
4. *Statistic*, published in Rock the Vote pamphlet, 1992.

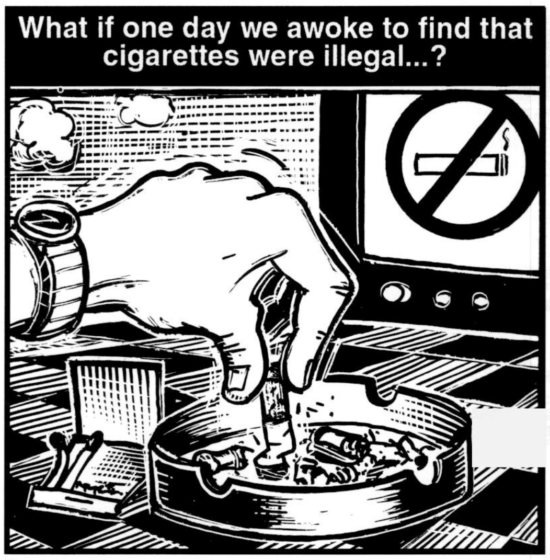
What if one day we awoke to find that cigarettes were illegal...?

3

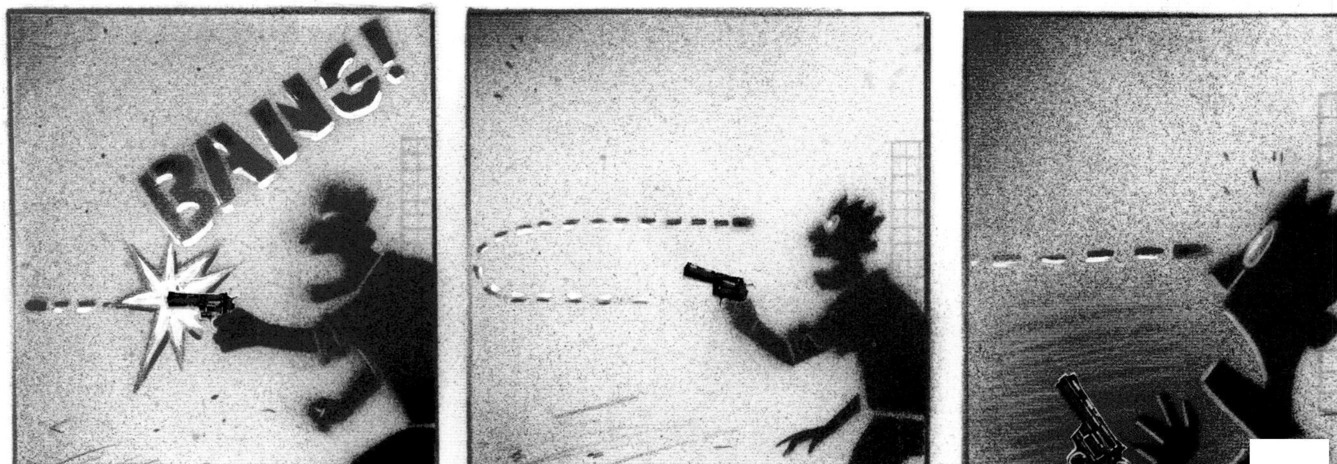
BANG!

4

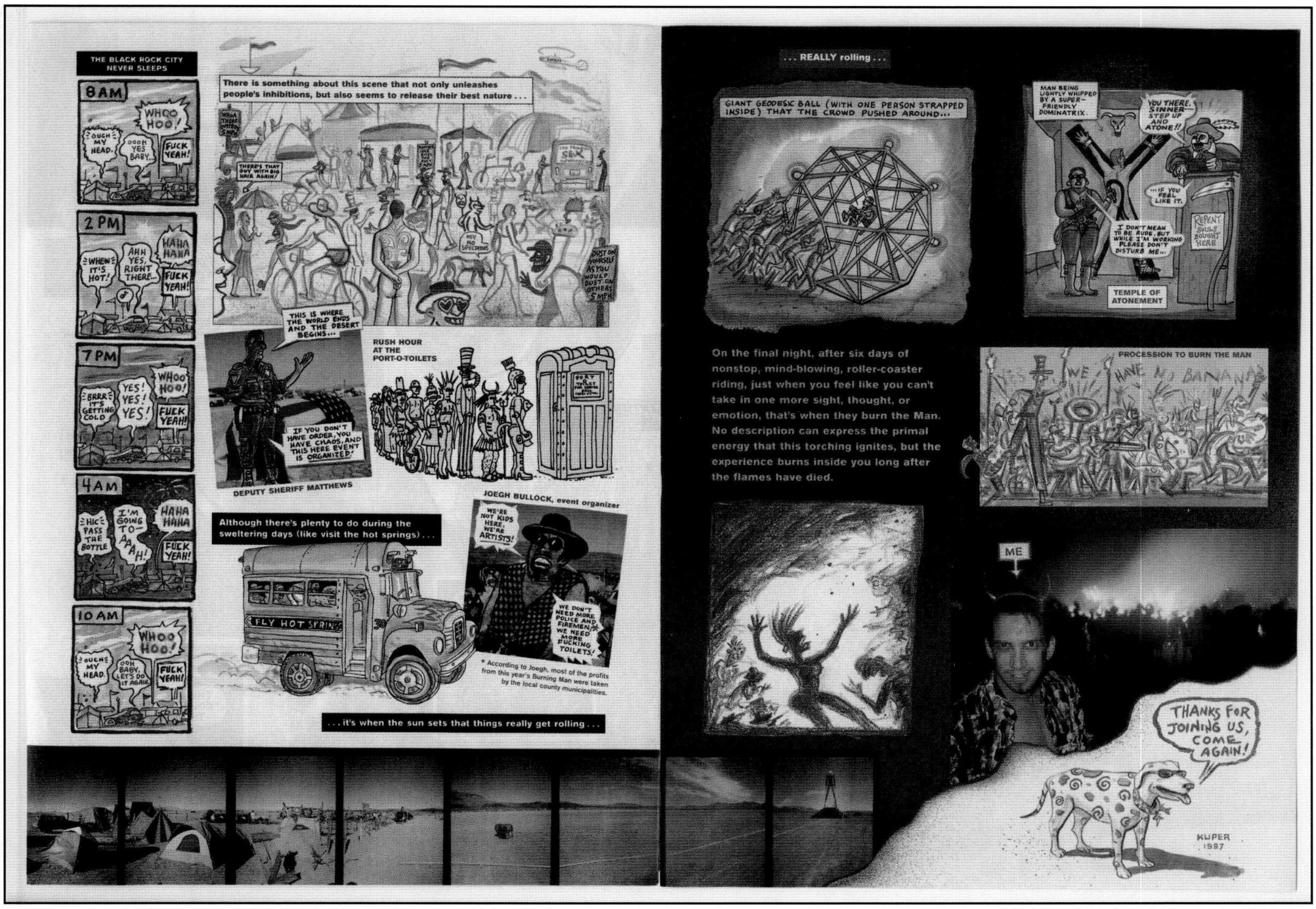

THE BLACK ROCK CITY NEVER SLEEPS
8AM
OUCH MY HEAD.
OOOH YES BABY...
WHOO HOO!
FUCK YEAH!
2PM
WHEW IT'S HOT!
AHH YES, RIGHT THERE...
HAHA HAHA
FUCK YEAH!
7PM
BRRR IT'S GETTING COLD
YES! YES! YES!
WHOO HOO!
FUCK YEAH!
4AM
HIC PASS THE BOTTLE
I'M GOING TO AAAH!
HAHA HAHA
FUCK YEAH!
10AM
OUCH MY HEAD.
OOH BABY, LET'S DO IT AGAIN.
WHOO HOO!
FUCK YEAH!
There is something about this scene that not only unleashes people's inhibitions, but also seems to release their best nature . . .
THERE'S THAT GUY WITH BIG HAIR AGAIN!
HEY NO SPECTATORS
DUST ON YOURSELF AS YOU WOULD DUST ON OTHERS 5 MPH
THIS IS WHERE THE WORLD ENDS AND THE DESERT BEGINS...
IF YOU DON'T HAVE ORDER, YOU HAVE CHAOS, AND THIS HERE EVENT IS ORGANIZED!
DEPUTY SHERIFF MATTHEWS
RUSH HOUR AT THE PORT-O-TOILETS
Although there's plenty to do during the sweltering days (like visit the hot springs) . . .
FLY HOT SPRINGS
JOEGH BULLOCK, event organizer
WE'RE NOT KIDS HERE, WE'RE ARTISTS!
WE DON'T NEED MORE POLICE AND FIREMEN,* WE NEED MORE FUCKING TOILETS!
* According to Joegh, most of the profits from this year's Burning Man were taken by the local county municipalities.
. . . it's when the sun sets that things really get rolling . . .
. . . REALLY rolling . . .
GIANT GEODESIC BALL (WITH ONE PERSON STRAPPED INSIDE) THAT THE CROWD PUSHED AROUND...
MAN BEING LIGHTLY WHIPPED BY A SUPER-FRIENDLY DOMINATRIX.
YOU THERE, SINNER— STEP UP AND ATONE!!
...IF YOU FEEL LIKE IT.
I DON'T MEAN TO BE RUDE, BUT WHILE I'M WORKING PLEASE DON'T DISTURB ME...
REPENT SOULS BOUGHT HERE
TEMPLE OF ATONEMENT
On the final night, after six days of nonstop, mind-blowing, roller-coaster riding, just when you feel like you can't take in one more sight, thought, or emotion, that's when they burn the Man. No description can express the primal energy that this torching ignites, but the experience burns inside you long after the flames have died.
PROCESSION TO BURN THE MAN
ME
THANKS FOR JOINING US, COME AGAIN!
KUPER 1997

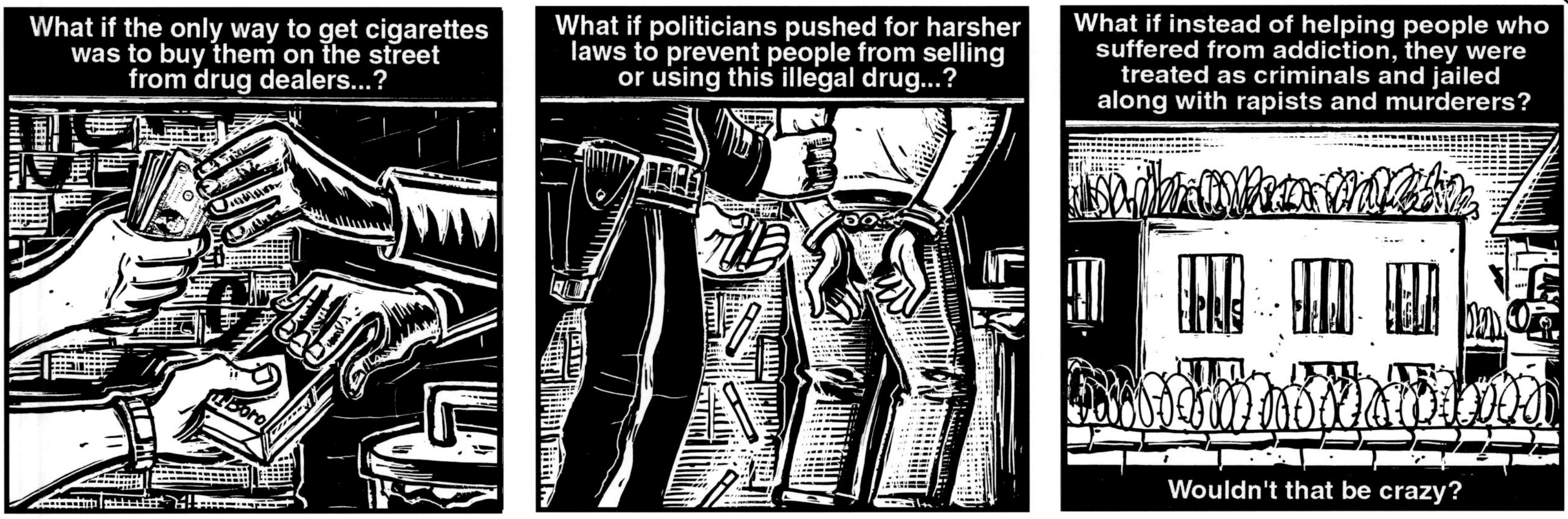

What if the only way to get cigarettes was to buy them on the street from drug dealers...?
What if politicians pushed for harsher laws to prevent people from selling or using this illegal drug...?
What if instead of helping people who suffered from addiction, they were treated as criminals and jailed along with rapists and murderers?
Wouldn't that be crazy?

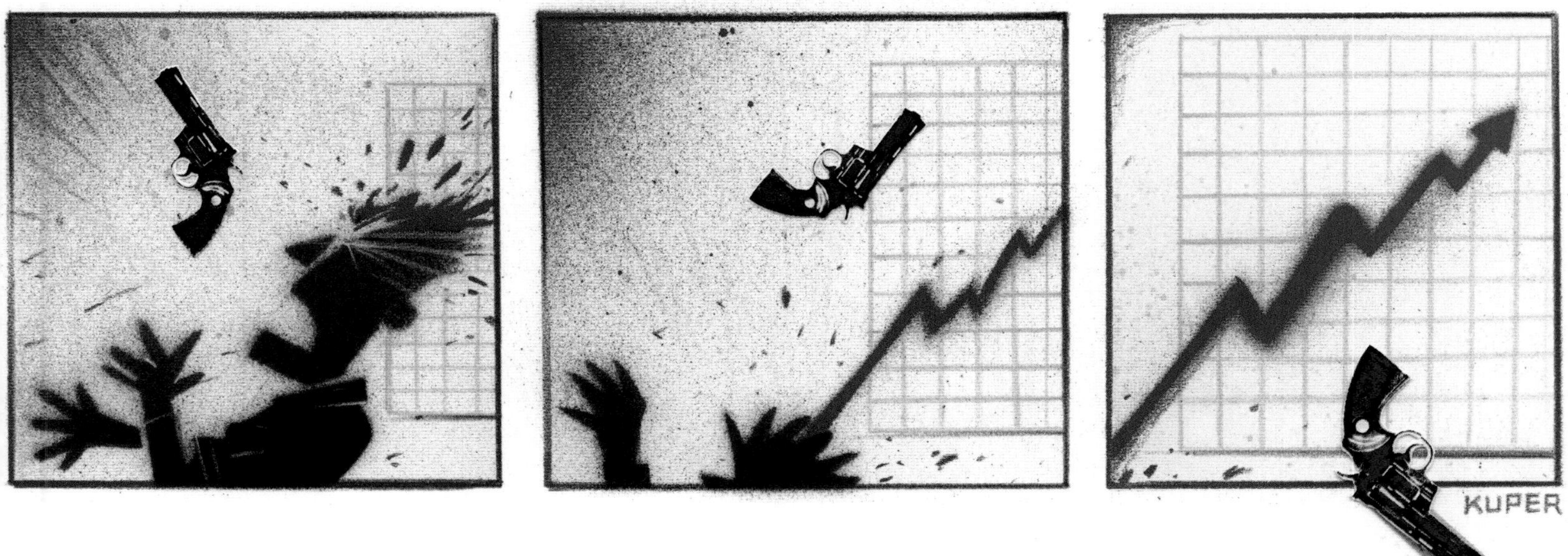

KUPER

I SPY

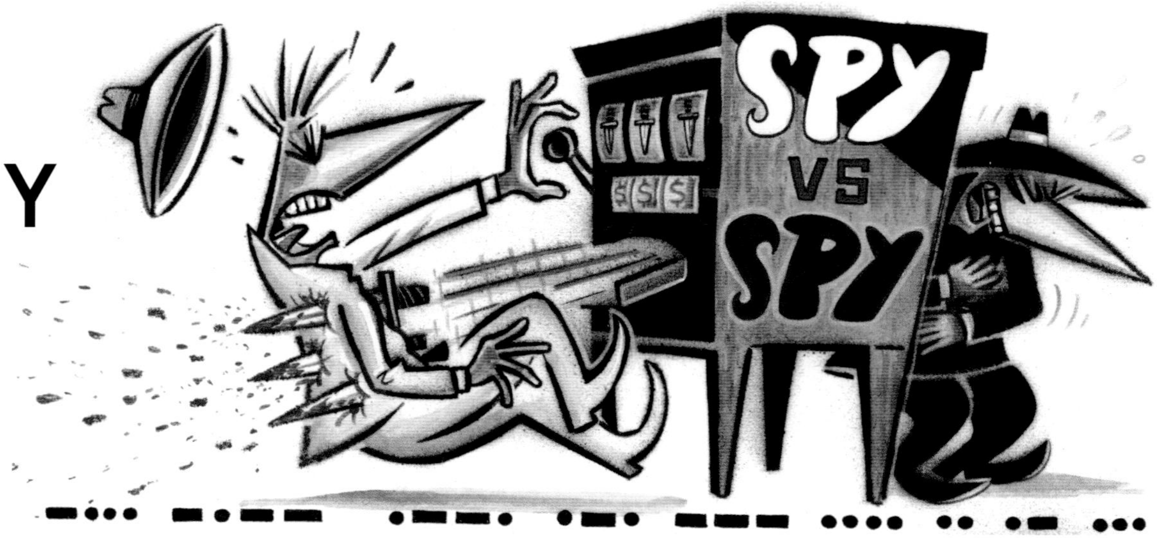
SPY
VS
SPY

1

In 1996, when the editors of *MAD* first approached me about taking over *Spy vs. Spy*, I almost passed. The idea of drawing these characters created in 1961 by the great Antonio Prohias wasn't part of my plans, but I figured it couldn't hurt to take a stab at it. What I immediately rediscovered was the huge influence the strip had on me with its bold, black and white, wordless trickery. I even convinced myself that the cold war sub-text was in keeping with my political commentary. Fact is, *Spy vs. Spy* is more *Itchy and Scratchy* than Kennedy and Kruschev, but it's a hoot to have them destroy each other every month. Also, I've got a whole new audience of kids I can now subvert...

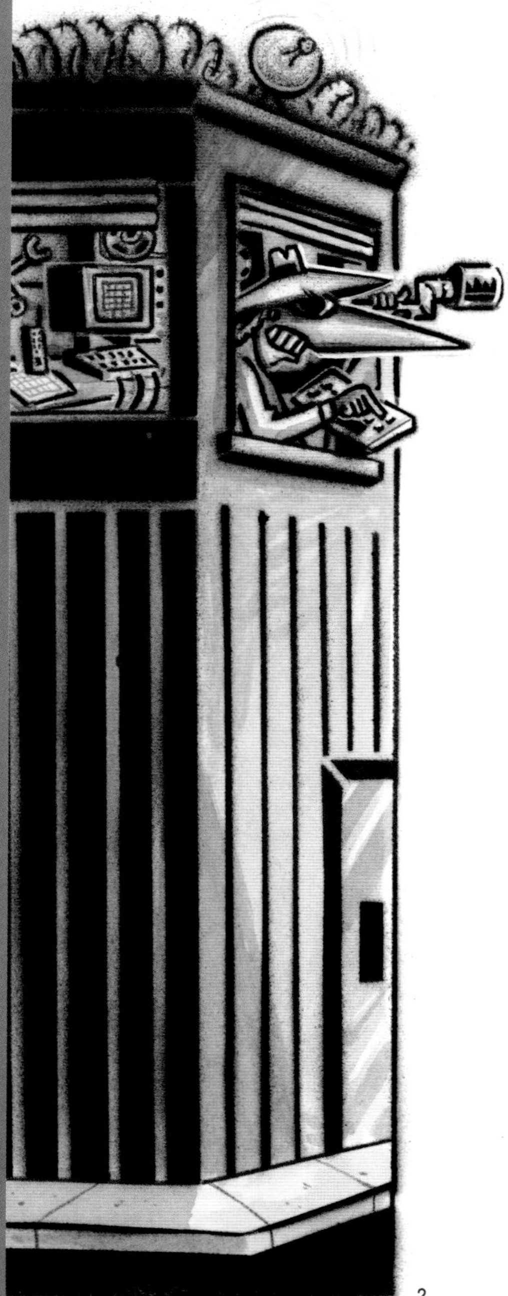

2

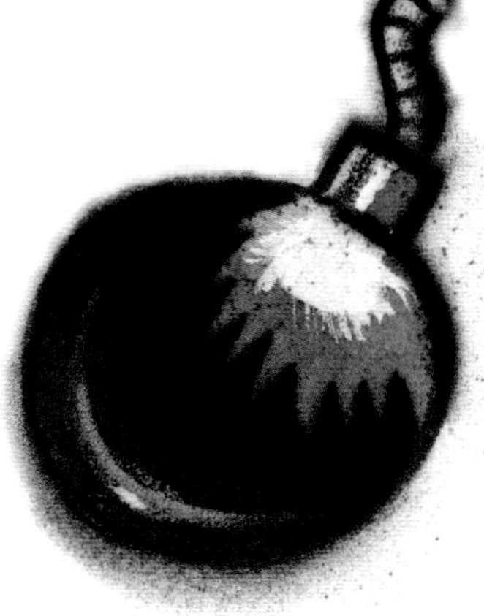

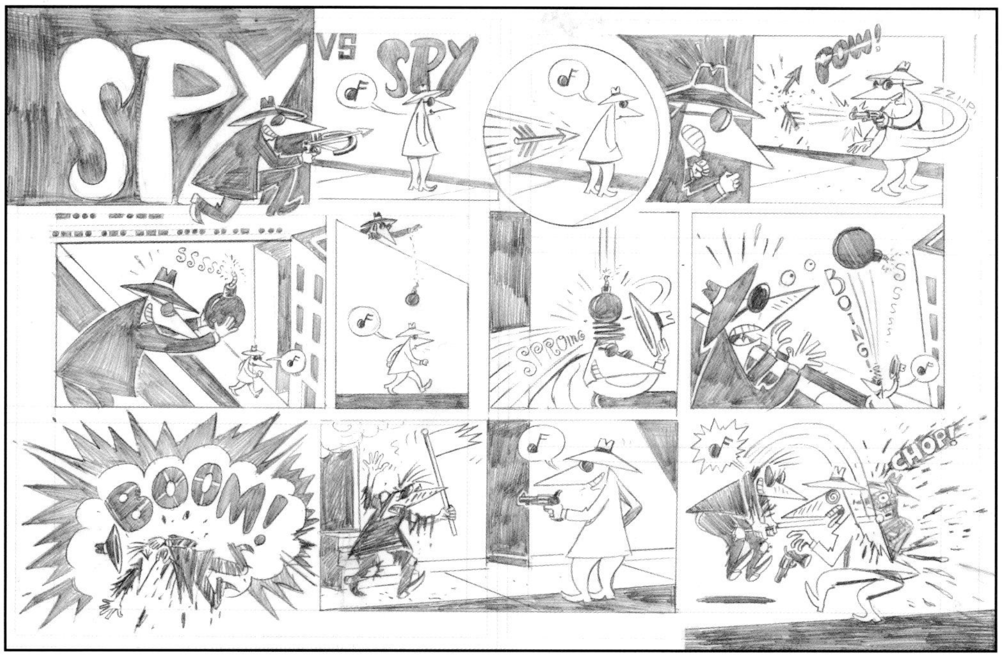
SPY VS SPY
POW!
BOOM!
CHOP!
3

1. Logo for full color *Spy* strip. Note: The Morse code spells out "by Prohias." *Mad* #379, 1999.
2. Illustrations published with an article on espionage in the *New York Times*, 1999.
3. Pencil sketch ready to be cut as stencil for *Spy* strip, 1997.
4. Illustration on corporate spying commissioned by *Forbes Magazine*, 1999.

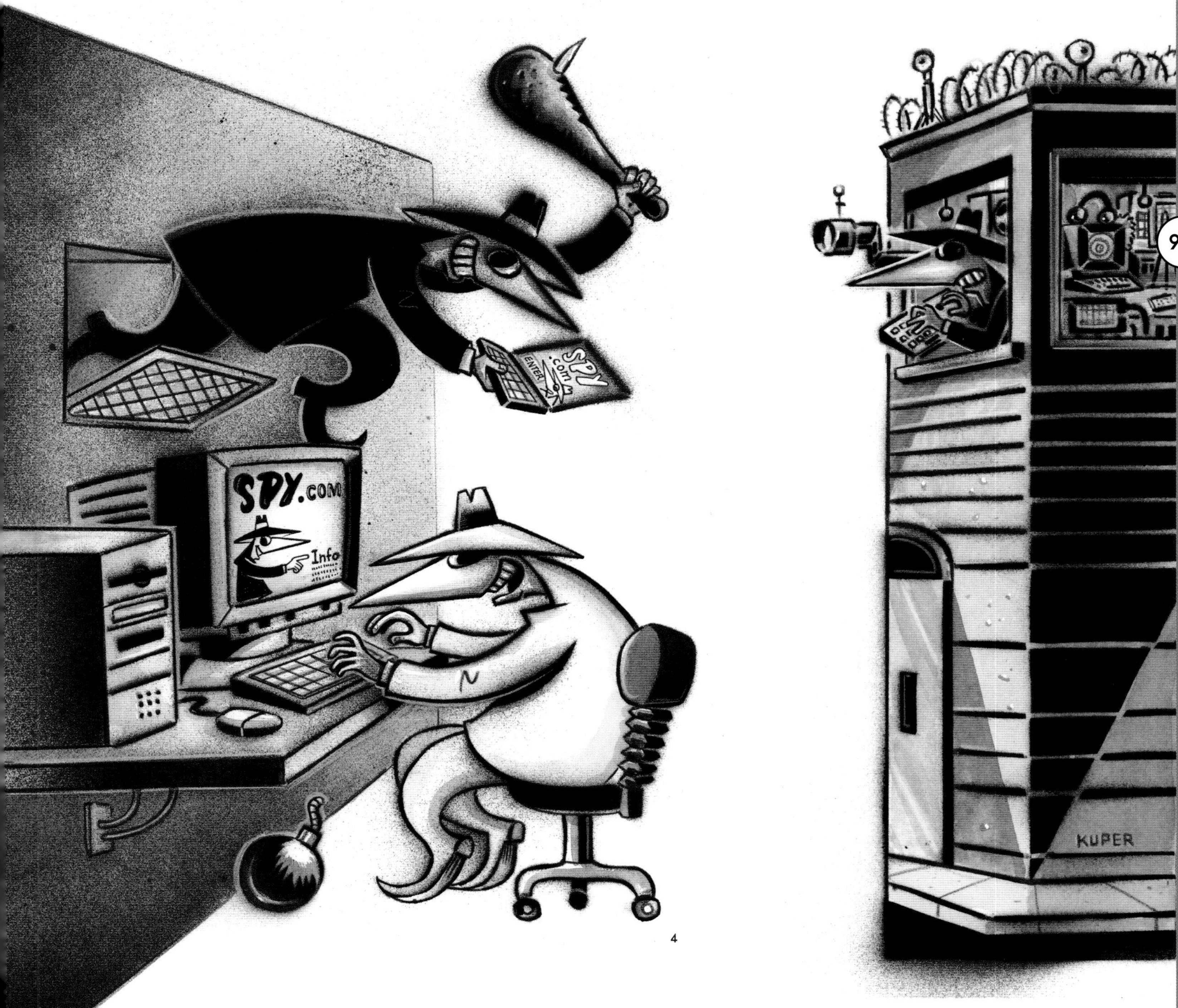
SPY.com
ENTER
SPY.com
Info
KUPER
4

IT'S OBSCENE

The following essay was published in *Print Magazine's* Cold Eye column in their May/June issue, 1994.

94

In the graphics field we are often asked to distinguish good art from bad. It's far less common that one is required to determine whether something is art at all. But that is exactly what I was asked to do last March as a comix and illustration witness in a Florida obscenity trial.

The works in question were two issues of *Boiled Angel*, a 'zine (loosely defined as a small self-published magazine) produced by 24-year-old Michael Diana between 1989 and 1991. Diana had photocopied a grand total of 300 copies of each of the eight issues of *Boiled Angel* and now was faced with the possibility of three years in jail and a $3,000 fine based on violating the "Community Standards" law of Pinellas County, Florida.

What was so obscene that it could send an artist to jail? Michael Diana depicted priests molesting children, parents sexually abusing their kids, men shooting up and raping their girlfriends—all in comic strip form. Instead of referring to such activities through the customary formats of nightly news programs, daily newspaper headlines, radio or TV talk shows, or national magazine articles, he used a "children's medium," one usually reserved for Garfield and Batman, to create images of our society's underbelly without gags or punchline endings.

He also demonstrated an interest in serial killers (according to a recent *Time* magazine article, this fascination puts him squarely among the majority of Americans) by publishing articles and interviews with a number of convicted murderers as well as publishing comics, illustrations, and writings by an array of contributors from around the country.

To be honest, much of the work in *Boiled Angel* doesn't sit too well with me. It disturbs and depresses, and often actually nauseates me. Oddly enough, I have the same reaction when I watch the local news or read the *New York Times*.

The saga of how Michael Diana came to find himself in front of a Pinellas County jury is perhaps even more twisted than some of the strips he published in *Boiled Angel*. It went something like this: In 1990, Florida State officials chanced upon a copy of the 'zine while chasing down leads in the Gainesville serial murder case. They located Diana, and gave him a blood test to determine whether his blood type matched that of the killer. Although the test verified that Diana had a different blood type, the officials passed a copy of *Boiled Angel* along to the local sheriff's office where it fell into the hands of one of Pinellas County's "intelligence" officers. The officer took it upon himself to correspond with Diana, posing as a fan of the 'zine, and ordered the next two issues of *Boiled Angel*. Nearly two years after the sheriff's office received its first copy, it suddenly concluded that *Boiled Angel* was obscene.

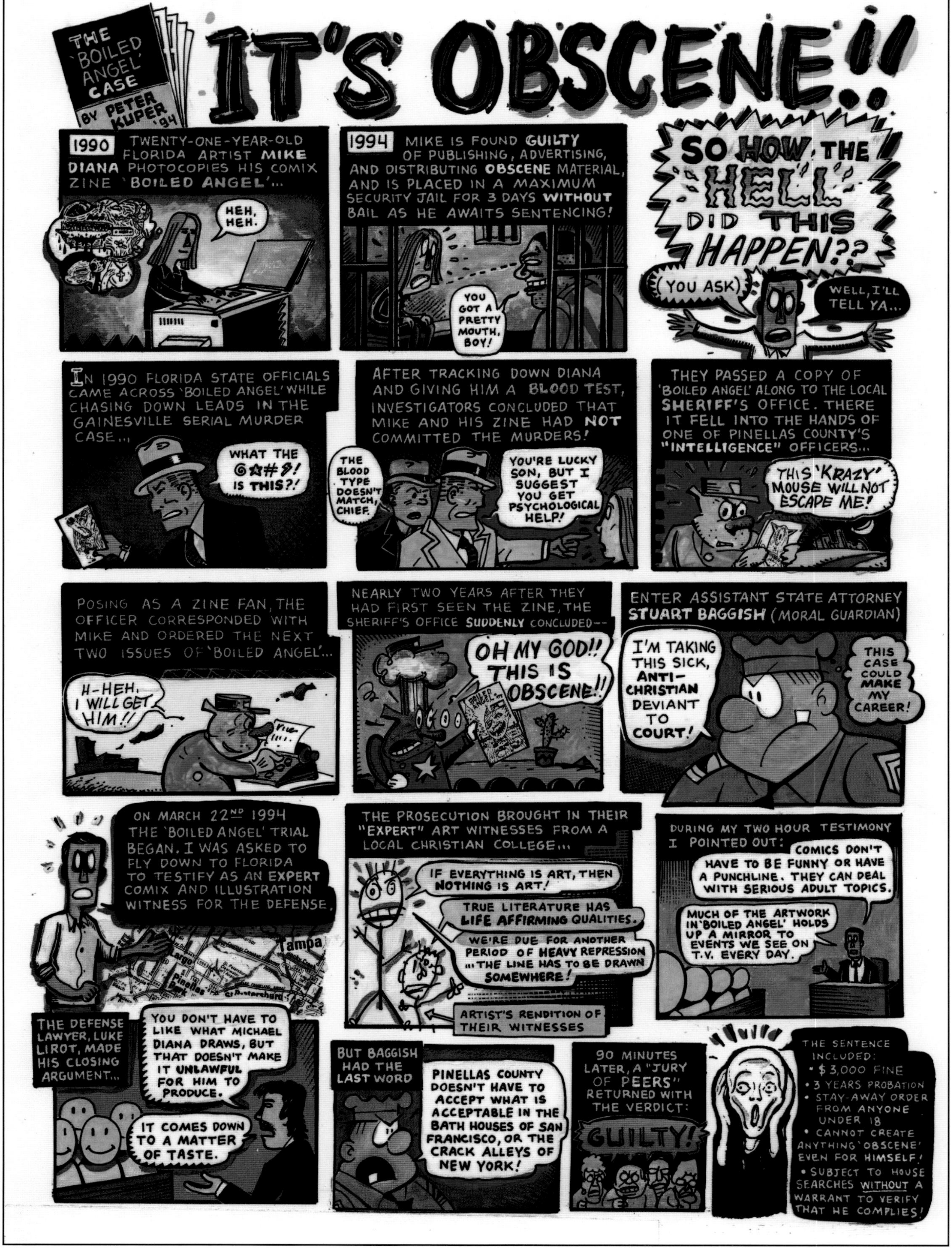

THE 'BOILED ANGEL' CASE
BY PETER KUPER '94
IT'S OBSCENE!!
1990 TWENTY-ONE-YEAR-OLD FLORIDA ARTIST MIKE DIANA PHOTOCOPIES HIS COMIX ZINE 'BOILED ANGEL'...
HEH, HEH.
1994 MIKE IS FOUND GUILTY OF PUBLISHING, ADVERTISING, AND DISTRIBUTING OBSCENE MATERIAL, AND IS PLACED IN A MAXIMUM SECURITY JAIL FOR 3 DAYS WITHOUT BAIL AS HE AWAITS SENTENCING!
YOU GOT A PRETTY MOUTH, BOY!
SO HOW THE HELL DID THIS HAPPEN??
(YOU ASK)
WELL, I'LL TELL YA...
IN 1990 FLORIDA STATE OFFICIALS CAME ACROSS 'BOILED ANGEL' WHILE CHASING DOWN LEADS IN THE GAINESVILLE SERIAL MURDER CASE...
WHAT THE @☆#$! IS THIS?!
AFTER TRACKING DOWN DIANA AND GIVING HIM A BLOOD TEST, INVESTIGATORS CONCLUDED THAT MIKE AND HIS ZINE HAD NOT COMMITTED THE MURDERS!
THE BLOOD TYPE DOESN'T MATCH, CHIEF.
YOU'RE LUCKY SON, BUT I SUGGEST YOU GET PSYCHOLOGICAL HELP!
THEY PASSED A COPY OF 'BOILED ANGEL' ALONG TO THE LOCAL SHERIFF'S OFFICE. THERE IT FELL INTO THE HANDS OF ONE OF PINELLAS COUNTY'S "INTELLIGENCE" OFFICERS...
THIS 'KRAZY' MOUSE WILL NOT ESCAPE ME!
POSING AS A ZINE FAN, THE OFFICER CORRESPONDED WITH MIKE AND ORDERED THE NEXT TWO ISSUES OF 'BOILED ANGEL'...
H-HEH. I WILL GET HIM!!
NEARLY TWO YEARS AFTER THEY HAD FIRST SEEN THE ZINE, THE SHERIFF'S OFFICE SUDDENLY CONCLUDED--
OH MY GOD!! THIS IS OBSCENE!!
ENTER ASSISTANT STATE ATTORNEY STUART BAGGISH (MORAL GUARDIAN)
I'M TAKING THIS SICK, ANTI-CHRISTIAN DEVIANT TO COURT!
THIS CASE COULD MAKE MY CAREER!
ON MARCH 22ND 1994 THE 'BOILED ANGEL' TRIAL BEGAN. I WAS ASKED TO FLY DOWN TO FLORIDA TO TESTIFY AS AN EXPERT COMIX AND ILLUSTRATION WITNESS FOR THE DEFENSE.
Tampa
THE PROSECUTION BROUGHT IN THEIR "EXPERT" ART WITNESSES FROM A LOCAL CHRISTIAN COLLEGE...
IF EVERYTHING IS ART, THEN NOTHING IS ART!
TRUE LITERATURE HAS LIFE AFFIRMING QUALITIES.
WE'RE DUE FOR ANOTHER PERIOD OF HEAVY REPRESSION ...THE LINE HAS TO BE DRAWN SOMEWHERE!
ARTIST'S RENDITION OF THEIR WITNESSES
DURING MY TWO HOUR TESTIMONY I POINTED OUT:
COMICS DON'T HAVE TO BE FUNNY OR HAVE A PUNCHLINE. THEY CAN DEAL WITH SERIOUS ADULT TOPICS.
MUCH OF THE ARTWORK IN 'BOILED ANGEL' HOLDS UP A MIRROR TO EVENTS WE SEE ON T.V. EVERY DAY.
THE DEFENSE LAWYER, LUKE LIROT, MADE HIS CLOSING ARGUMENT...
YOU DON'T HAVE TO LIKE WHAT MICHAEL DIANA DRAWS, BUT THAT DOESN'T MAKE IT UNLAWFUL FOR HIM TO PRODUCE.
IT COMES DOWN TO A MATTER OF TASTE.
BUT BAGGISH HAD THE LAST WORD
PINELLAS COUNTY DOESN'T HAVE TO ACCEPT WHAT IS ACCEPTABLE IN THE BATH HOUSES OF SAN FRANCISCO, OR THE CRACK ALLEYS OF NEW YORK!
90 MINUTES LATER, A "JURY OF PEERS" RETURNED WITH THE VERDICT:
GUILTY!
THE SENTENCE INCLUDED:
• $3,000 FINE
• 3 YEARS PROBATION
• STAY-AWAY ORDER FROM ANYONE UNDER 18
• CANNOT CREATE ANYTHING 'OBSCENE' EVEN FOR HIMSELF!
• SUBJECT TO HOUSE SEARCHES WITHOUT A WARRANT TO VERIFY THAT HE COMPLIES!

It's Obscene, published in the *Village Voice*, 1994.
It was later made into a poster to raise money for the Comic Book Legal Defense Fund.

Opposite page: Illustration, published in the *Progressive*, 1993.

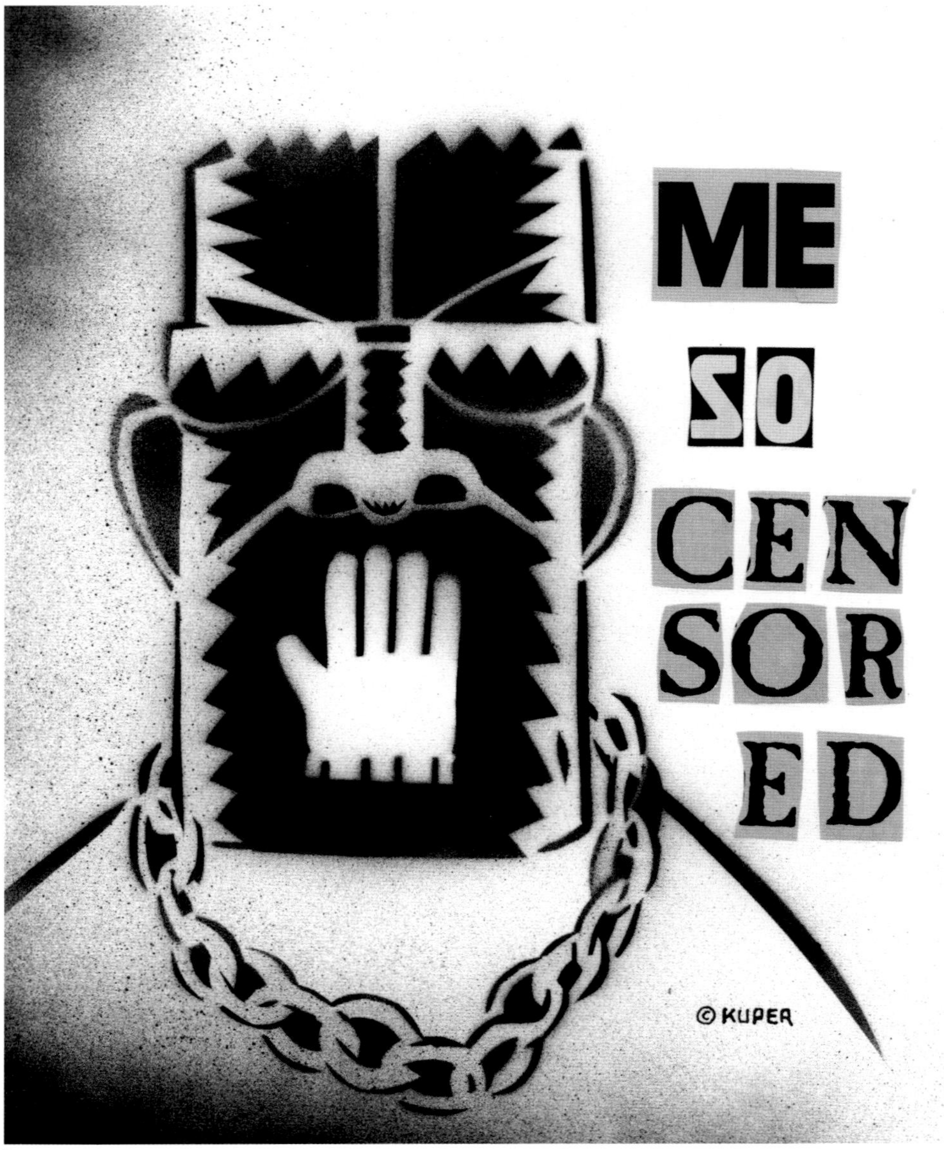
ME
SO
CEN
SOR
ED
©KUPER

1

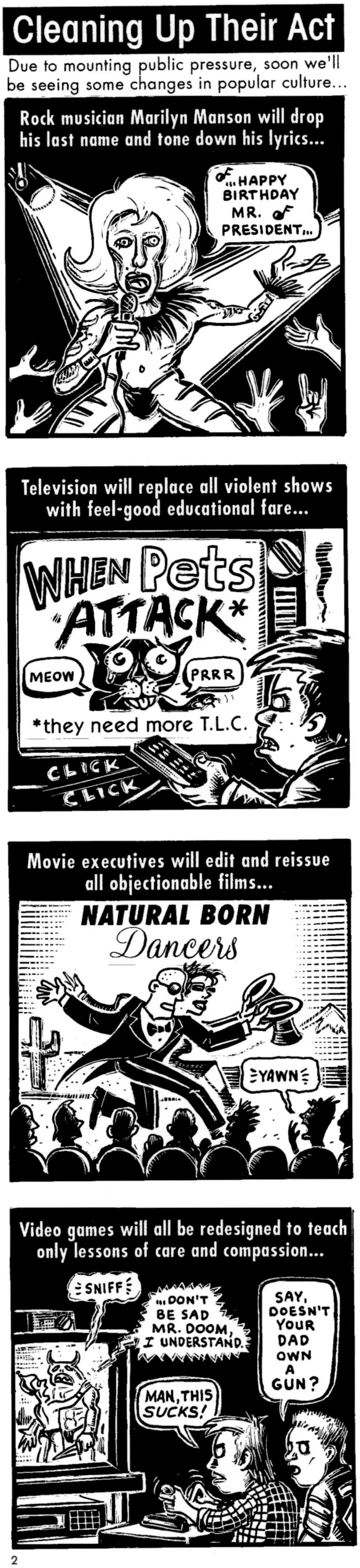
Cleaning Up Their Act
Due to mounting public pressure, soon we'll be seeing some changes in popular culture...
Rock musician Marilyn Manson will drop his last name and tone down his lyrics...
...HAPPY BIRTHDAY MR. PRESIDENT...
Television will replace all violent shows with feel-good educational fare...
WHEN Pets ATTACK*
MEOW
PRRR
*they need more T.L.C.
CLICK
CLICK
Movie executives will edit and reissue all objectionable films...
NATURAL BORN
Dancers
YAWN
Video games will all be redesigned to teach only lessons of care and compassion...
SNIFF
...DON'T BE SAD MR. DOOM, I UNDERSTAND.
SAY, DOESN'T YOUR DAD OWN A GUN?
MAN, THIS SUCKS!

2

Enter Assistant State Attorney Stuart Baggish. Baggish charged Diana with three counts: publishing obscene material, distributing it, and advertising it. (The "advertisement" was part of the editorial of Issue #7 in which Diana had written: "In order for me to do a *Boiled Angel* #8, I need money, so send a donation if you can spare it.")

The case came to trial a year after the charges were brought, at which point The Comic Book Legal Defense Fund, an organization established in 1986 to fight censorship and uphold the First Amendment in the comic book industry, asked me to testify for the defense. I had not seen *Boiled Angel* before this point, but I was aware of Diana's work, having published "Grasshopper Boy," a story of sexual abuse, and "Suffer the Innocent" a strip dealing with his then upcoming obscenity trial, in the 'zine I co-edit, *World War 3*.

1. *Me so Censored*, appeared in a 2 Live Crew comic book, published by Fantagraphics Books, 1991.
2. *Cleaning up Their Act*, the *New York Daily News*, 1999.
3. *Censorship is the Obscenity*, T-shirt design for Comic Book Legal Defense Fund, 1999.
4. *...No Evil*, the *New York Daily News*, 2000.

The prosecution's witnesses included a forensic psychologist and two professors from a local Christian college. The psychologist, Sidney Merin, (who, according to the prosecutor was paid nearly $4,000 for his testimony) concluded that, "*Boiled Angel* was designed for and primarily disseminated to clearly defined deviant sexual groups, to that segment of society generally which finds perverted sexuality to be stimulating and appealing." James Crane and Stirling Watson, professors from Eckerd College, served as art experts, respectively concluding that "if the 'arts community' hasn't heard of it, or you can't hang it on a wall, it's not art," and "true art has life affirming qualities."

During my nearly two-hour cross-examination I tried to give the jury a crash course in "alternative comics" (a subject I teach at the School of Visual Arts in New York) and dissuade them from the assumption that comics are necessarily restricted to children, or should avoid tackling personal, social, or political content. I cited such examples as Art Spiegelman's Pulitzer Prize-winning *Maus*, which explored the tragedy of the Holocaust using the comic strip medium. I also pointed out that although *Boiled Angel* deals with gruesome, disturbing topics, it only mirrors what takes place in society. A priest molesting a child is criminal; writing about it or drawing it is not.

Another expert witness called by the defense was *Factsheet Five* editor, R. Seth Friedman, who reviews roughly 7000 'zines each year. He estimated that nearly 50,000 are in circulation in this country, and that *Boiled Angel* is among many comic book 'zines dealing graphically with social topics that are aimed at other 'zine fans.

CENSORSHIP IS THE OBSCENITY

3

From Eminem to South Park to Dr. Laura and on and on. Where will it end?
...NO EVIL
If only we could ban all those hateful talk-radio shows...
If only we could eliminate those distasteful television shows...
If only we could silence the barrage of offensive music lyrics...
ECORDS • CDS
What a wonderful world it would be?

4

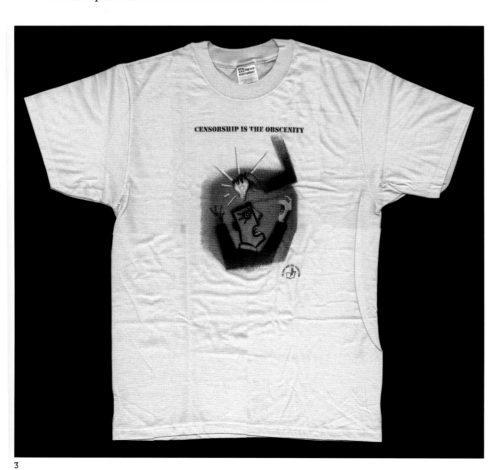

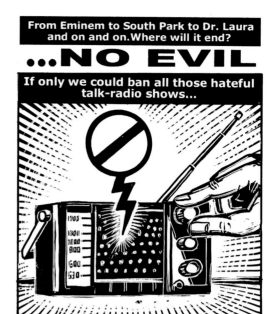

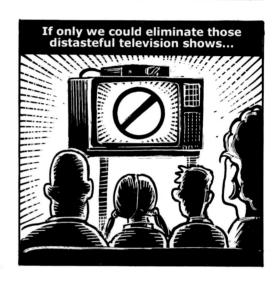

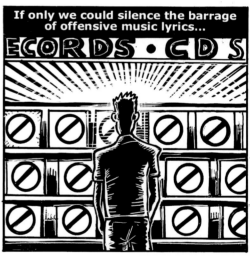

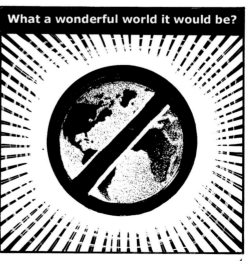

In his summation, Diana's attorney, Luke Lirot, pointed out that whether or not the jury liked what Michael Diana created, the work remained protected by the First Amendment. This was a "matter of taste" and not a criminal offense. He also noted that *Boiled Angel* was not sold in stores, and that the only copies sold in Pinellas County had been ordered by an undercover police officer through the mail.

The prosecution, however, was able to throw all of the defense's testimonies out the window by appealing to the jury's irrational fears. Stuart Baggish's summation identified Diana as a serial killer in the making. "This is how Danny Rolling [the confessed Gainesville serial killer who, ironically, had been sentenced to the electric chair the morning of Diana's trial] got started. Step one, you start with the drawings. Step two, you go on to the [pornographic] pictures. Step three is the movies. And step four, you're into reality. You're creating these scenes in reality." He presented this completely unsubstantiated scenario as fact and offered only innuendo to counter the validity of the defense's testimonies. Baggish concluded [Pinellas County] "doesn't have to accept what is acceptable in the bathhouses of San Francisco or the crack alleys of New York."

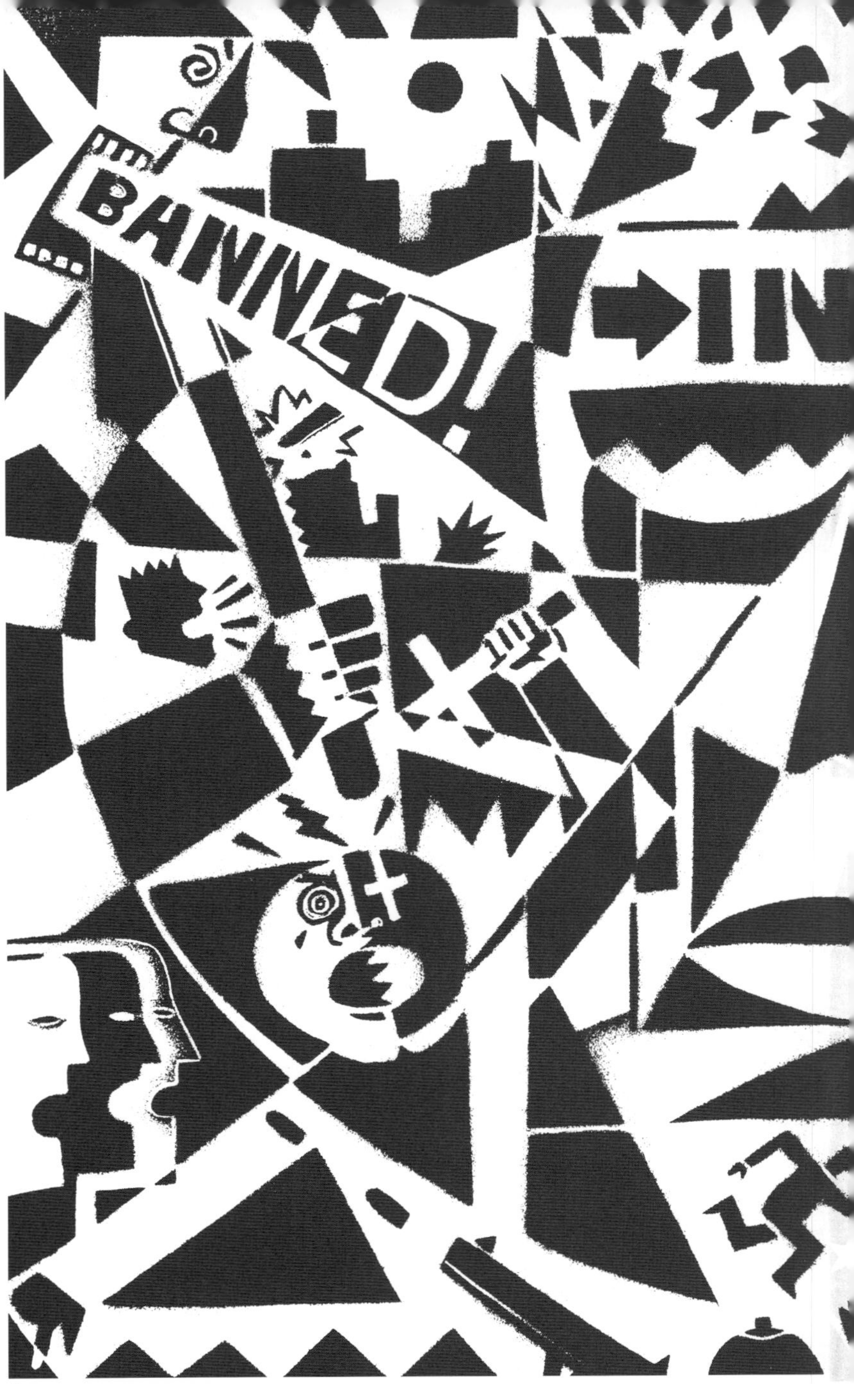
BANNED!
IN

1

Consider what a hazy point of law *obscenity* is. After all, one can determine only after the fact that the law has been broken. In the 1973 landmark case, Miller vs. California, the Supreme Court determined that something can be ruled obscene only if it satisfies all three of these points: 1. The work appeals primarily to prurient interests, 2. It is patently offensive as determined by "community standards," 3. Taken as a whole, it lacks serious literary, artistic, political or scientific value.

Ultimately, short of libel, can any pen-and-ink drawing on paper be so harmful that it should be banned? Should any artist be required to predetermine exactly why he or she chooses a particular type of imagery or subject matter? Isn't the freedom to create art unfettered by law primary to our First Amendment rights?

Considering the many debatable issues involved in a case of this nature, one would have expected a fair degree of deliberation before any jury could reach a verdict. All this Florida jury of three men and three women required were ninety minutes to conclude Michael Diana was guilty on all three counts.

When I heard the verdict I felt as though I had been punched in the stomach. I wondered whether had I chosen different words or said something more, I might have swayed the jury's decision. As a 'zine publisher myself, I felt a particular horror at the notion that Diana's fate could easily have been my own.

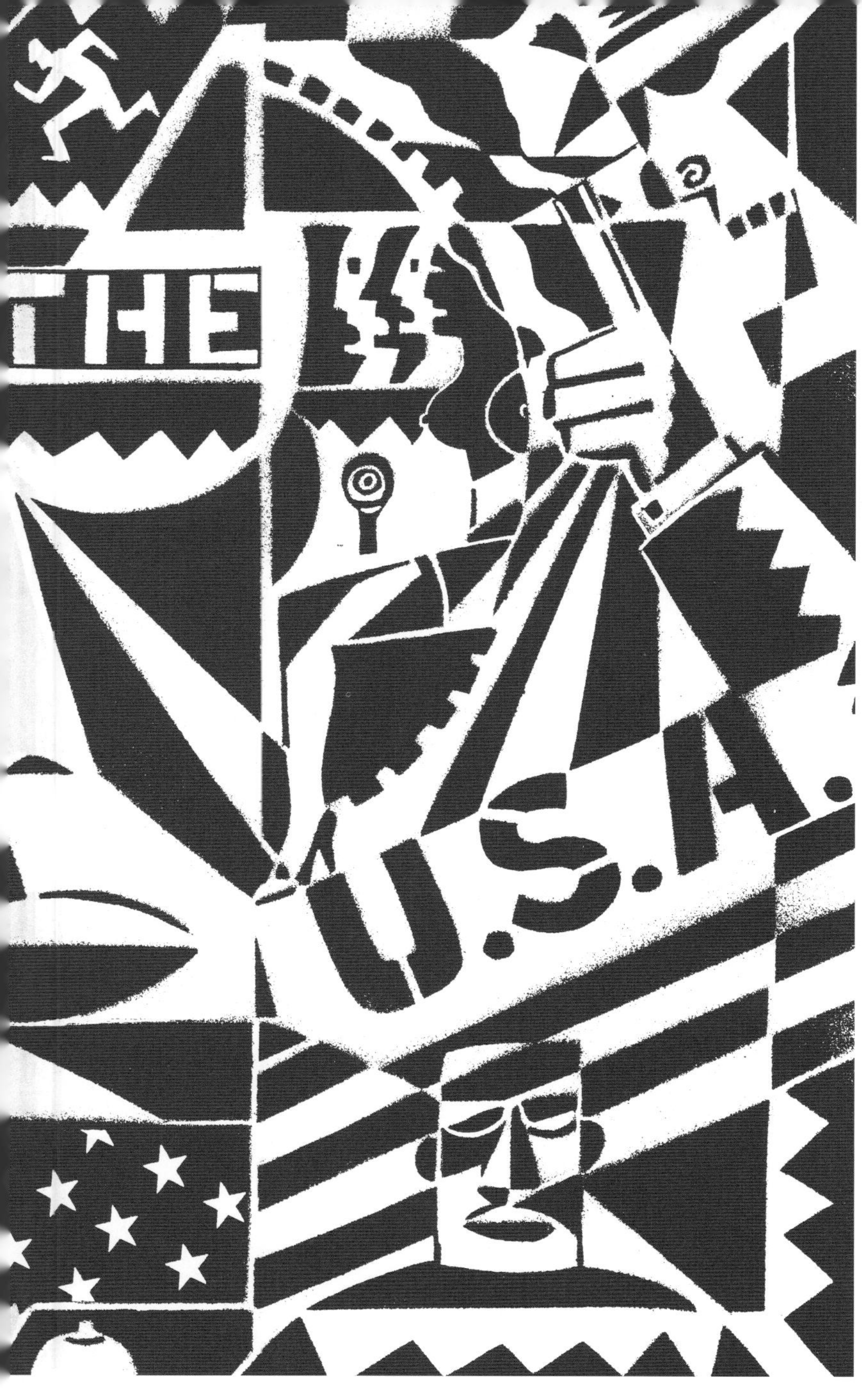
THE
U.S.A.

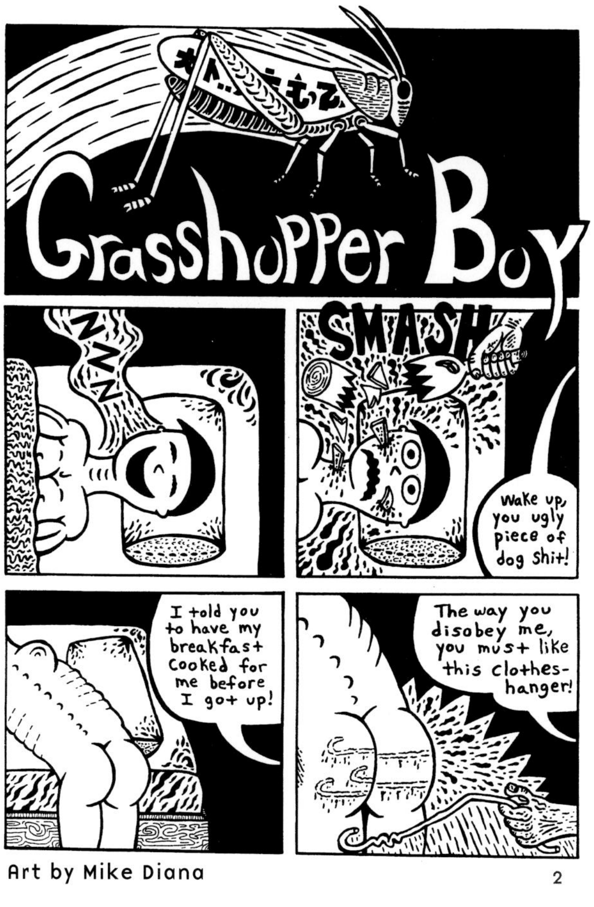
Grasshopper Boy
SMASH
Wake up, you ugly piece of dog shit!
I told you to have my breakfast cooked for me before I got up!
The way you disobey me, you must like this clothes-hanger!
2

Art by Mike Diana

Immediately following the verdict, Judge Walter Fullerton ordered Diana sent to the maximum security section of the county jail, to be held without bail over the weekend until Monday's sentencing. With one rap of the gavel, Michael Diana became the first 'zine publisher and cartoonist in the twentieth century to be imprisoned for his creations. But that was only the beginning.

On Monday, the judge announced the sentence: three years probation, 1,248 hours of community service, a $3,000 fine, mandatory psychological evaluation at Diana's own expense (the cost was ultimately $1,250), and a mandatory course in "journalism ethics." He must stay away from anyone under 18, and he is prohibited from publishing anything that in the judge's words "could be considered obscene." The judge went on to say that Diana could not create such work even for his own personal use in his home. Diana's probation officer is authorized to make unannounced house searches without a warrant to verify that Diana is not doodling "obscenities." The judge closed by ordering Diana to spend a fourth night in jail—presumably just for good measure.

If it was the intent of the prosecutor and judge to silence Michael Diana and to suppress work they have decided should be kept from public view, they have failed. The more than $50,000 of taxpayer's money spent on this case so far has bought an audience for Diana's work far greater than the artist himself, with his limited resources, could ever have hoped for (though he may find this of little consolation unless his conviction is overturned).

Perhaps it is easy to look at all this and say, "Well, I'd never create anything so obscene I'd get put in jail for it." But every time an artist like Diana is found guilty, the line separating art from obscenity is harder to make out. Are you sure you know on which side you'll be found?

1. *Banned in the U.S.A.*, appeared in the 2 Live Crew comic book, published by Fantagraphics Books, 1991.

2. *Grasshopper Boy*, by Mike Diana, published in *World War 3*, 1994.

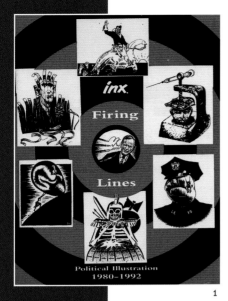

inx.
Firing
Lines
Political Illustration
1980–1992
1

INX

Kisangani
ZAIRE
Ubundu
RWANDA
2

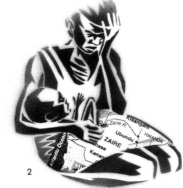

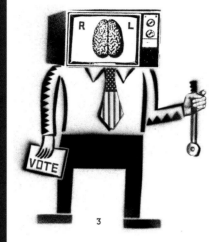

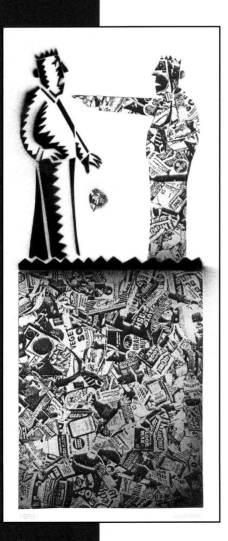

In 1980, Ronald Reagan was elected president and John Lennon was assassinated, among other tragic events. The same year a group of New York based illustrators decided to form the first artist-run syndicate for editorial illustration. Rather than awaiting the assignments, they produced images that subscribing newspapers could place with appropriate articles. They called the group INX, and the artists worked for no pay—in fact they all contributed money to get the syndication service off the ground. They succeeded in getting nearly 30 subscribers, including the *Washington Post*, the *Boston Globe*, and the *Atlanta Journal Constitution*.

The following is a modified version of an essay published in the catalog for a retrospective show of INX at Parsons School of Design in New York, 1992.

R
L
VOTE
3

After three years of self-syndication (and exhaustion), INX negotiated a contract with United Feature. Under this arrangement, artists were to be paid a flat fee for each drawing and freed from the process of promotion and sales of the service.

I began contributing illustrations to INX in 1984, and since 1988, have also been one of the art directors. This responsibility involves picking pertinent topics from the week's news, and commissioning illustrators to produce corresponding images. Artists are chosen for their ability to create strong conceptual pieces, and are given a lot of latitude in this process.

Often in the illustration field, artists' strongest images are rejected by art directors and editors as too offensive, too opinionated and too expressive. After years of this struggle, many artists start to pre-censor themselves and reject images even before they put pencil to paper. For 20 years, INX has combated this situation by giving illustrators the opportunity to bring strong content to their work, and has found opinion pages willing to publish drawings as powerful as their articles.

4

5

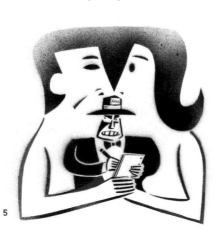

1. *Inx: Firing Lines*, catalog cover, 1992.
2. *Rwandan Refugees*, 1997.
3. *American Voter*, 1996.
4. *Litterbug*, 1993.
5. *Privacy and the Media*, 1999.
6. *Gas Prices*, 1991.
7. *Dividing the Pie*, 1998.
8. *India and the Bomb*, 1999.

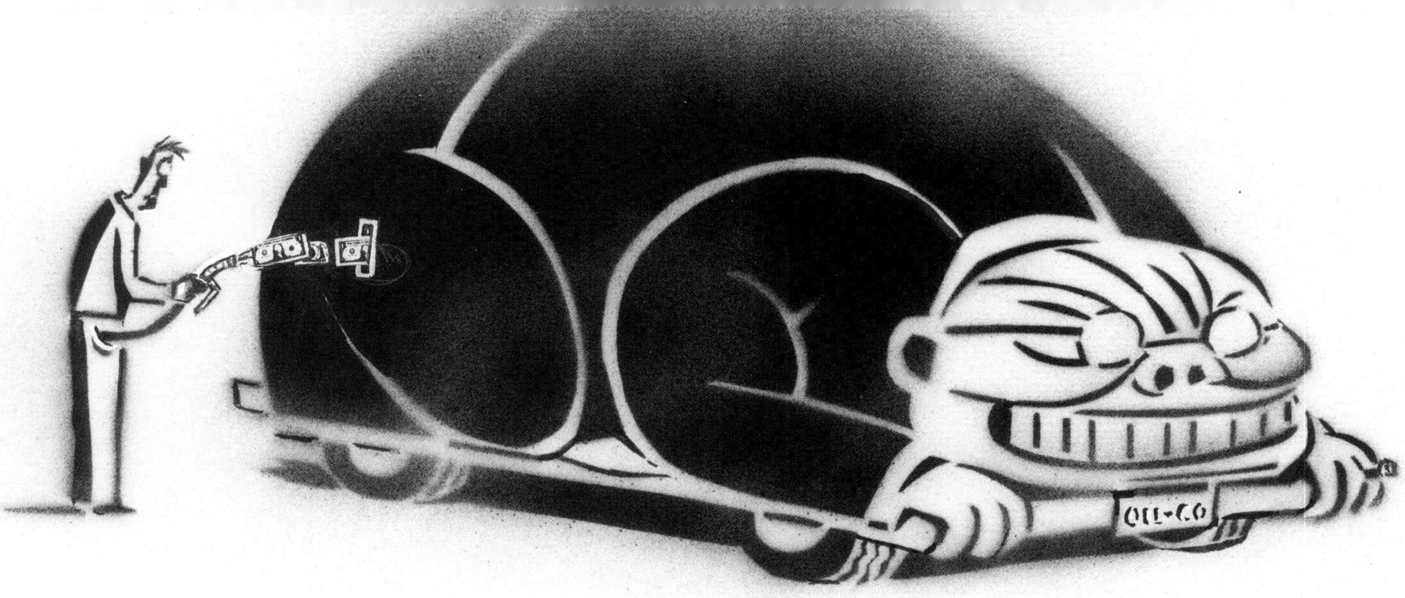
OIL-CO

6

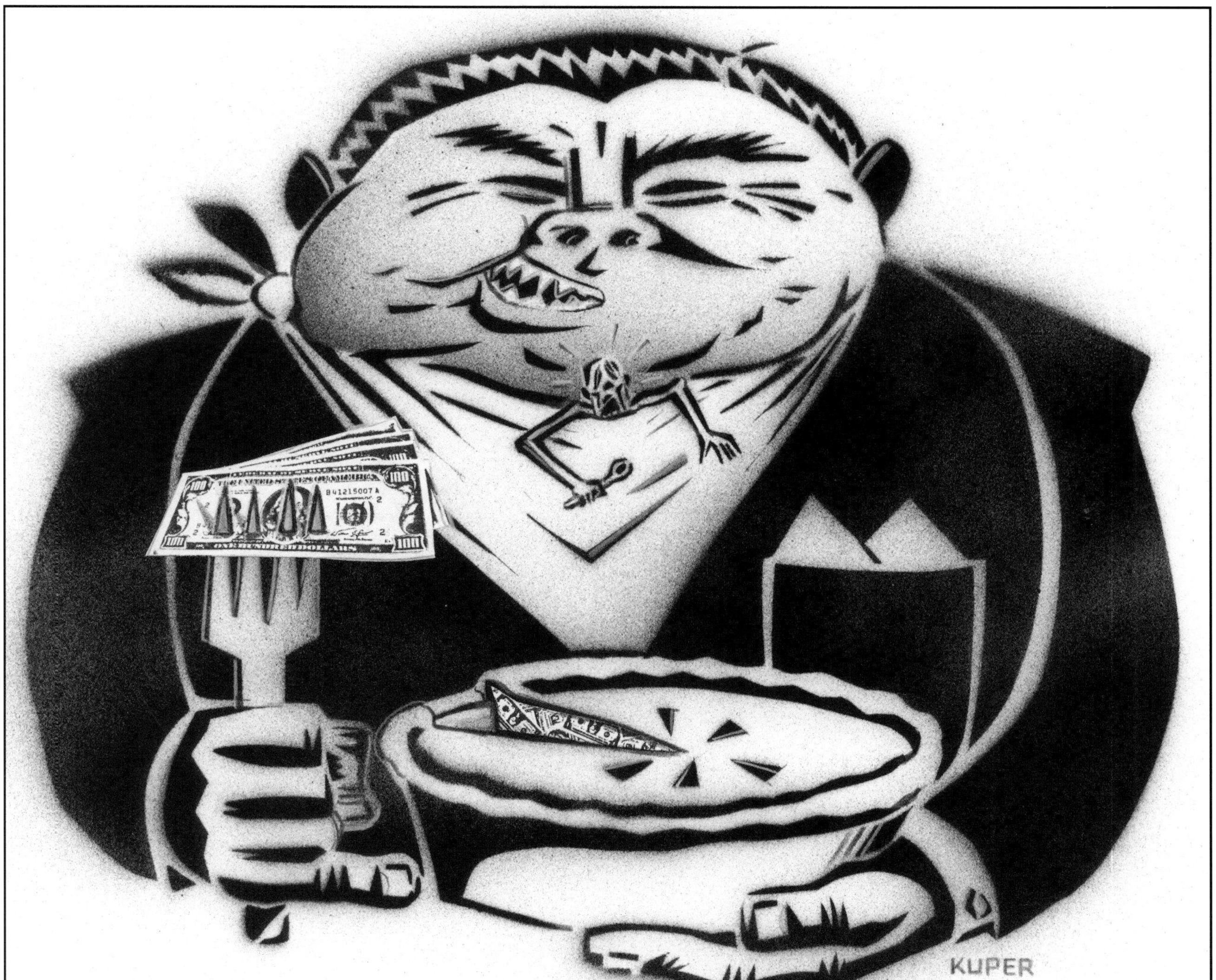
KUPER

7

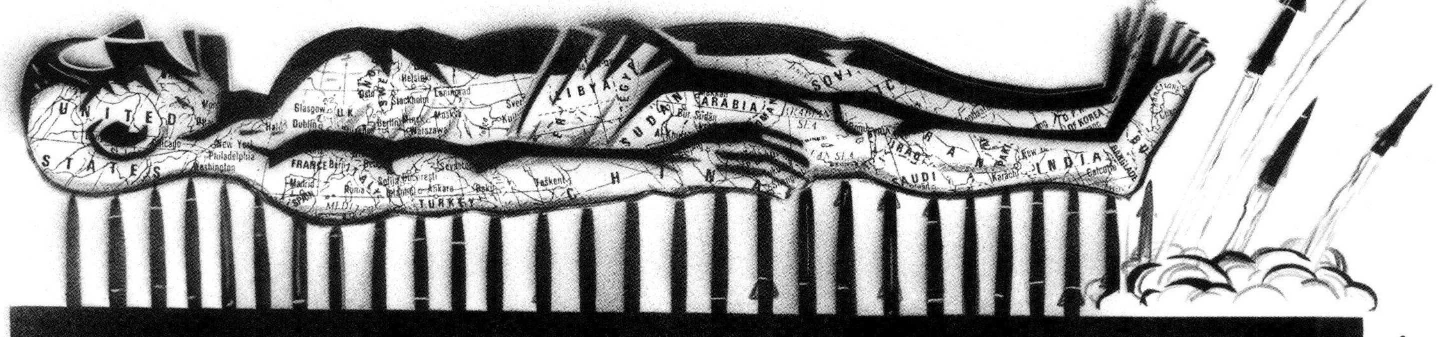
UNITED
STATES
LIBYA
ARABIA
INDIA
FRANCE
TURKEY

8

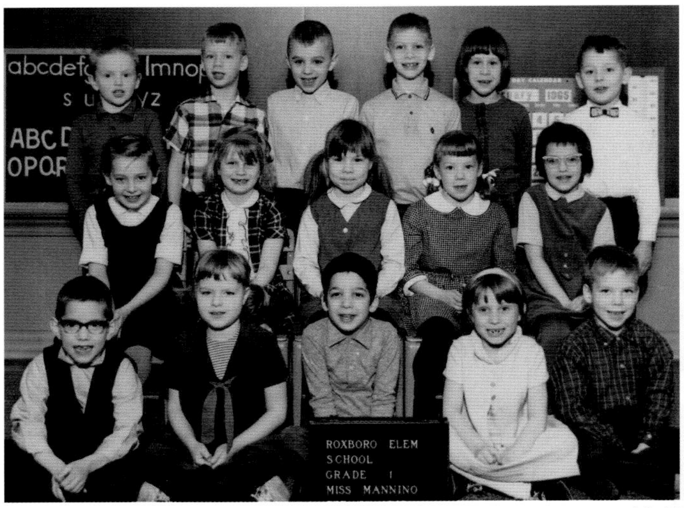

ROXBORO ELEM
SCHOOL
GRADE 1
MISS MANNINO

Front row, center: Peter Kuper
Back row, third from right:
Seth Tobocman.

1964

TIMELINE

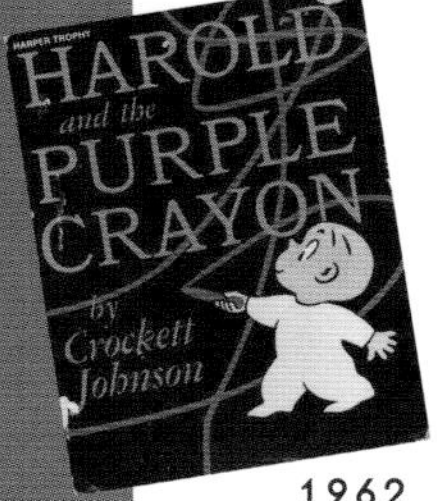

HAROLD and the PURPLE CRAYON
by Crockett Johnson

1962

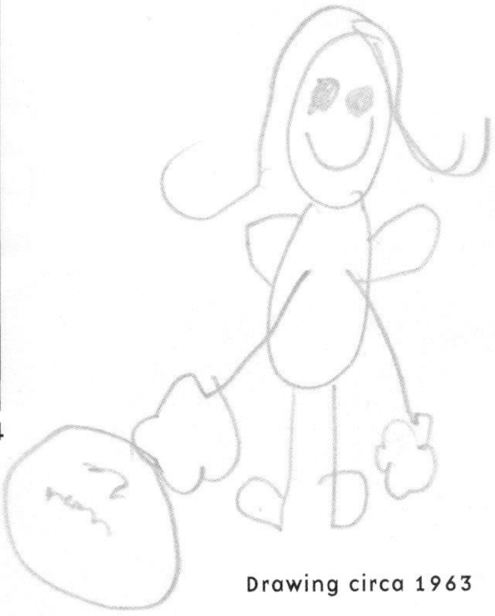

Drawing circa 1963

1958 Born September 22 in Summit, New Jersey, to Alan and Virginia Kuper, with older sisters Holly and Kate.

1962 Reads Crockett Johnson's *Harold and the Purple Crayon* and decides to be an artist.

1963 Catches first butterfly, and changes career track deciding that entomology is the way to go.

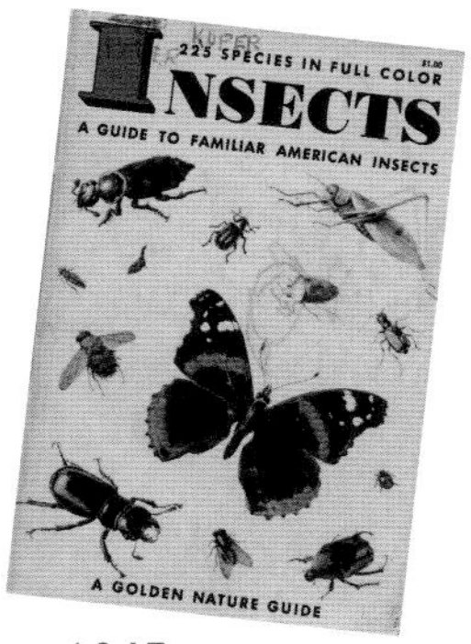

225 SPECIES IN FULL COLOR
INSECTS
A GUIDE TO FAMILIAR AMERICAN INSECTS
A GOLDEN NATURE GUIDE

1963

1964 Moves to Cleveland, Ohio, and becomes friends with classmate Seth Tobocman.

1965 Buys first comic book, *Thor* by Stan Lee and Jack Kirby.

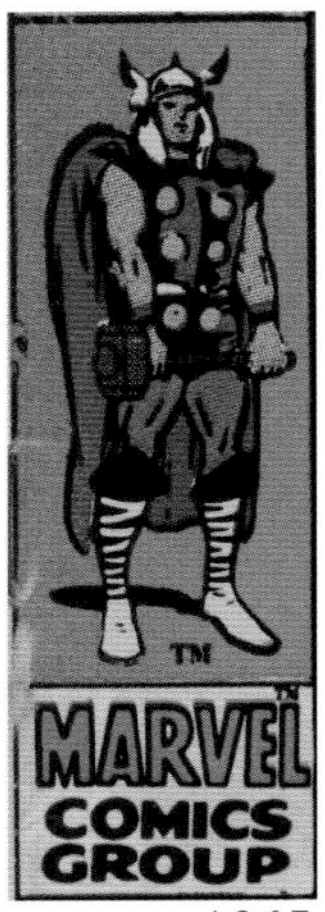

MARVEL COMICS GROUP

1965

1968 Visits New York City to see uncle in Broadway version of *Fiddler on the Roof* and decides to move to N.Y. at the first opportunity.

1969–70 Family takes a one-year sabbatical, traveling by VW camper van through Europe (England, Belgium, Luxembourg, France, Italy, Greece), living for a year in Israel, then camping through Europe again (Yugoslavia, Austria, Switzerland, Denmark, England).

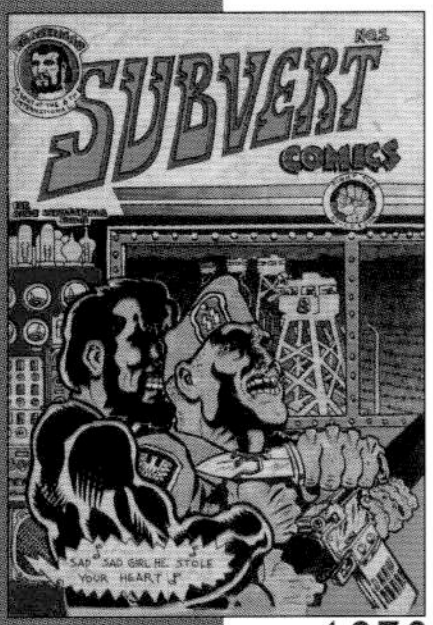

SUBVERT COMICS

1970

1970 Returns to U.S.A. Attends first comic book convention in Detroit.

Sees first underground comix, Spain Rodriguez's *Subvert.*

Co-publishes first comic fanzine, *Phanzine*, with Tobocman.

Decides not to be an entomologist.

Cover of *Phanzine*
1970

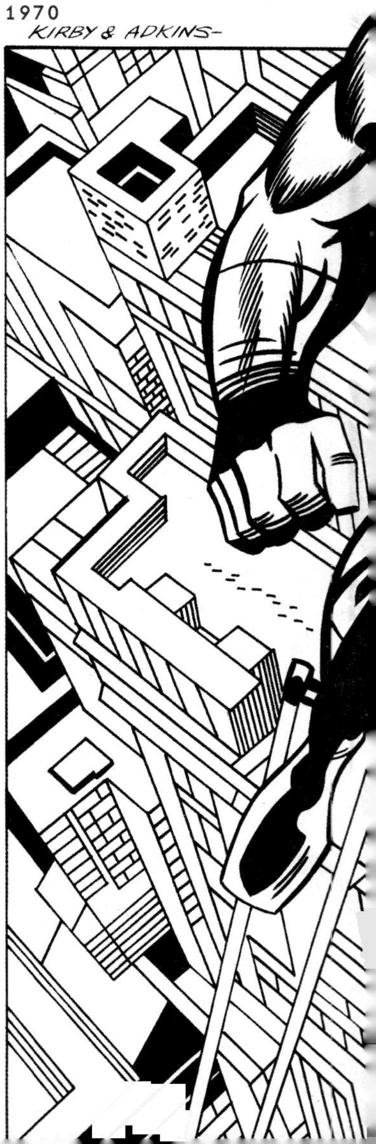

KIRBY & ADKINS-

1971 Meets Clevelander Harvey Pekar through Tobocman, who is his newspaper delivery boy. Makes trade of 78 rpm records for art and interview with Pekar's friend, R. Crumb.

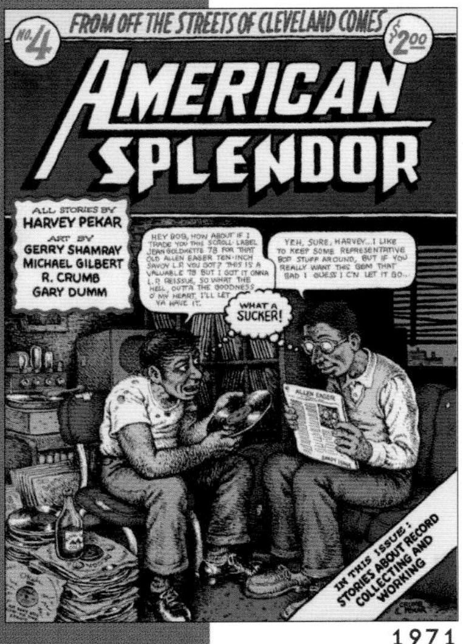

No. 4
FROM OFF THE STREETS OF CLEVELAND COMES
$2.00
AMERICAN SPLENDOR
ALL STORIES BY HARVEY PEKAR
ART BY GERRY SHAMRAY MICHAEL GILBERT R. CRUMB GARY DUMM
WHAT A SUCKER!
IN THIS ISSUE: STORIES ABOUT RECORD COLLECTING AND WORKING

1971

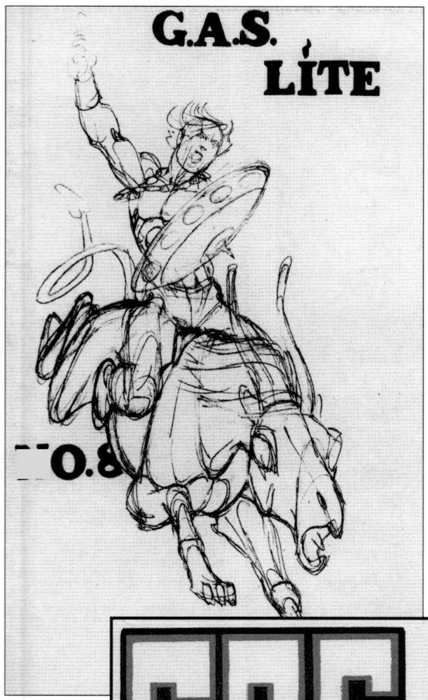
G.A.S.
LITE

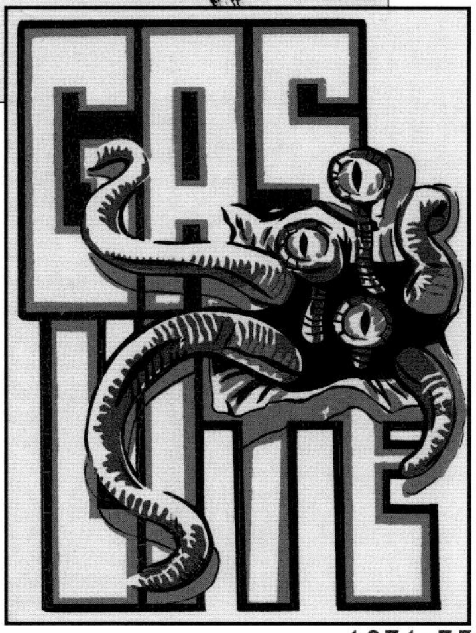

1971-73

With Tobocman, edits and publishes fanzine, *G.A.S. Lite*, the official magazine of the Cleveland Graphic Arts Society (a small group of local comics fans), and produces three issues between 1971–73. First issue includes interview with R. Crumb, subsequently publishes interviews with Isaac Asimov, William Gaines, Vaughn Bode, and Jack Kirby, among others.

Attends first comic convention in New York.

1972 R. Crumb visits Pekar, and drops by Kuper's for tea and trades more art for 78 rpm records.

Publishes *Melotoons* #1, including a collection of pages photocopied from an R. Crumb sketchbook and *G.A.S. Lite* interview.

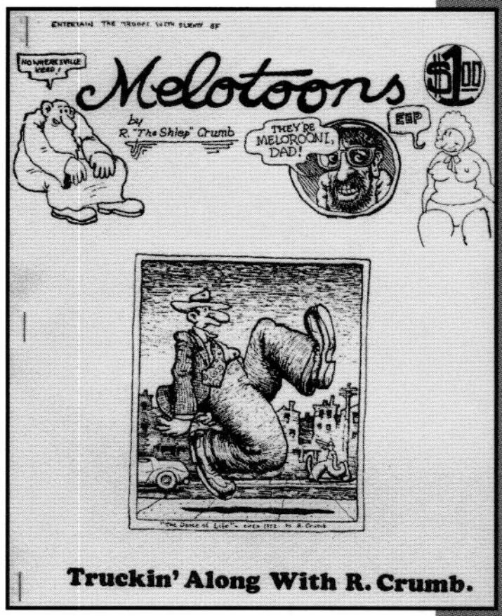
Melotoons
$1.00
Truckin' Along With R. Crumb.

1972

1973-74 Aimless adolescent hell.

Begins to lose interest in comics.

1975 Sick in bed with mononucleosis for a month, rekindles interest in comics and drawing and decides firmly on career as cartoonist.

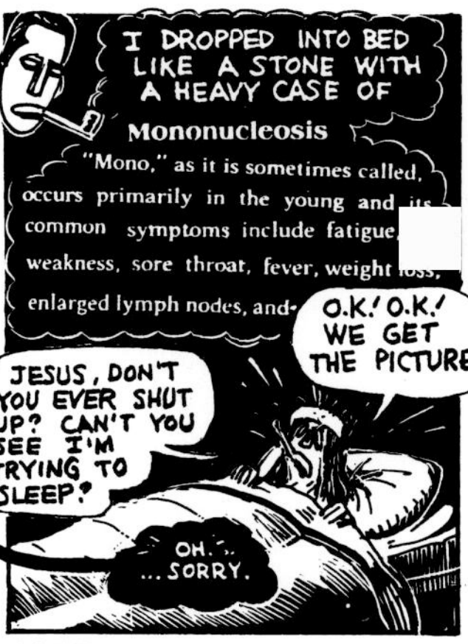
I DROPPED INTO BED LIKE A STONE WITH A HEAVY CASE OF
Mononucleosis
"Mono," as it is sometimes called, occurs primarily in the young and its common symptoms include fatigue, weakness, sore throat, fever, weight loss, enlarged lymph nodes, and-
O.K.! O.K.! WE GET THE PICTURE!
JESUS, DON'T YOU EVER SHUT UP? CAN'T YOU SEE I'M TRYING TO SLEEP?
OH... ...SORRY.

1975

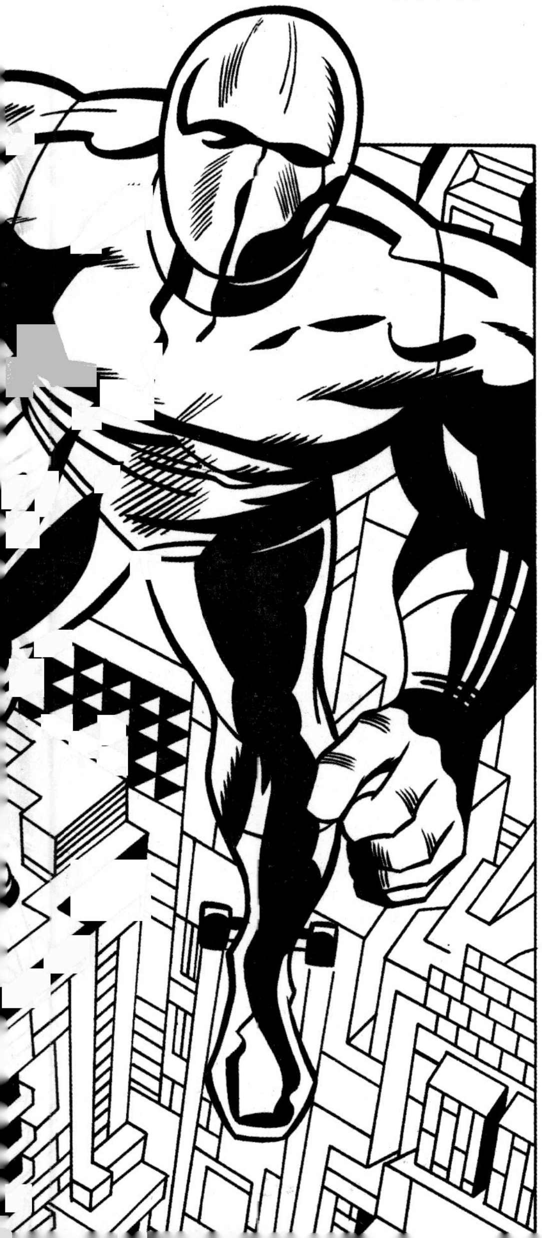

1976 Does drawings for high school year book and enormous Mickey Mouse on adhesive paper which is attached to school clock for several years.

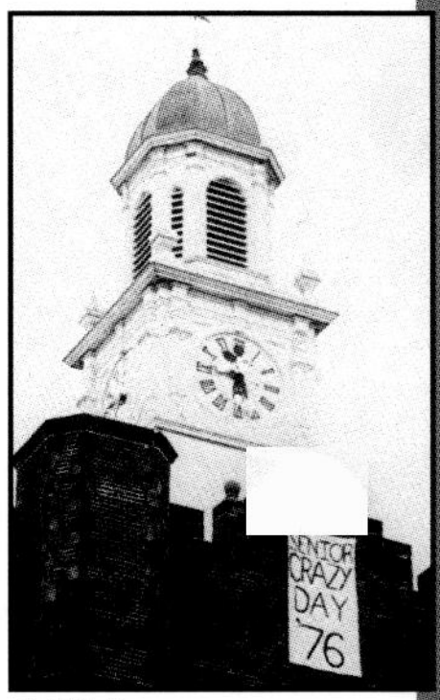
CRAZY
DAY
'76

1976

Publishes *Melotoons* #2.

1976-77 Attends Kent State and gets very depressed, fearing limited career prospects with a Bachelor of Fine Arts degree.

1977 Visits New York on Spring Break, uses sketchbook as a portfolio, hoping to find work in any area of art.

Offered employment by Zander Animation working on *Raggedy Anne and Andy* film.

Moves to New York for promised animation job that summer, but animation is complete and Zander says call in a couple of weeks.

1977-78 Calls Zander every two weeks for six-to-eight months to no avail.

Attends night classes at Art Students' League.

Earns money drawing caricatures of passers-by on city streets.

First magazine assignment illustrating articles for *Close Encounters* magazine, publishers of *Gasm*, *Death of Elvis*, and *Ancient Astronauts*, among others.

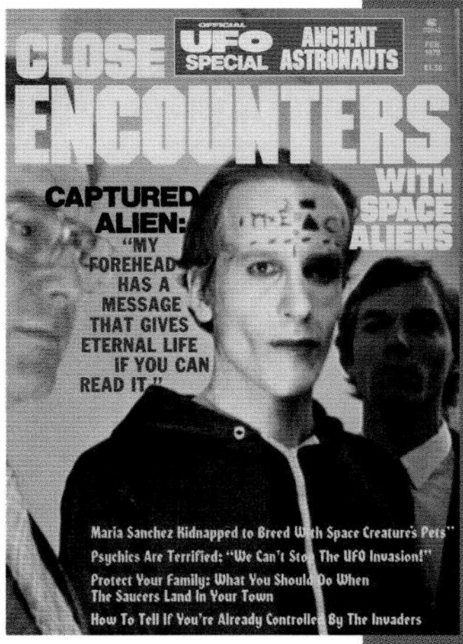
CLOSE
UFO SPECIAL
ANCIENT ASTRONAUTS
ENCOUNTERS
WITH SPACE ALIENS
CAPTURED ALIEN: "MY FOREHEAD HAS A MESSAGE THAT GIVES ETERNAL LIFE IF YOU CAN READ IT"
Psychics Are Terrified: "We Can't Stop The UFO Invasion!"
How To Tell If You're Already Controlled By The Invaders

1977-78

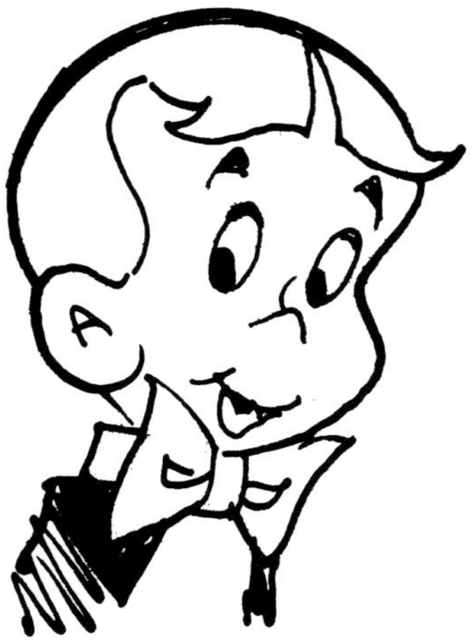

1978

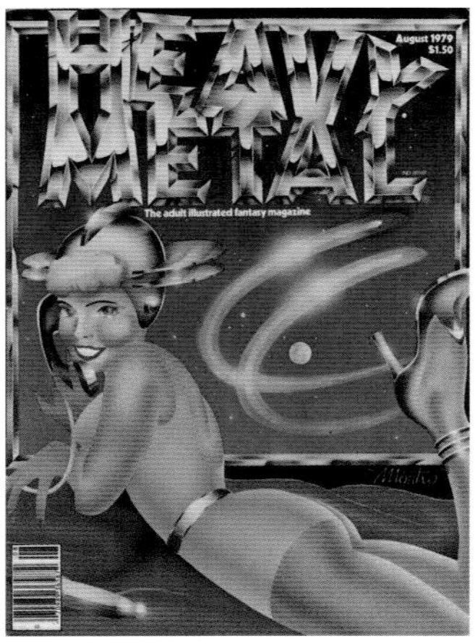
HEAVY METAL
August 1979
$1.50
The adult illustrated fantasy magazine

1979

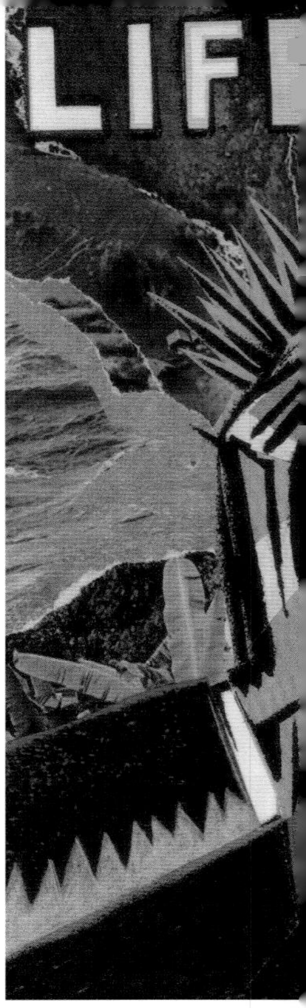
LIF

1978 Begins inking for Harvey Comics' *Richie Rich* (continuing on and off through 1980).

Travels to England, France, and Israel, working on a kibbutz for two months as a banana picker.

Attends Pratt Institute in a work studies program.

1979 Hired as an assistant to comic book artist and illustrator Howard Chaykin (from '79–'82) in Upstarts Studio, which is shared by cartoonists Walter Simonson, Val Mayerik, Jim Starlin, and later, Frank Miller and James Sherman.

First comic strip publication in *Heavy Metal* Magazine, August 1979 issue; continues appearing periodically through 1994.

Joined at Pratt by Seth Tobocman; with Tobocman, co-founds, edits, and publishes first issue of *World War 3 Illustrated*, which continues publication to this day.

1980 First underground strip "Shiver and Twitch" appears in *Commies from Mars* #3, published by Last Gasp.

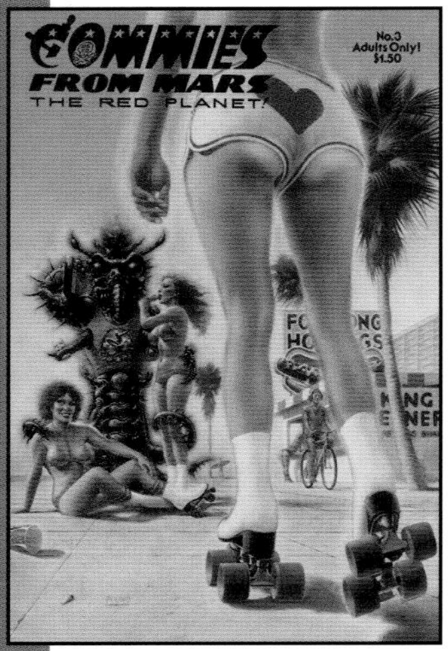
COMMIES FROM MARS
THE RED PLANET
No.3
Adults Only!
$1.50

1980

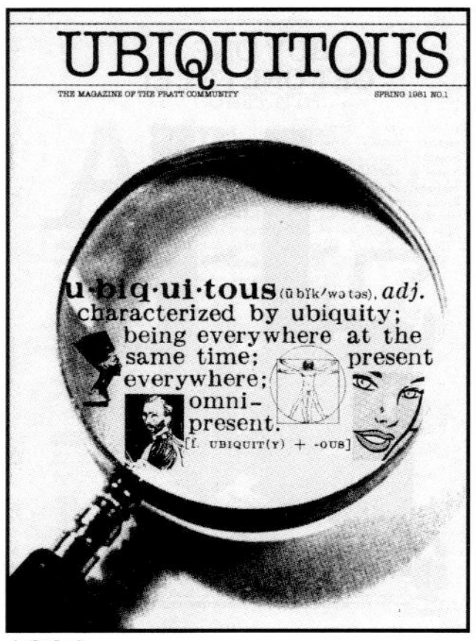
UBIQUITOUS
THE MAGAZINE OF THE PRATT COMMUNITY
SPRING 1981 NO.1
u·biq·ui·tous adj.
characterized by ubiquity;
being everywhere at the
same time; present
everywhere; omni-
present.

1981

1981 Founds, edits, and publishes *Ubiquitous*, an arts magazine for the Pratt Institute community.

First book illustrated (interior only), Philip Jose Farmer's *Stations of the Nightmare*, published by Tor Books.

1982 Publishes second issue of *Ubiquitous*; it continues publication by incoming students to the present.

First *New York Times* illustration assignment from art director Steven Heller in the Book Review section.

1983 Travels in Mexico and draws first travel comic strip.

First illustrations for INX, syndicated by United Media.

1984 Illustrates Robert E. Howard's essay "Beast from the Abyss," published as a paperback by Dodd Mead under the title *The Last Cat Book*.

Travels in England, Scotland, France, Spain (meeting future wife Betty Russell in Madrid), and Israel.

Begins regularly incorporating maps and other collages into illustrations.

1985 Travels in England and Scotland.

1986 Travels in France and Holland.

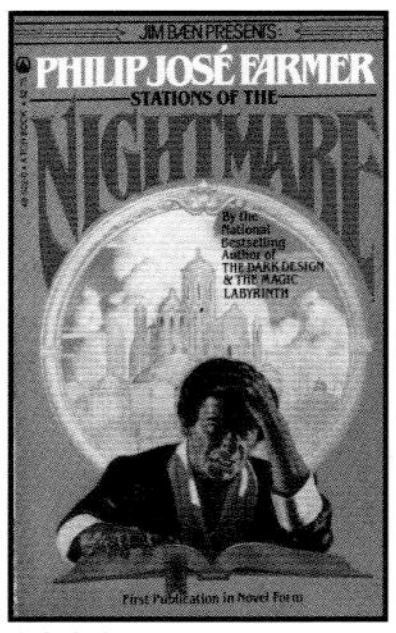
PHILIP JOSÉ FARMER
STATIONS OF THE
NIGHTMARE
First Publication in Novel Form

1981

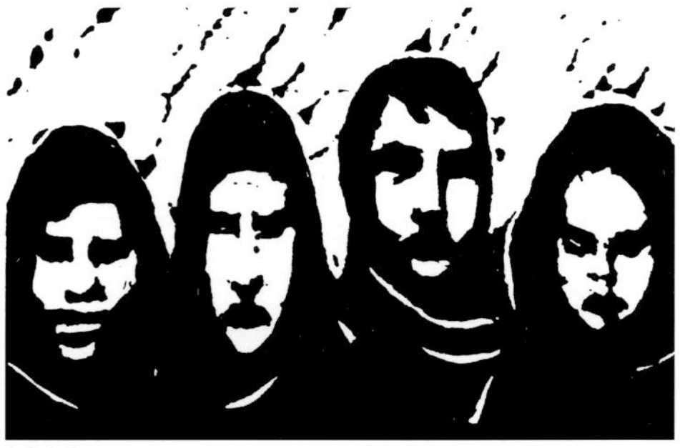

1982

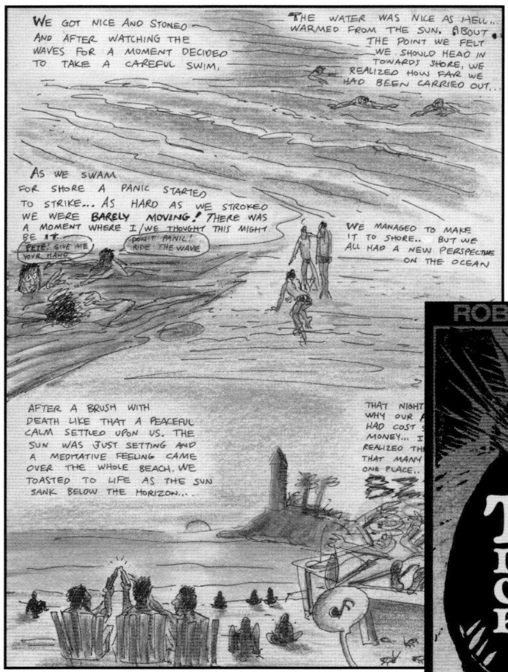
WE GOT NICE AND STONED AND AFTER WATCHING THE WAVES FOR A MOMENT DECIDED TO TAKE A CAREFUL SWIM.
THE WATER WAS NICE AS HELL.. WARMED FROM THE SUN. ABOUT THE POINT WE FELT WE SHOULD HEAD IN TOWARDS SHORE, WE REALIZED HOW FAR WE HAD BEEN CARRIED OUT..
AS WE SWAM FOR SHORE A PANIC STARTED TO STRIKE... AS HARD AS WE STROKED WE WERE BARELY MOVING! THERE WAS A MOMENT WHERE I/WE THOUGHT THIS MIGHT BE IT..
PETE GIVE ME YOUR HAND
DON'T PANIC! RIDE THE WAVE
WE MANAGED TO MAKE IT TO SHORE.. BUT WE ALL HAD A NEW PERSPECTIVE ON THE OCEAN
AFTER A BRUSH WITH DEATH LIKE THAT A PEACEFUL CALM SETTLED UPON US. THE SUN WAS JUST SETTING AND A MEDITATIVE FEELING CAME OVER THE WHOLE BEACH. WE TOASTED TO LIFE AS THE SUN SANK BELOW THE HORIZON...

1983

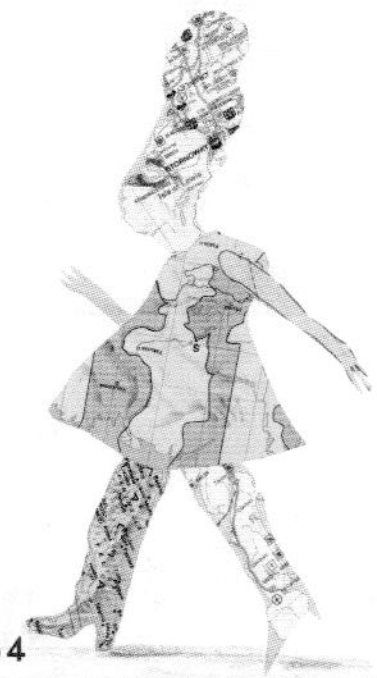

1984

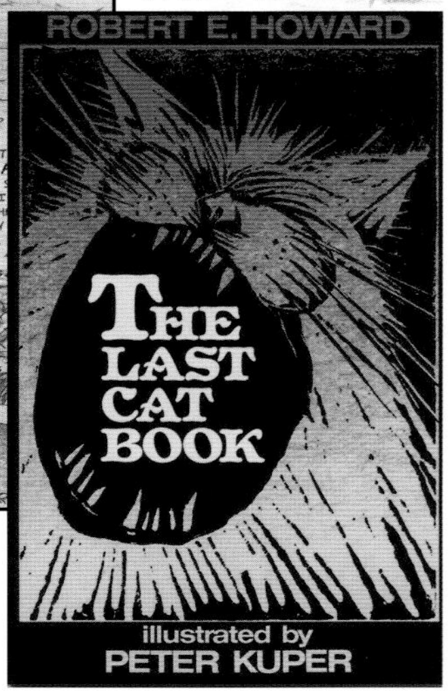
ROBERT E. HOWARD
THE LAST CAT BOOK
illustrated by
PETER KUPER

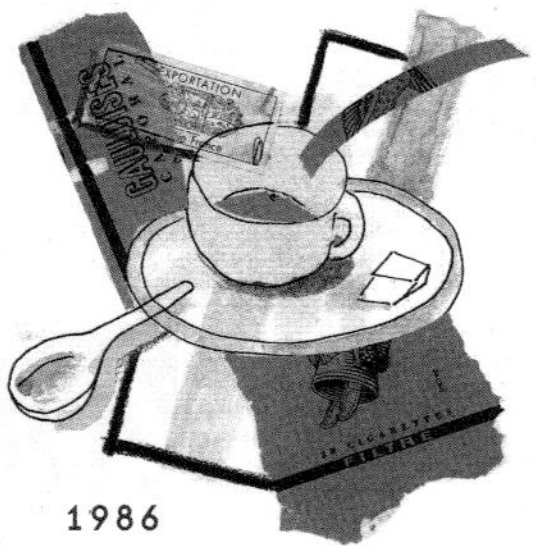

1986

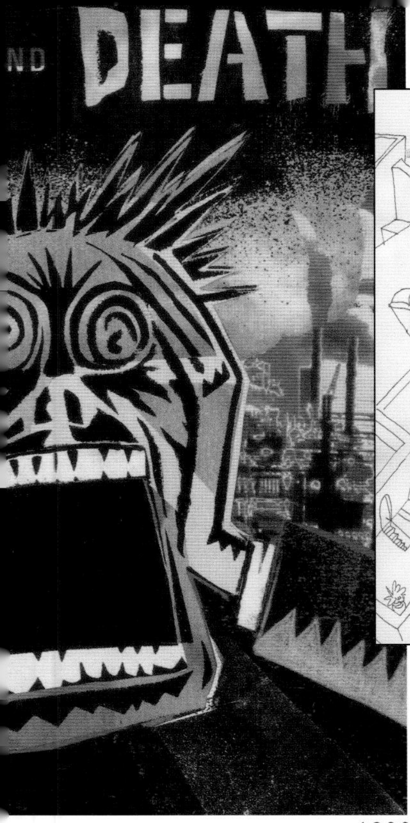
DEATH

1988

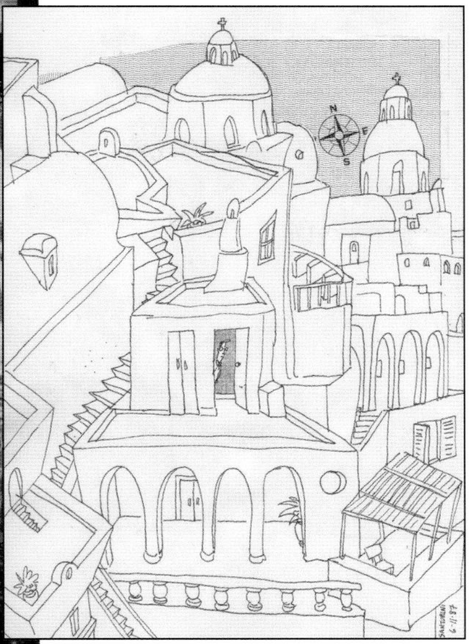

1987

1987 Travels in Mexico.

Fantagraphics Books publishes *New York, New York,* Kuper's first comics collection.

Marries Betty Russell.

Travels with Betty in Greece.

Begins teaching a comix course at New York's School of Visual Arts that continues through 1996.

Travels to Germany, visits Berlin Wall.

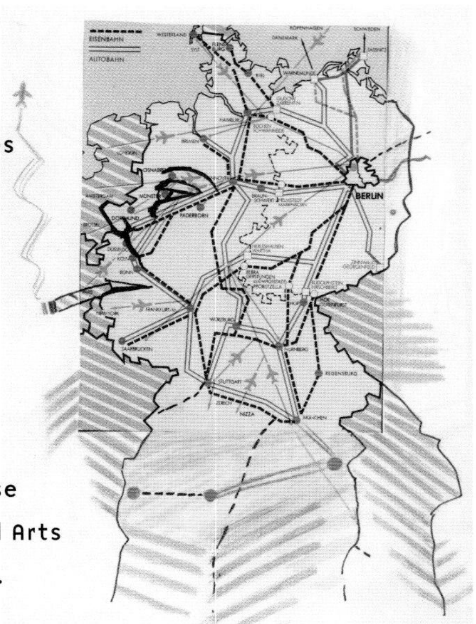

1987

1988 Fantagraphics Books publishes second collection, *It's Only a Matter of Life and Death.*

Begins co-art directing INX.

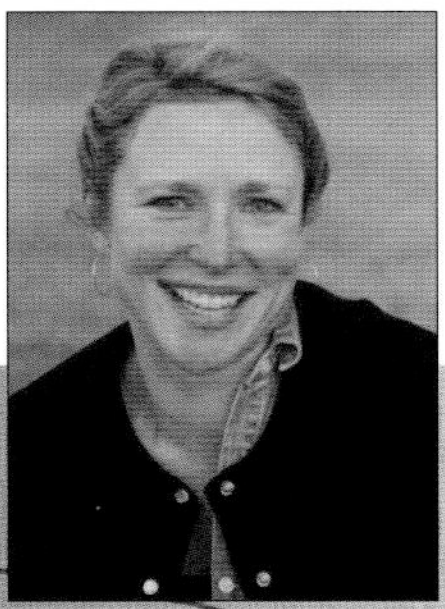

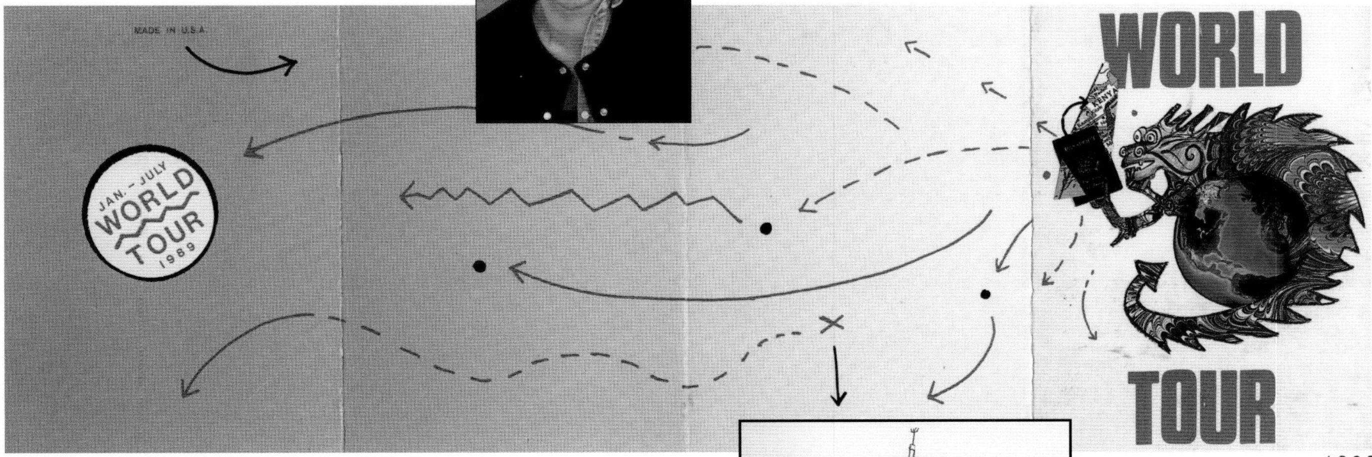
MADE IN U.S.A.
JAN.–JULY WORLD TOUR 1989
WORLD
TOUR

1989

1989 Travels with Betty for eight months through Kenya, Tanzania, Rwanda, Egypt, Israel, India, Thailand, Malaysia and Indonesia, keeping sketchbook diary. Meets and travels with photographer Mark E. Owen.

Fantagraphics Books publishes first anthology collection of early issues of *World War 3 Illustrated.*

1990 Travels with Seth Tobocman to Poland with tickets won in a radio contest. Visits Auschwitz, Czechoslovakia, and Amsterdam.

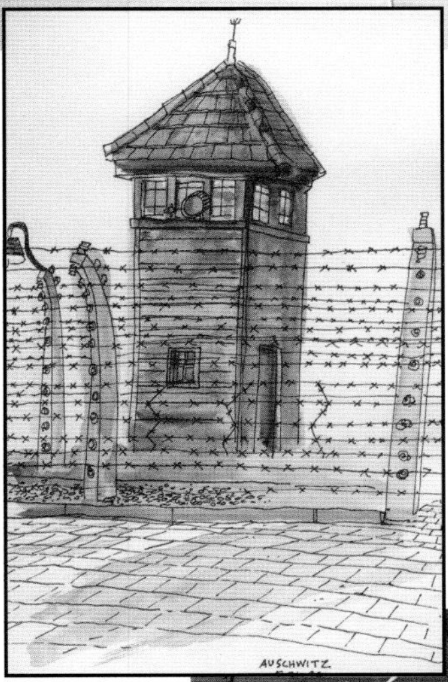
AUSCHWITZ

1990

Returns to Eastern Europe and visits Hungary.

World War 3 gets National Endowment for the Arts grant for group retrospective show in San Francisco.

1991 Adapts Upton Sinclair's *The Jungle* with writer Emily Russell, published by First/Classics Illustrated.

Fantagraphics Books begins publishing *Bleeding Heart*, a five-issue comic series (1991–1993).

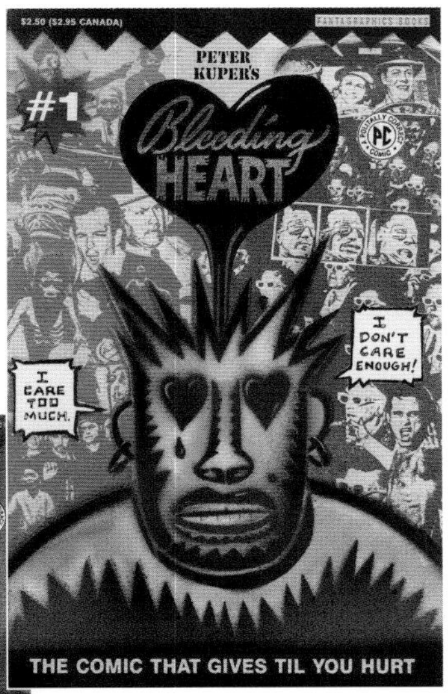
$2.50 ($2.95 CANADA)
FANTAGRAPHICS BOOKS
#1
PETER KUPER'S
Bleeding HEART
I CARE TOO MUCH.
I DON'T CARE ENOUGH!
THE COMIC THAT GIVES TIL YOU HURT

1991

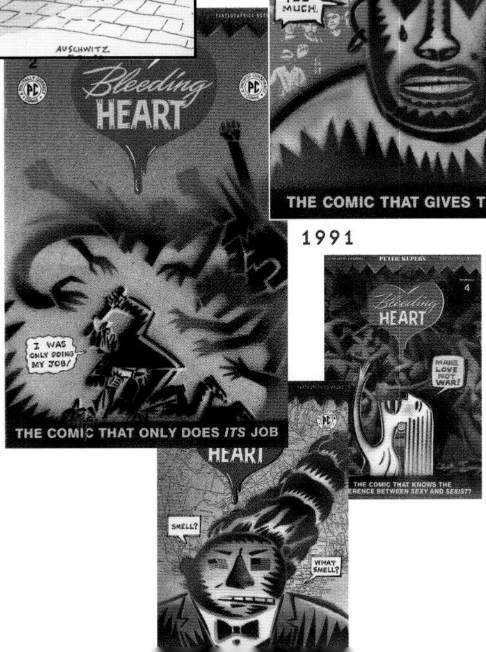
Bleeding HEART
I WAS ONLY DOING MY JOB!
THE COMIC THAT ONLY DOES ITS JOB
PETER KUPERS
Bleeding HEART
MAKE LOVE NOT WAR!
SMELL?
WHAT SMELL?

1992 *Comics Trips*, a collection of sketches and comics from 1989 Africa/Southeast Asia trip is published by Tundra (a company founded by Ninja Turtle co-creator Kevin Eastman); later reissued by NBM.

Travels to Guatemala, Honduras and Belize with Betty and photographer Mark E. Owen.

Co-organizes, with Martin Kozlowski, retrospective show of INX artists at Parsons School of Design in New York City.

1993 Travels to Ecuador and the Galapagos Islands.

First of a series of paintings on windows.

"Eye of the Beholder" appears in the *New York Times'* City Section, the first comic strip to ever appear regularly in that paper.

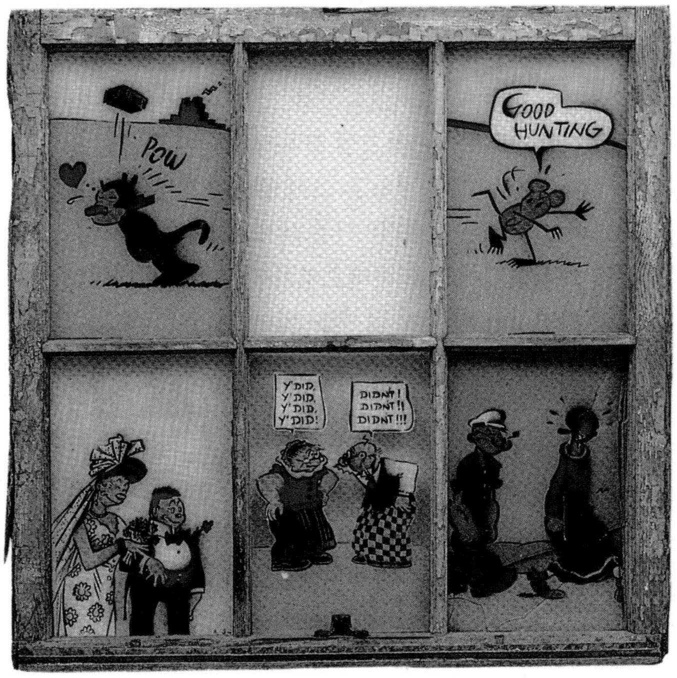
POW
GOOD HUNTING
Y'DID, Y'DID, Y'DID, Y'DID!
DIDN'T! DIDN'T!! DIDN'T!!!
1993

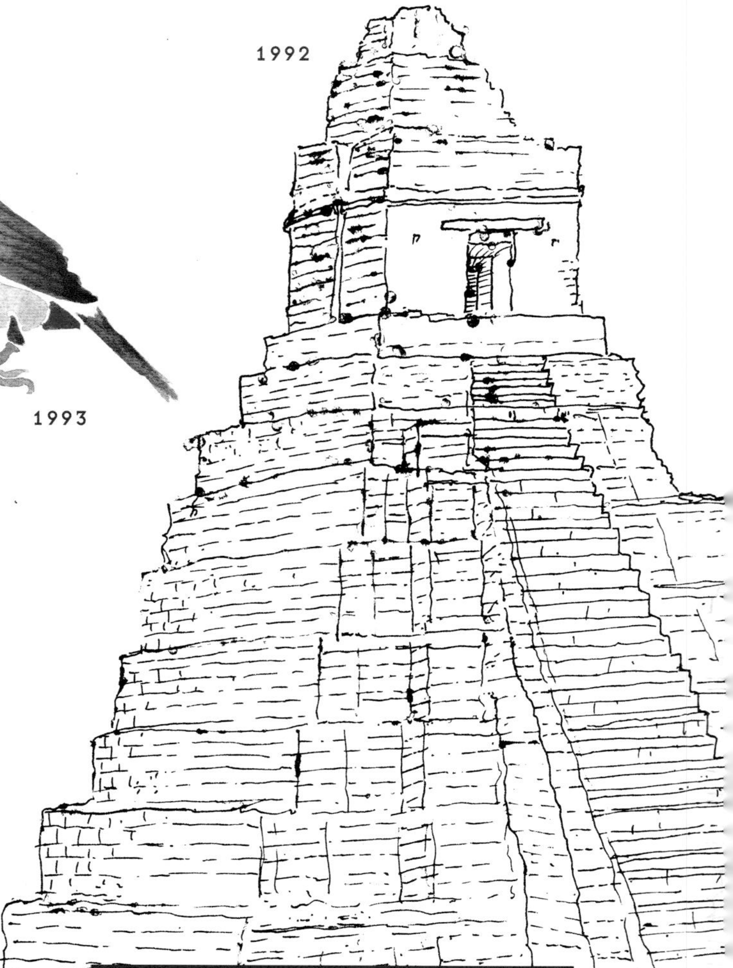
1992

1993–94 Fantagraphics Books publishes *Wild Life*, a series of autobiographical stories in comic form.

1994 Begins self-syndicating "Eye of the Beholder" to: *Tucson Weekly*, *Funny Times*, and *San Diego Reader*, among others.

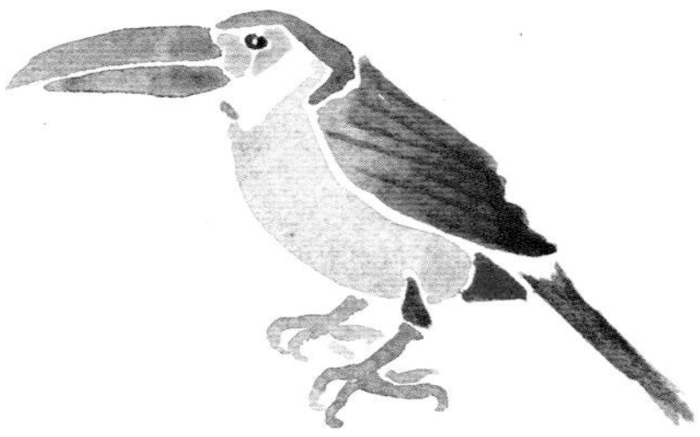
1993

Illustrates covers for *Time*, *Business Week*, *Newsweek*, and *Boston Globe Magazine*, among others.

Travels to Portugal for show of window paintings and comics.

Testifies as expert defense witness for the Comic Book Legal Defense Fund in obscenity trial of cartoonist Mike Diana in Florida.

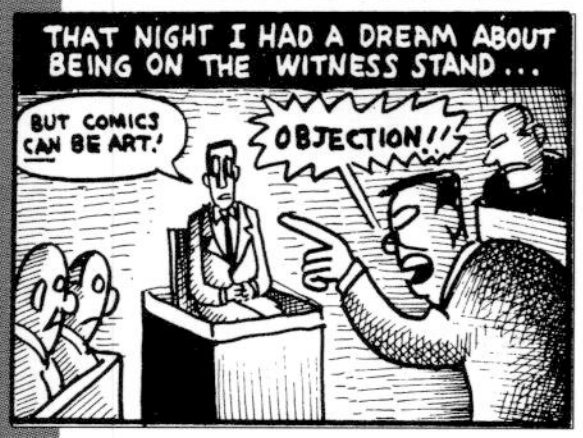
THAT NIGHT I HAD A DREAM ABOUT BEING ON THE WITNESS STAND...
BUT COMICS CAN BE ART!
OBJECTION!!
1994

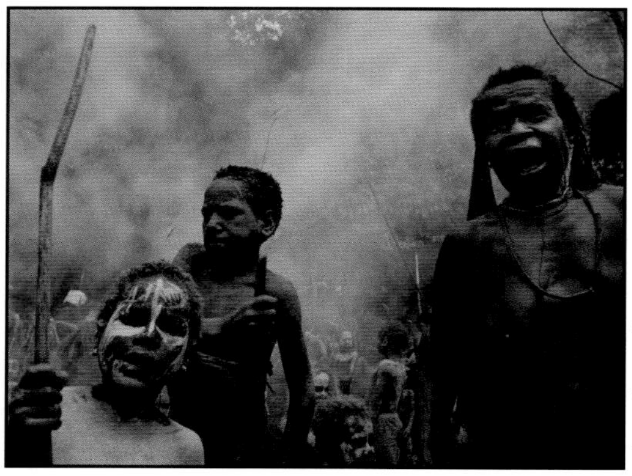
Photo by Mark E. Owen
1995

1995 Returns to Indonesia with Mark E. Owen, visiting Bali and trekking in Irian Jaya, New Guinea.

Fantagraphics Books publishes *Stripped, An Unauthorized Autobiography*, which includes comics from *Bleeding Heart* and *Wild Life*, among others.

NBM publishes *Give it Up!*, a hardbound collection of Franz Kafka comic strip adaptations. German, Portuguese and Swedish editions follow over the next few years.

Four Walls Eight Windows publishes second anthology collection, *World War 3, Confrontational Comics*, co-edited with Scott Cunningham, Sabrina Jones and Seth Tobocman.

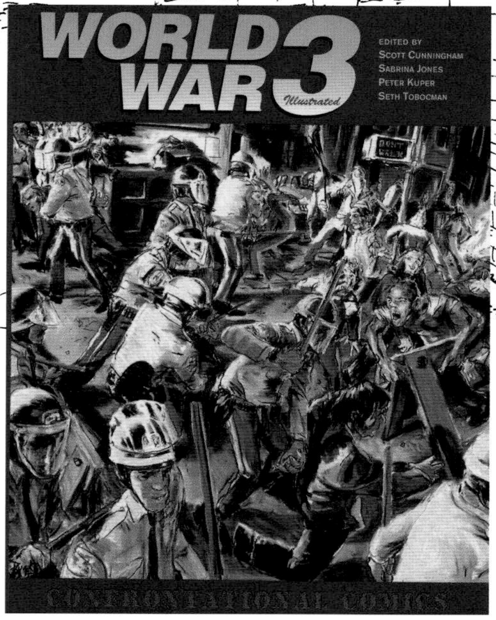
WORLD WAR 3 Illustrated
EDITED BY
SCOTT CUNNINGHAM
SABRINA JONES
PETER KUPER
SETH TOBOCMAN
CONFRONTATIONAL COMICS
1995

1995 Named "Hot Cartoonist of the Year" by *Rolling Stone* magazine.

Co-organizes retrospective show of *World War 3* at Parsons School of Design, with Scott Cunningham, Sabrina Jones and Seth Tobocman.

1996 DC/Vertigo publishes *The System* in 3 comic book formatted issues.

NBM publishes first collection of *Eye of the Beholder*.

Daughter Emily Russell Kuper born.

1997 *The System* is collected into a softbound book form by DC/Vertigo. Italian, Greek, and Brazilian editions published over next few years.

Takes over illustrating Antonio Prohias' "Spy vs. Spy" for *Mad Magazine*.

Sent by *Details* magazine to cover "Burning Man," a six day arts festival in the Nevada desert, with photographer Mark E.Owen. *Details'* first feature journal comic with new editor Art Spiegelman.

1998 Interlink, a Japanese company, produces a CD-ROM based on travel book *Comics Trips*.

1999 World War 3 included in *Urban Encounters*, a retrospective of political artists, at the New Museum of Contemporary Art in New York.

Begins producing a weekly strip for a new opinion section of the *New York Daily News* titled "New York Minute."

2000 NBM publishes a second collection of "Eye of the Beholder," titled *Mind's Eye*, and reissues the first collection, both in hardcover.

Self-publishes collection of Daily News Strips titled *Topsy Turvy*.

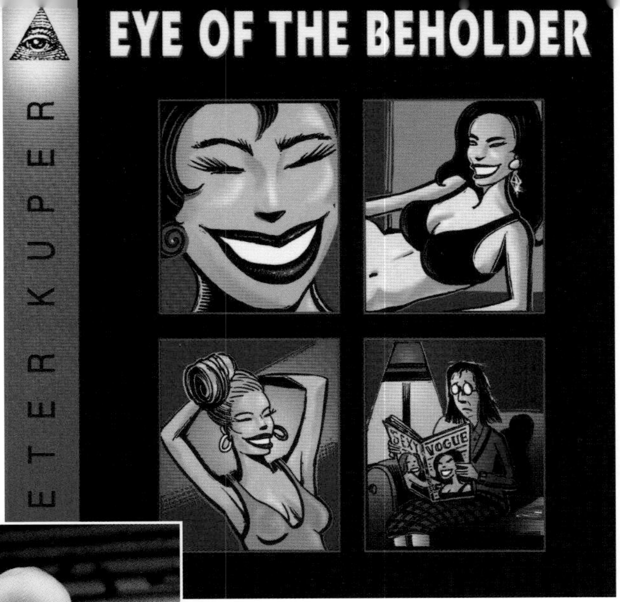
EYE OF THE BEHOLDER
PETER KUPER
VOGUE

1996

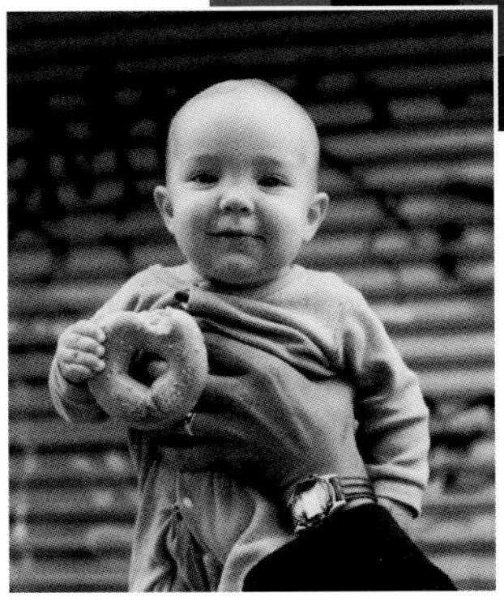

Photo by Holly Kuper

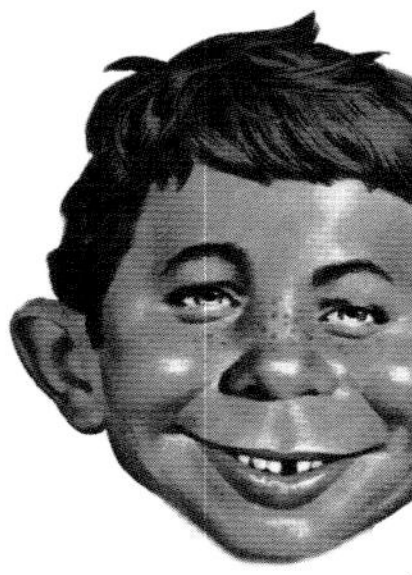

1997

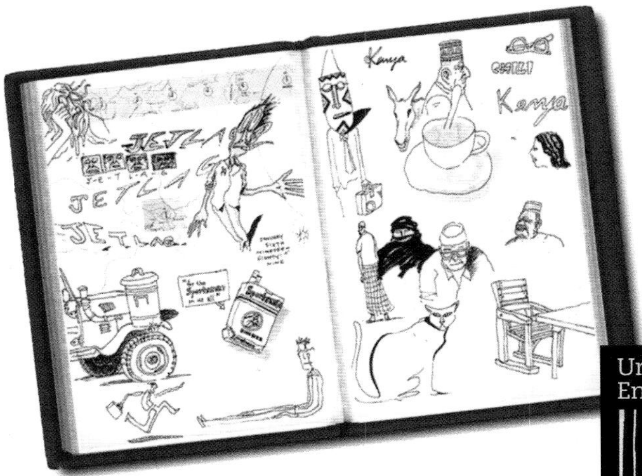
JETLAG
Kenya

1998

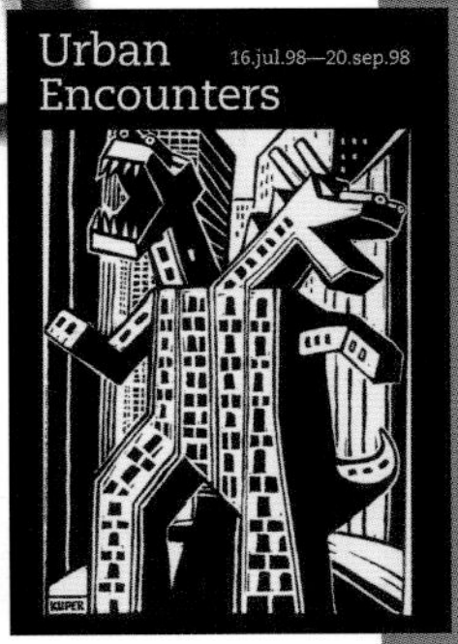
Urban Encounters
16.jul.98—20.sep.98

1999

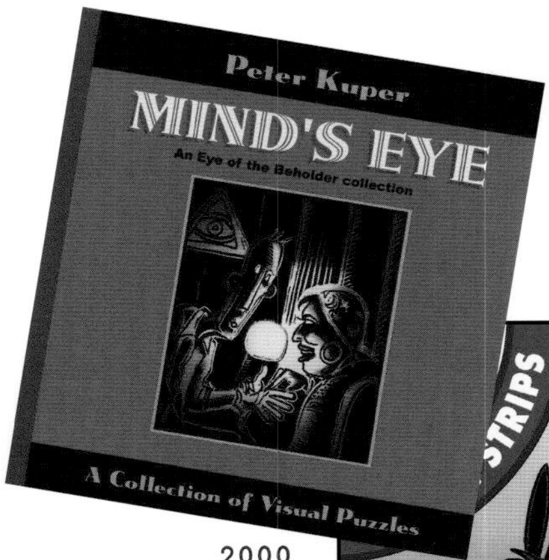
Peter Kuper
MIND'S EYE
An Eye of the Beholder collection
A Collection of Visual Puzzles

2000

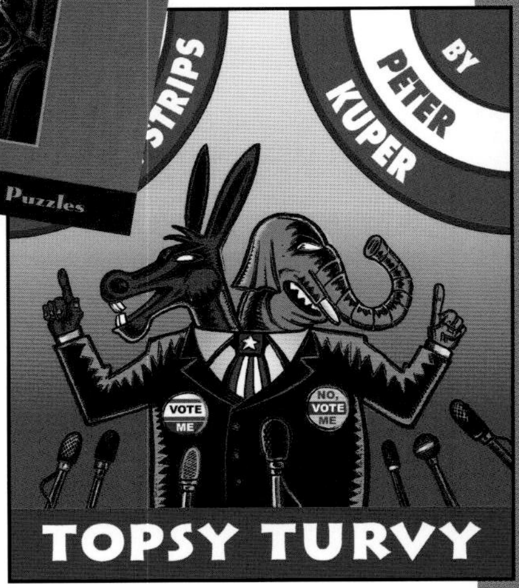
STRIPS
BY PETER KUPER
VOTE ME
NO VOTE ME
TOPSY TURVY

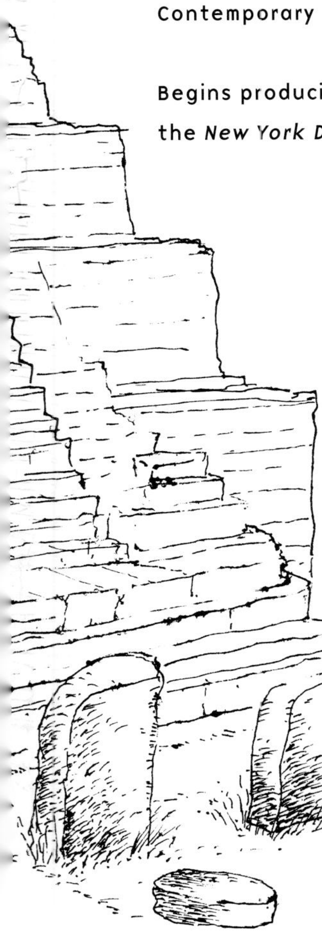

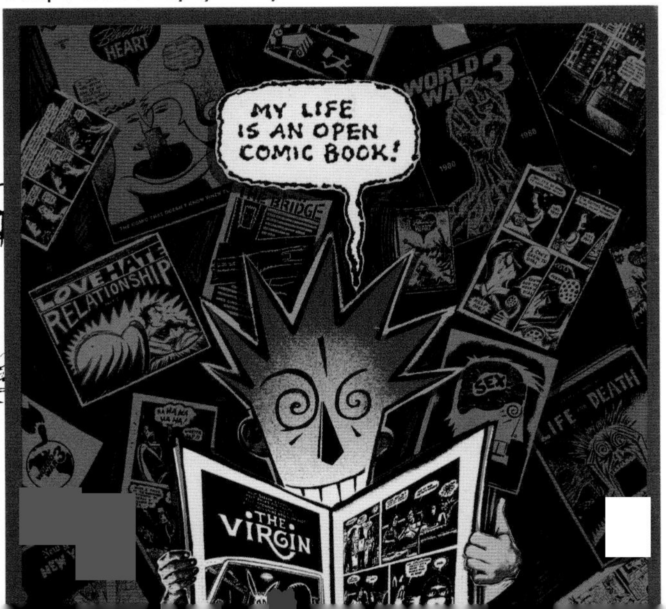
MY LIFE IS AN OPEN COMIC BOOK!
WORLD WAR 3
LOVE-HATE RELATIONSHIP
SEX
LIFE DEATH
THE VIRGIN

First signs of impending mid-life crisis.

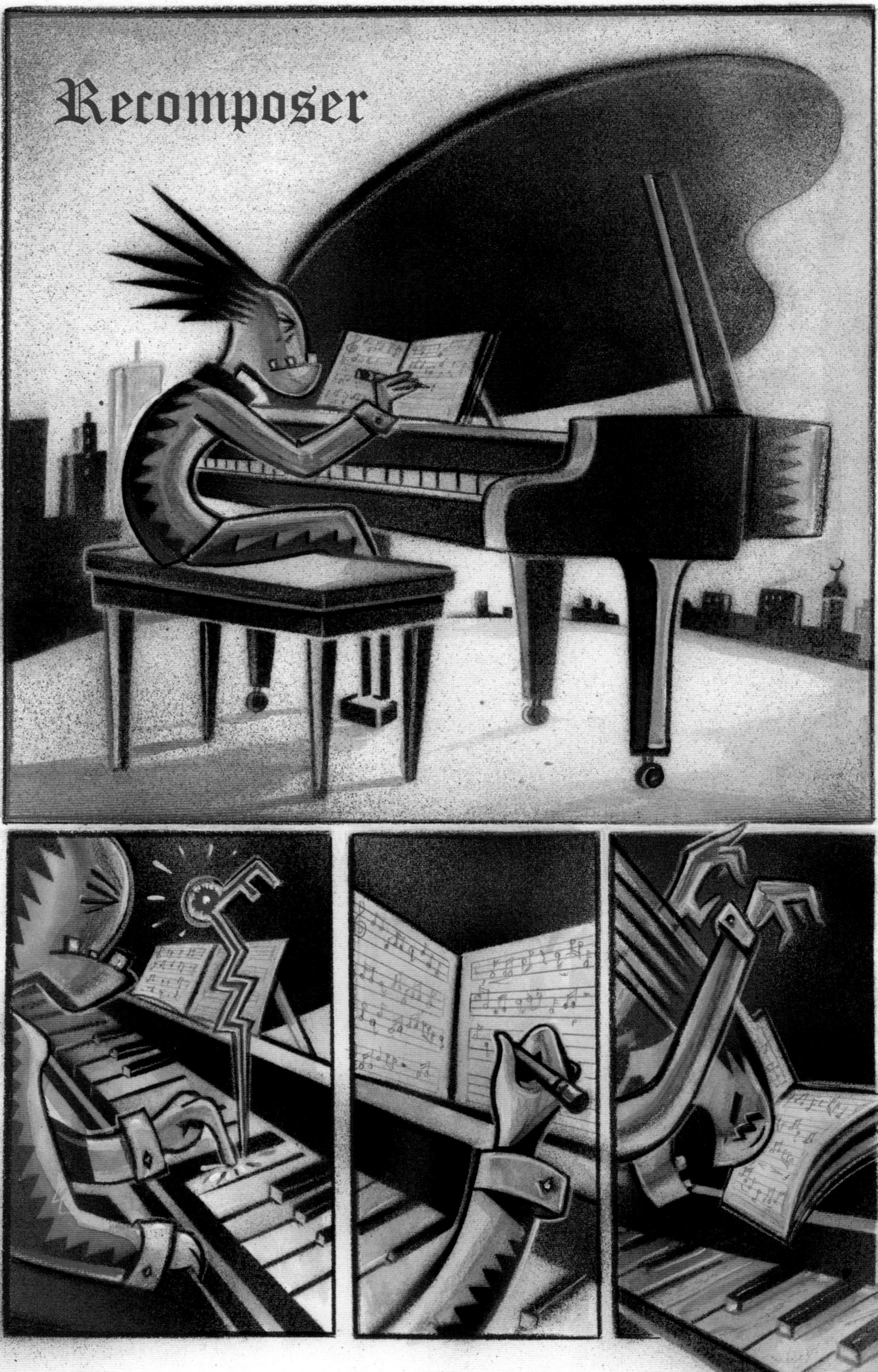
Recomposer

Recomposer, Unpublished, 2000.

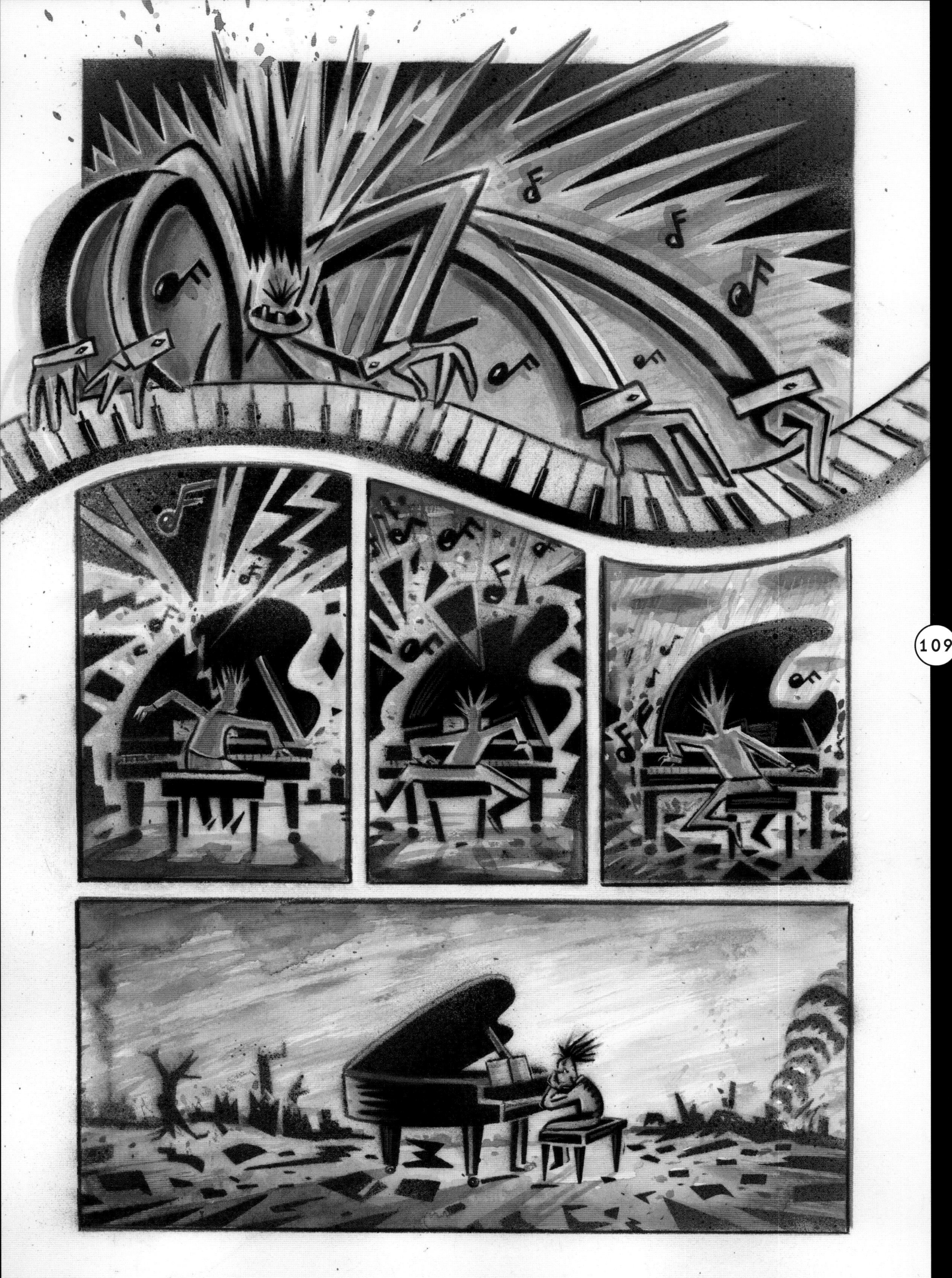

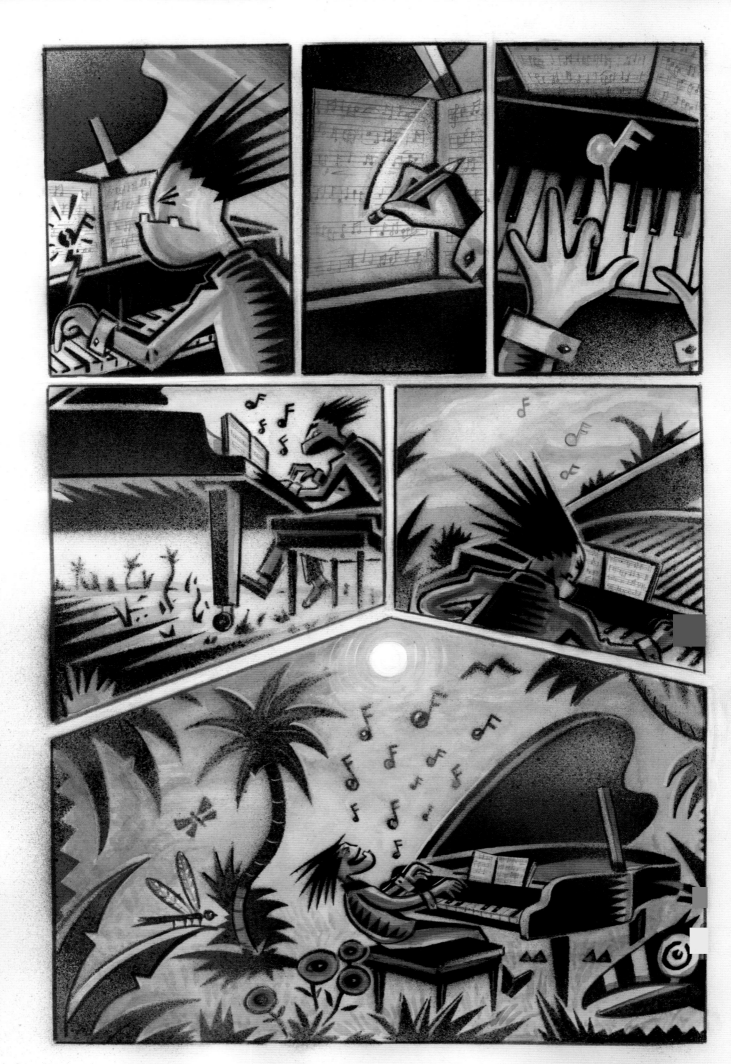

The End.

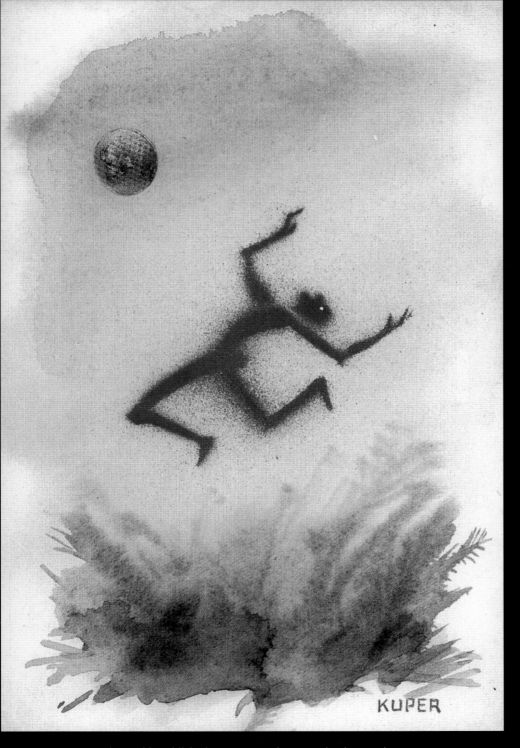

See The World, published as a postcard announcing lecture by Kuper
at School of Visual Arts in New York, 1990.

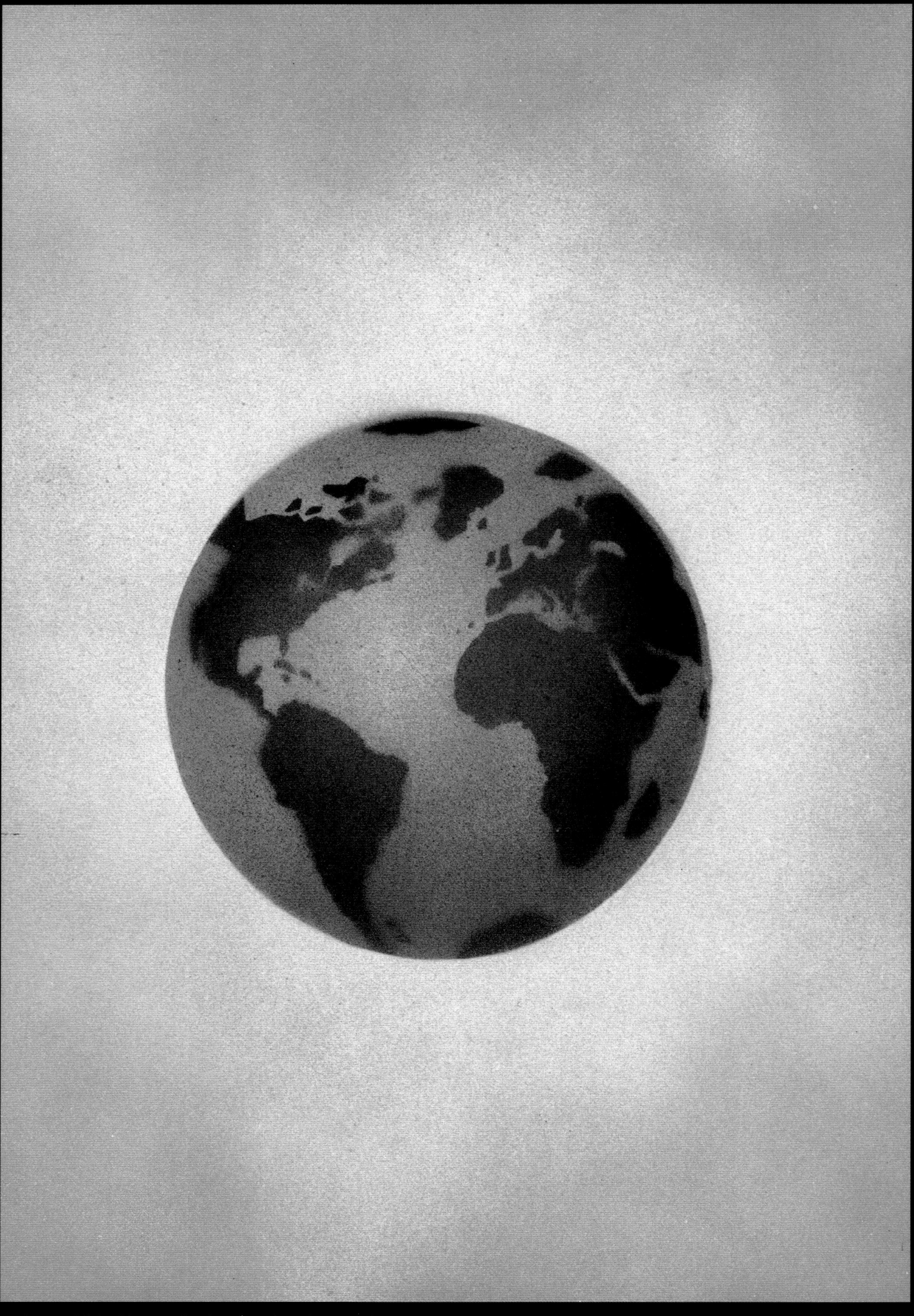

Mother, published in recycling brochure by Take It Back, 1992.